AF837681

Sustainable Development Goals Series

The **Sustainable Development Goals Series** is Springer Nature's inaugural cross-imprint book series that addresses and supports the United Nations' seventeen Sustainable Development Goals. The series fosters comprehensive research focused on these global targets and endeavours to address some of society's greatest grand challenges. The SDGs are inherently multidisciplinary, and they bring people working across different fields together and working towards a common goal. In this spirit, the Sustainable Development Goals series is the first at Springer Nature to publish books under both the Springer and Palgrave Macmillan imprints, bringing the strengths of our imprints together.

The Sustainable Development Goals Series is organized into eighteen subseries: one subseries based around each of the seventeen respective Sustainable Development Goals, and an eighteenth subseries, "Connecting the Goals", which serves as a home for volumes addressing multiple goals or studying the SDGs as a whole. Each subseries is guided by an expert Subseries Advisor with years or decades of experience studying and addressing core components of their respective Goal.

The SDG Series has a remit as broad as the SDGs themselves, and contributions are welcome from scientists, academics, policymakers, and researchers working in fields related to any of the seventeen goals. If you are interested in contributing a monograph or curated volume to the series, please contact the Publishers: Zachary Romano [Springer; zachary.romano@springer.com] and Rachael Ballard [Palgrave Macmillan; rachael.ballard@palgrave.com].

Alessandro Crimi

Innovate for Impact

A Roadmap to Sustainable Technology Beyond AI

Springer

Alessandro Crimi
AGH University of Krakow
Krakow, Poland

ISSN 2523-3084 ISSN 2523-3092 (electronic)
Sustainable Development Goals Series
ISBN 978-3-032-21562-8 ISBN 978-3-032-21563-5 (eBook)
https://doi.org/10.1007/978-3-032-21563-5

© The Editor(s) (if applicable) and The Author(s), under exclusive license to Springer Nature Switzerland AG 2026

Color wheel and icons: From https://www.un.org/sustainabledevelopment/, Copyright © 2020 United Nations. Used with the permission of the United Nations.

The content of this publication has not been approved by the United Nations and does not reflect the views of the United Nations or its officials or Member States.

This work is subject to copyright. All rights are solely and exclusively licensed by the Publisher, whether the whole or part of the material is concerned, specifically the rights of translation, reprinting, reuse of illustrations, recitation, broadcasting, reproduction on microfilms or in any other physical way, and transmission or information storage and retrieval, electronic adaptation, computer software, or by similar or dissimilar methodology now known or hereafter developed.
The use of general descriptive names, registered names, trademarks, service marks, etc. in this publication does not imply, even in the absence of a specific statement, that such names are exempt from the relevant protective laws and regulations and therefore free for general use.
The publisher, the authors and the editors are safe to assume that the advice and information in this book are believed to be true and accurate at the date of publication. Neither the publisher nor the authors or the editors give a warranty, expressed or implied, with respect to the material contained herein or for any errors or omissions that may have been made. The publisher remains neutral with regard to jurisdictional claims in published maps and institutional affiliations.

This Springer imprint is published by the registered company Springer Nature Switzerland AG
The registered company address is: Gewerbestrasse 11, 6330 Cham, Switzerland

If disposing of this product, please recycle the paper.

To my parents Carmelo and Marianna, and to my son David, I will always be there for you, despite the lies.

Acknowledgements This book is the culmination of a series of ideas lingering in my head for a long time, combined with contemporary issues such as AI and sustainability. I have always been fascinated by why certain countries or groups of people flourish and others remain poor. Why do people need to emigrate to fulfill themselves and why certain things never change in the good and bad way. I hope this will serve as an input for people to invent new policies or to avoid failures while doing it. Above all, I believe in changes from the bottom, where entrepreneurs and activists fill the gaps left from their governments. This is for you and dedicated to those grassroots heroes, you have been the main inspirations.

I would like to thank the editor who followed this work, Habiba Kalantarova, for the tremendous support and guidance during the book development. I also want to thank the anonymous reviewers and early readers Orestis Vantzos and Irene Paniccia, who I met during what seems like another life in Germany and are now coming to help me. Your comments have been extremely valuable. Davey Groothoff for the insights about system thinking.

At some point in our lives, we become a bit apathetic or resign ourselves to our limits. We might become tired of fighting lobbyists, politics, and financial limitations. Even science or activism might appear as just 90% bureaucracy and 10% changing the world. However, if this 10% saves a life or improves it, it might still be worthwhile. I hope that at least one of the ideas in this book might actually provide new insight to someone who is actually creating some sustainable impact. Therefore, I thank anyone who would take some actions.

All drawings are from the author realized using the open source software Krita.

Competing Interests The author has no competing interests to declare that are relevant to the content of this manuscript.

Praise for *Innovate for Impact*

"This book exemplifies engaged scholarship: analytically sharp, normatively bold, and policy-relevant. Crimi turns innovation into a matter of governance, offering a refreshing and much-needed guide to shaping it for the public good.

This book exemplifies what engaged scholarship should be: analytically sharp, normatively bold, and policy-relevant. Crimi succeeds in making innovation a matter of governance, not just markets. By weaving system thinking with concrete cases, this book speaks directly to regulators, scholars, and practitioners eager to turn innovation into inclusion and challenges us to look beyond buzzwords and see innovation as a tool of empowerment. A rigorous yet accessible guide to how innovation can be governed for the public good."

—Alberto Alemanno, *Jean Monnet Professor in EU Law at HEC Paris, Author of "Lobbying for Change"*

"I can summarize my understanding of this book as follows: if you are a grassroots organizer, NGO practitioner, or public policymaker with a strong desire to tackle persistent public challenges, this book is for you. Professor Crimi offers an alternative way of approaching complex social problems through a systems-thinking perspective. He encourages readers to understand the broader environment surrounding a problem, identify its key elements and components, and examine the internal and external relationships that govern its dynamics. From there, he emphasizes defining precise, measurable indicators of impact, collecting relevant data, and continuously evaluating and refining interventions through iterative feedback loops. Within this data-driven framework, AI enters the picture with unprecedented potential for accurate measurement, insight, and prediction.

To ground these ideas, Crimi takes on a bold and ambitious case study on a grandiose challenge: poverty in the Global South. He confronts its deep-rooted complexity and demonstrates how AI-enabled systems thinking can accelerate progress toward poverty reduction. At the same time, he is careful not to oversell the technology. The book clearly acknowledges that AI can also reinforce historical injustices, perpetuate existing biases, and amplify societal "garbages" if left unchecked. Crimi explicitly warns against these risks and offers thoughtful strategies to mitigate them.

The book is scholarly yet written in clear, accessible language. It is rich with vivid examples–both inspiring humane stories, successful interventions and cautionary tales of failure. Overall, it serves as a practical roadmap for how AI, when used responsibly and ethically, can drive sustainable, inclusive, and scalable innovation in addressing some of society's most enduring challenges."

—Abdo Elnasar Degoot, *Researcher at the London School of Hygiene and Tropical Medicine*

Introduction

In movies, we sometimes see grotesque cyberpunk scenes of urban societies dominated by computer technology. Despite those dystopian fantasies, many of us believe in a potential bright future of humanity where technology is still our friend. The last centuries have seen a steep decrease in infant mortality [1], malaria is not the same unknown killer as years ago, and now people are endowed with affordable solutions [2]. The future looks like a mosaic of infinite potential, instead of fantasies of grotesque scenes as body modification, robots in crowded street markets, or tech junkyard from pessimistic cinematography. We might live in a tapestry of automation, wealth, and freedom, submerged by organic and sustainable infrastructures.

Yet, new technologies have introduced novel issues. Mental health issues are on the rise related to overconnectivity [3]. We are entering cloud-feudalism, or techno-feudalism [8], with people not owning but sharing on platforms which are owned by corporations sometimes valuated more than small countries. People have longer life expectancy, and societies face burdens related to the aging population, with more and more cases of dementia and tumors, and younger generations are paying the price. Artificial intelligence (AI) infrastructures are the fastest way to introduce innovation, but they consume a lot of electricity, solving challenges on the one hand, but introducing new ones environmentally [4]. In addition, one might think that the world is in the hands of a small group of people who influence or take advantage of everything, and most of the efforts are vain or pure luck. Unfortunately, as we will discuss in this book, there are unfair advantages and they actually make things complicated, but it is not that simple; there is still hope, or actually "many hopes".

Looking for innovations, even deserts like the Sahara can have blooming flowers. South Asian countries are not just a kaleidoscope of spices, with culinary notes. Moreover, Latin America, even if adorned with the colors of resilience and the melodies of ancient wisdom, could also host particles of novelty. Those places can have innovators, entrepreneurs, pioneers, and activists. As we embark on a quest to explore the fusion of AI and novel technologies with the soulful beats of the Sustainable Development Goals (SDGs). Those are "Global Goals", where we are invited to dance with innovation, following the rhythm and harmonies given by tradition, sustainability, and progress.

Those goals were introduced in 2015 by the United Nations as a universal call to action to end poverty, protect the planet, and ensure that by 2030 all people enjoy peace and prosperity. The first goal is focused on the fight against poverty, though the other goals indirectly also address it. You cannot fight poverty in an abstract manner, you have to do it by promoting empowerment, sustainability, and technology. With this in mind, this book is focused on three major issues, considering three aspects that, in my opinion, can help the fight against poverty and inequality: social change (from a bottom-up perspective of NGOs and entrepreneur), education, and healthcare. The impact of healthcare on poverty reduction is known, but in this text we consider healthcare issues with AI due to the need of data.

More specifically, in Chap. 1, we revise some general issues related to what it takes to run projects in the global south. This might be for academics, for start-uppers, or activists. When your government is not acting by providing effective policies, it is time to provide those changes from the bottom.

Chapter 2 explores the persistence of poverty, framed as self-reinforcing "traps" related to health, conflict, resources, and governance. Here, although education has historically been seen as an equalizer, the chapter warns that emerging technologies such as AI could either exacerbate or alleviate inequalities depending on their design and implementation. Successful interventions require integrating technology with local customs and authority structures, as shown in case studies like a prenatal telemedicine project in Ghana. The chapter concludes that sustainable poverty reduction requires combining targeted human capital investments, deliberate policy safeguards against technological disruption, and institutional reforms to create inclusive pathways out of poverty.

In Chap. 3, there is particular emphasis on educational approaches and conducting research projects. Indeed, there is a divergence in educational and research, both inside and outside academia, between the Global North and the Global South. This reflects all the undertones of the realities given by history, economy, ideologies, and cultures. We also focus more on educating the new generations toward the necessary changes and reducing the gaps between the Global North and South. In the Global North, education systems often emphasize specialized fields and technology-driven curricula, fostering a strong foundation for entrepreneurship and scientific innovation, still benefiting from the previous unfair advantage of the Industrial Revolution. In contrast, while new technologies allow leapfrogs, the Global South faces challenges related to access, infrastructure, and resource disparities, may this be generated by bad governments, local mindsets or other reasons we will discuss together, but there education often grapples with limited resources, and the emphasis may lean towards addressing immediate socio-economic needs rather than prioritizing long-term scientific and entrepreneurial goals. However, the Global South increasingly recognizes the importance of promoting entrepreneurship and science as catalysts for a better and more sustainable future. Independently, they are supported by their local governments; there is for sure a new generation of thinkers and doers. Some of the issues described in this part will also be present for spreading AI and biotech in the Global South, not just for education.

Indeed, AI can orchestrate a symphony of solutions across multiple SDGs. First and foremost, AI is supercharged education, since with chatbots now we can access a huge amount of knowledge. Given internet availability, it becomes a 24 h available tutor, offering personalized learning experiences to bridge gaps and ensure that no one is left behind. In healthcare, machine learning algorithms and robotics allow for competitive predictive diagnosis, or aid surgeons in outstanding ways. The potential in other fields to accelerate social change is also almost infinite.

In Chap. 4, we discuss how AI sharpens the societal lenses on healthcare care and agriculture. In addition, we discuss how climate data contribute to more effective conservation and disaster response. Without even thinking of blockchain, in the realm of Goal 16 (Peace, Justice, and Strong Institutions), new technologies and AI can pave the way for more secure and traceable digital infrastructure, which can reduce corruption and foster trust in our society. Goal 7 is centered on affordable and clean energy. Here we are initiating an alchemy of renewable energy technologies. Solar panels, wind turbines, and advanced energy storage systems are the spellcasters transforming sunlight and wind into clean, accessible power, but also less consuming algorithms and more efficient devices, because we have to deal with increasing technology, but also reducing its impact. Lastly, in Chap. 5 we discuss issues that are more general, such as whether there are alternatives to intellectual property, what the relationship is between tax, innovation, and governmental revenue, and whether while we were focused on deploying the Global North model into the Global South, we forgot the Global East. After Chap. 5 we review the main topics discussed, and we look for a hopeful realistic vision for the future.

In summary, I propose a roadmap to sustainable technology, based on social change, promotion of education, healthcare, and nutrition, backed by new technologies and AI as depicted in Fig. 1.

Perhaps it is time to decolonize cloud-feudalism with local innovations. Those can be frugal at first, but with time, they will allow more uniform wealth in both the Global North and South. Given the speed of current innovation, predicting the future is even more difficult, but we can do our best to facilitate the quest toward a more sustainable world. Things do not come easily. If you are a scientist, an activist, or an entrepreneur, you know this very well. If you are a timid student embarking on bigger challenges than you, you should not make the mistake of climbing Mount Everest in flip-flops. Most of the things we try go wrong or work, and introduce additional challenges. Very often the reasons for failure are not related to technology. Maybe we already have all the answers to most of the problems. We need system thinking [5]. Often failures are related to human nature, such as resistance to change [6], or interest groups creating strong entry barriers to newcomer activists, startups, or scientists who put some effort into translating from the lab to the real world [7]. I want to reassure the reader, and not discourage him/her. As Shakespeare said in his play The Merry Wives Of Windsor: 'The world is your oyster; it is up to you to find the pearl' [9]. In this book, some of those aspects related to system thinking will be revised as well, empowering the reader and allowing them to find those pearls.

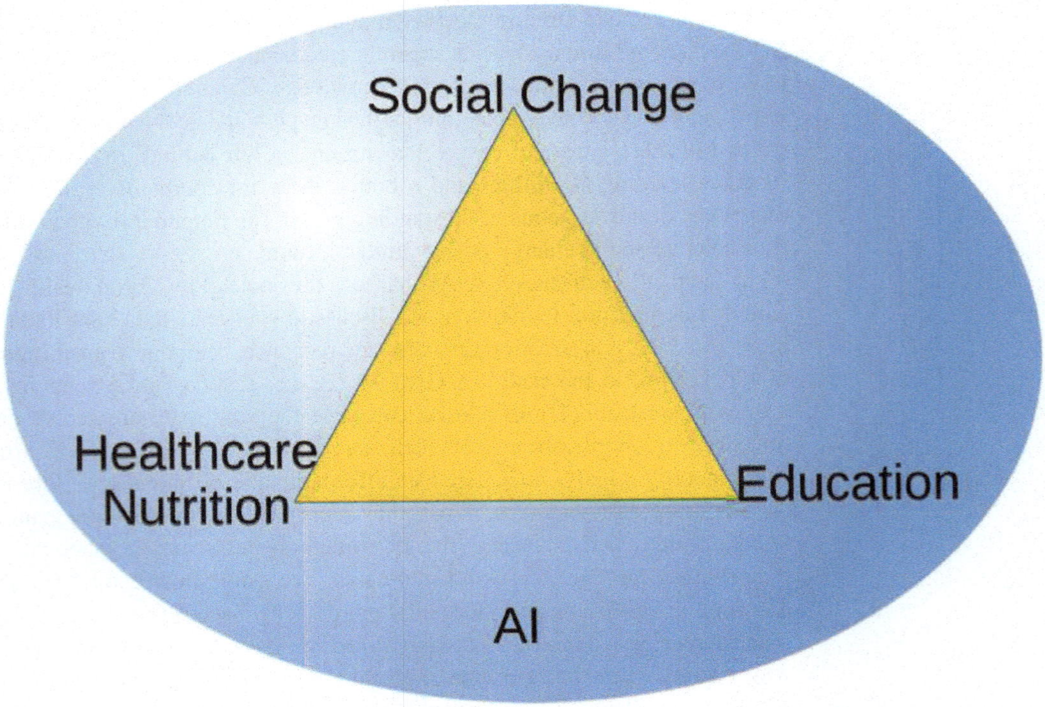

Fig. 1 The basis of improving well-being and reducing poverty: social change, healthcare and nutrition, and education. AI is shown in the background to indicate its general supporting role

References

1. Sartorius, Benn KD, and Kurt Sartorius. "Global infant mortality trends and attributable determinants–an ecological study using data from 192 countries for the period 1990–2011." Population Health Metrics 12 (2014): 1–15.
2. Nájera, José A. "Malaria control: achievements, problems and strategies." Parassitologia 43.1-2 (2001): 1–89.
3. Berryman, Chloe, Christopher J. Ferguson, and Charles Negy. "Social media use and mental health among young adults." Psychiatric quarterly 89 (2018): 307–314.
4. Strubell, Emma, Ananya Ganesh, and Andrew McCallum. "Energy and policy considerations for modern deep learning research." Proceedings of the AAAI conference on artificial intelligence. Vol. 34. No. 09. 2020.
5. World Health Organization. "Everybody's business–strengthening health systems to improve health outcomes: WHO's framework for action." (2007).
6. Centola, Damon. Change: How to make big things happen. Hachette UK, 2021.
7. Tusk, Bradley. The fixer: my adventures saving startups from death by politics. Penguin, 2018.
8. Varoufakis, Y. (2024). Technofeudalism: What killed capitalism. Melville House.
9. Shakespeare, William. The merry wives of Windsor. Oxford University Press, USA, 1998.

Contents

1 Changes for Impact

The world's biggest problems are complex, interconnected, and persistent. Persistent because change is really hard, and for decades, huge efforts, massive government aid and passionate grassroots campaigns have struggled to create lasting change.

In this chapter, we do not discuss why those efforts failed. We will point out some issues related to change, such as system thinking and lobbying to help the new generation of activists, entrepreneurs, and policymakers. Indeed, change is hard; it is very hard. We will discuss in this chapter some critical aspects to change.

1.1 The Landscape of Inequality and the Search for Solutions

As technology advances, it generally promises greater equality, but often creates greater inequality, and this is because it disproportionately rewards certain people of a certain status or from certain geographical areas. Across the globe and within our society, we have unfair advantages. Becoming a rich family or living in a wealthy country can make your life is much easier than if you are born in a low-income country (Eliazar and Cohen 2014). Wealth is unequally distributed. According to the World Bank, there are still eight countries where more than 60% of the population lives below the poverty line (World Bank Open Data n.d.). Nevertheless, United Nations reports say that in 2021 nearly USD$2.15 billion in investment capital was directed to the tech startup sector in Africa (Akiwumi 2023). Even in our constantly evolving society, every year poverty kills millions of people around the world (Zhou and Liu 2022).

Many people in the last 50 years have tried to address these issues, the fight against poverty is not a new topic. In fact, we live in a post-humanitarian age. For decades, governmental and non-governmental humanitarian organizations have addressed these issues by flooding areas with aid in the most disadvantaged areas in the hope that this spark will ignite further social improvements (Sachs 2006). An approach that has been highly criticized since it creates dependencies, is not sustainable and, apart from a couple of cases, has not produced long-term effects (Moyo 2009; Easterly 2014). In fact, some more neutral views have pointed out that the issues are not related to giving or not giving aid in an inconsiderate way, but rather to how an individual government uses the available resources (Robinson and Acemoglu 2012).

From the failures of those top-to-bottom approaches, recent scholars have proposed bottom-up approaches to reduce poverty and create wealth. Those bottom-up approaches propose to relatively

© The Author(s), under exclusive license to Springer Nature Switzerland AG 2026

A. Crimi, *Innovate for Impact*, Sustainable Development Goals Series,
https://doi.org/10.1007/978-3-032-21563-5_1

ignore external aids, and to improve society starting from grassroots organizations (Hopkins 2011; Alemanno 2017), or by introducing companies that indirectly have to fix infrastructure or create jobs, improving the economy better than governmental policies (Christensen et al. 2019). Assuming that those companies act in their interest but still ethically and in the way they build the necessary infrastructures.

This chapter starts from those conclusions. Policymakers should take into account a more scientific approach to improving general issues, education and research, reducing loneliness introduced by new technology, and supporting young businesses (Goldin 2016). Those who are not policymakers should consider bottom-up approaches when their institutions and government do not support them by creating grassroots movements (Hopkins 2011; Alemanno 2017) or impactful startups (Christensen et al. 2019). This circumstance will be more pronounced in the Global South, from Africa, Southeast Asia, and Latin America, but valid elsewhere on our planet as well.

We often refer to "poverty" reduction as the ultimate goal. However, this is an abstract definition. Poverty is often relative, and not directly addressable. It is more the emerging behavior stemming from other issues, such as lack of education, poor productivity, or diseases in turn affecting education and productivity. If we fix one of those issues, indirectly we will fight poverty. It is more a fractal scenario than a straightforward way. Often, things do not improve or even worsen until there is a societal change, or an action with impact. This is easier said than done, and we need many innovations that do that. Lasting change is hard because problems are systemic. The reasons why an innovation does not spread or scale can be related to multiple factors. For example, a startup might have an innovative idea, but there is little feasibility or interest from the market (Feinleib 2012), or an activist might need a larger team. Beyond those organizational aspects, it will be beneficial to all readers to understand why certain things have been difficult to change so far, at least to be aware of what will be encountered when changing the world. Let us pause for a second and think about societal changes. We will come back to fighting poverty and the underlying causes later.

1.2 Activists, Start-Uppers, and Other Ordinary Heroes

In the 1970s, the international community started a large-scale initiative to end river blindness in West Africa. To eradicate black flies that were spreading the disease, helicopters would swoop above towns and spray larvicide. It was a logistical marvel, but it failed (Crump et al. 2001). The flies developed resistance, the chemicals harmed other wildlife, and the program did not empower local communities to maintain the fight. This is a classical case which is considered a failure. In practice, social improvements are not even starting due to clogged gears somewhere in the system. Those narratives have been repeating themselves in many places, at the point that people lost hope in change. There is now another narrative emerging, which is not written by aid or humanitarian agencies, but by grassroots activists, moral businesspeople, and involved academics who are bringing about change from the ground.

People choose to act for various reasons. Some entrepreneurs start businesses not to change the world, but likely out of a desire for independence. Although, starting a business in certain geographic regions could already be seen as very transformative (Bornstein 2007). Beyond the idea of social entrepreneurship (Kamaludin et al. 2024), just starting any business promotes wealth, since new ideas are incorporated into the social environment and new jobs are created (Christensen et al. 2019), assuming that the new entrepreneurs are acting ethically and sustainably. Christensen and colleagues (Christensen et al. 2019) more specifically coined the expression "prosperity paradox", where poverty is not reduced by aid and humanitarian donations, but rather by legitimate business opportunities which create jobs, indirectly wealth, and therefore addressing poverty issues.

Academics who aim to contribute to low-income countries often strive to bring about changes through education, research, and sustainable development initiatives should be aware of the aspects involved in cooperation. Indeed, it is even possible to encounter the expression *academic activism* (Davids and Waghid 2021). In these views, teaching is not just sharing knowledge, but ensuring that students are becoming aware of the world around them and the impact that their actions can have, a sort of educational leadership (Waghid 2020). Likewise, research and publishing can be oriented to matters of social issues, the relationship between a scientist and a journalist raising attention on pivotal topics for the Global South. For instance, increasing attention on the dynamics of poverty (Nogales and Oldiges 2024), diseases usually ignored in high-income countries (Frangoul et al. 2024), and more.

From the point of view of civil society, several tools are available. The least activists can do is raise awareness on a specific topic. Many people have launched campaigns and played a crucial role in driving social and political change. Across the globe, issues such as human rights, environmental sustainability, and access to education and healthcare have been largely advocated by non-governmental entities. For example, European and Indian laws have been shown to be affected by movements as an effect of grassroots actions on gender equality (Adhikari and Heller 2024), integration of immigrants (Alagna 2024), and food policies (Rana 2024). Awareness is nothing on its own; it is like the tiny spark in a dynamite fuse that does not reach the main tube. We need to act according to a strategy. We will discuss this later. Grassroots organizations can actually advance progress toward societal goals, especially at a local or subnational level (Flores and Samuel 2019; Qin 2023).

In the early 2000s, we started hearing the expression "social accountability", used to describe initiatives using new forms of civic engagement to promote reform (Maru 2010), especially in countries receiving foreign aid (Lyew et al. 2021). At a practical level, to be effective, a certain level of creativity is required, as simply distributing leaflets is not sufficient (Boyd and Mitchell 2013). In addition, there are novel tools such as mailing lists, social networks, and online petitions (Alemanno 2017). Lastly, there must be a shift in how the average people see activists and small active communities. We need to recognize that their importance in building the capacity to sustain social change efforts. Non-governmental organizations often conduct training programs, provide support to people in difficulties as women's counseling centers, and skill-building sessions to empower community members with the necessary knowledge and skills to address issues locally. Sometimes, they represent a breath of fresh air where people have lost trust in the government. Capacity building ensures long-term sustainability and strengthens grassroots movements (Smith et al. 2019). Not all heroes wear caps, and not all good comes from institutions.

Several step-by-step approaches for grassroots organizations have been proposed, and even frameworks exist. Some are related to community organizing and sustainability (Starhawk 2011; Brown 2007), others review direct action and activism strategies (Bond 2016; Boyd and Mitchell 2012; Kauffman 2017; Gibson 2017), and others offer practical guides for everyday activism (Shaw 1996; The Trapese Collective 2007; Loeb 2004). The possible steps to follow can be summarized in the diagram in Fig. 1.1.

Some of the steps mentioned to achieve a societal change require not being focused simply on an idea, but having a more holistic consideration, like focusing on aspects related to barriers to change, which we will discuss in the following sections. Regarding issues specific to education and the running of projects in low-income countries, we will dive into the second part of the book. In Chap. 4, after we have gone through many topics, I will come back to system thinking to provide a real case study using AI and health.

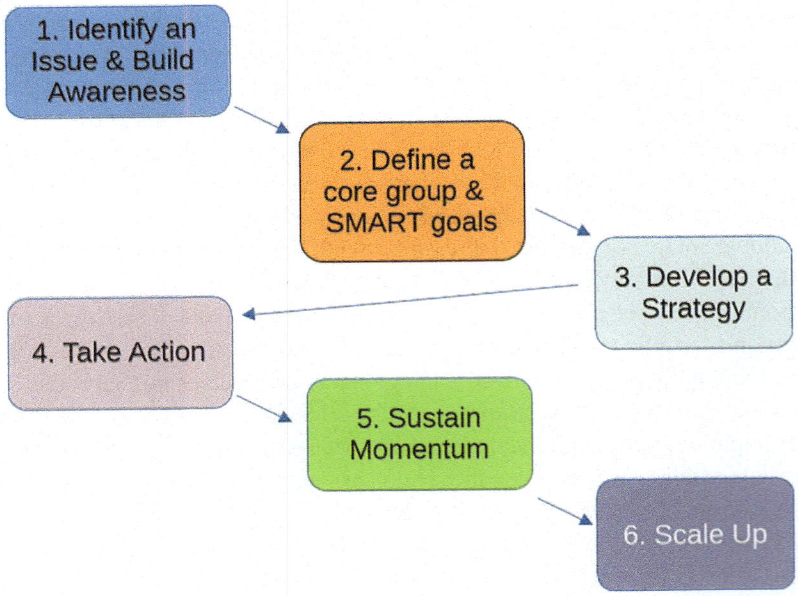

Fig. 1.1 The six major steps to follow by activists or organizations: (1) Connect with existing groups or gather like-minded people. Use narratives and storytelling to inspire action (Hopkins 2011). (2) A committed core team (5–10 people) is more effective than a loose crowd; also, clear roles are important. Use SMART goals (Specific, Measurable, Achievable, Relevant, and Time-bound). Will you focus on protests, policy, community projects, or cultural change? Bond (2016). (3) Strategy: Identify who has influence (allies, opponents, institutions), and where can pressure create the most change (Boyd and Mitchell 2012). (4) Take actions but start with low-risk steps: Petitions, teach-ins, or social media. Escalate strategically: Move to rallies, strikes, or civil disobedience if needed (Kauffman 2017). (5) Sustain Momentum by acknowledging progress to keep morale high, but also build long-term structures: Create cooperatives, local policies, or mutual aid networks (Hopkins 2011). (6) Scale Up: Network with other groups, train new leaders, institutionalize change into laws and policies (Gibson 2017)

1.3 What We Need to Know About System Thinking

Whether someone is an activist, an NGO, or a governmental policymaker, certain aspects related to performing a successful change are the same. Sometimes we need a broader view, sometimes we need to understand what the barriers to change are, sometimes we need to measure and evaluate whether the change is feasible.

A first starting point should be considering social issues or unmet needs in a holistic manner with what we can call *system thinking*. Conventional problem-solving frequently addresses problems in isolation. System thinking recognizes the interconnectedness of societal issues, and flips this approach (Stroh 2015). System thinking can be defined as a holistic approach that focuses on the way a system's parts interrelate and how systems work over time. A systems approach is essential to poverty reduction because it considers the interconnected factors that perpetuate poverty and develops comprehensive solutions that address these factors simultaneously, rather than blind donations to the poor.

Hence, applied to social change, system changes happen taking into account the interactions among several aspects of a social problem or an unmet need (such as poverty, opportunity gaps, sustainability, or education), similarly to inferring the proper movements of the lancets in a watch, the harmony of the gears inside the watch is needed. Or the famous figurative representation of experts of different fields, who are blindfolded and are touching an elephant. All touching a different part, and therefore

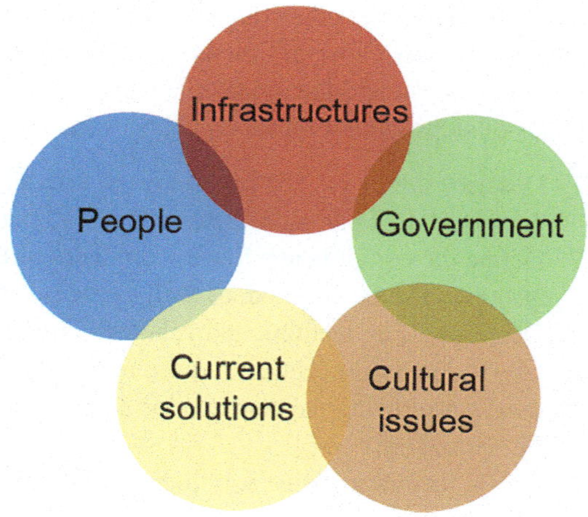

Fig. 1.2 Example of system thinking with different parts. The overlapping areas represent the interactions and relationships, and they are as important as the parts themselves

having a different idea of what an elephant is. One touching a foot, one touching the trunk, and one touching the tusk. Instead, an elephant is the combination of all these. In short, while focusing on solving an issue we should not focus only on a specific aspect we deem relevant, as other unforeseen barriers might appear from corners we did not know they existed. Building a school in a low-income neighborhood, for instance, may seem straightforward, but it might not address the underlying cause of poverty if it does not take into account issues such as transportation infrastructures or employment opportunities. Similarly, if we want to create a startup selling electric cars, we should not focus on the customers buying the car, but whether the government will subsidize enough the installation of the charging stations as well. Graphically, we can think of something like in the Fig. 1.2, where an NGO or a company would mostly focus on people/customers and current solutions/competitors, ignoring possible issues that can arise by other aspects of the "system", such as infrastructures that people should use or further regulations that can appear from the government. It is also important to bear in mind that the interactions (overlaps in the Venn diagram below) are as important as the elements.

Moreover, some parts of the system can be so convoluted as to represent a further subsystem with delicate interactions between its parts. An example of this is public administration, as shown in Fig. 1.3. Here, some hypothetical subparts are depicted, such as the city council, the district council, and the grants and funding committees.

More technically, the key aspects of any system are interconnectedness, emergence, and dynamics (Stroh 2015). There is an entire universe related to physics that studies systems, considering those elements, by using partial differential equations and producing relatively accurate predictions and simulations (Strogatz 2018). However, this is not a physics course, but rather a social change blueprint. In our context, we could define those key aspects as follows.

- Interconnectedness: The parts of a system are interconnected and changes in one part can affect the others.
- Emergence: Complex behaviors and patterns emerge from the interaction of simpler system components in ways that we cannot comprehend if we study the individual elements alone.
- Dynamics: A system changes over time, and its parts dynamically interact and can change as well.

Given those key aspects, a pivotal role is given to us by feedback loops (Stroh 2015). Parts interact with each other, understanding the cycles of cause and effect that can either amplify (positive feedback) or stabilize (negative feedback) changes within the system. This was originally used in environmental systems to evaluate changes in temperature. In our world of catalyzing social change, an example could be increasing education levels. In this case, there may be a positive feedback loop when better education raises earnings, allowing families to make larger investments in their kids' educations, and therefore boosting educational standards throughout generations. In the literature, we can also find a series of steps to address social changes, which can be summarized as follows.

1. Describe the issue: The first step is to give a clear formulation of the issue or problem that needs to be solved. It is pivotal to determine the underlying problems and symptoms that require attention.
2. Define the components: Each component of the system needs to be defined. The level of definition also needs to be clarified, as well as the people, procedures, materials, and data to be used.
3. Determine connections and relationships: The overlaps between parts, which in practice mean how the parts are related, require more in-depth understanding. It is probably beneficial to draw a diagram showing the connections and exchanges between the various parts (more advanced than a Venn diagram).
4. Create feedback loops: Any intervention in a system should be coupled with feedback loops. How changing one component impacts the system needs to be clarified, ideally by some key performance indicators (KPIs).
5. Examine behavior through time: The system should be tracked during a period of time to comprehend the dynamics, looking for patterns, trends, and behavioral changes.
6. Determine your leverage points: Using the feedback loops and the results from the short-term behavior tracking, adjustments and changes in the current plan should be made quickly when possible.
7. Create strategies and interventions: Given the previous steps, it should be possible to define a more general strategy to tackle the system.
8. Put into practice and monitor: It is now time to launch the strategy from a long-term perspective and to monitor it.

Following these steps should ensure a structured and comprehensive approach to effectively address social changes.

Furthermore, another interpretation of an actionable approach for system thinking considers social challenges as *"complex, large scale, and deep issues"* (Rayner and Bonnici 2021). *Complex* is what has already been discussed: Social issues are relationship-based. It is cumbersome to isolate the parts. *Large scale* refers to the fact that problems become bigger as efforts are made to solve them across larger geographies and populations. It might be possible for an NGO to solve the decay in a specific neighborhood, but can they solve it for all neighborhoods like that of the whole city? Or of the entire world? In this context, scale might refer to efficiency, where higher impacts can be reached by increasing throughput in a system. Or the size that will need to impact the system in a sustainable manner, and how the system will respond to such big changes. *Deep* refers to the related beliefs, values, and assumptions of the people who are the target of the social intervention. A system fails when it entrenches our beliefs and behaviors to the point that people cannot imagine or accept the change. Obviously, different cultures have different thresholds to those barriers to change, but it is common to all cultures. To be successful in a social change taking into account those elements, we have to, first of all, build a collective identity among the beneficiaries of the social intervention by fostering connections as broad as possible and ensure that primary actors are in the position of decision-making. An example of establishing connections can be Uptogether. They define themselves as "a systems change organization working to disrupt the status quo approach to ending poverty because it is not working". More specifically, they have shown that altering people's perceptions of themselves. From being alone to a sense of unity among them can have considerably more profound and long-lasting consequences than trying to modify individual behavior (Mcleod et al. n.d.). In practice, this is achieved by an online platform

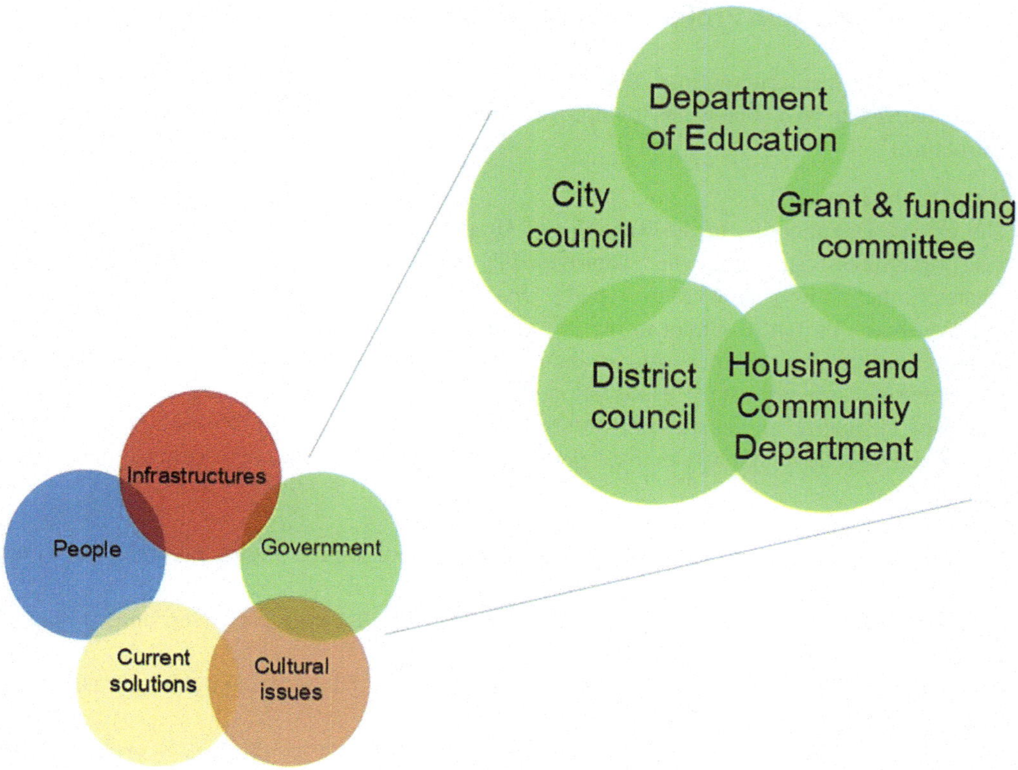

Fig. 1.3 Example of a subsystem within a larger system. Oversights in smaller subparts can undermine policies or interventions

aimed at attracting like-minded people, with the goal of keeping constant interaction for the process of change. Another organization focused on system thinking is the Democracy Fund. They are an independent and non-partisan private foundation that confronts deep-rooted challenges in American democracy. Their goal is to support the US political system in meeting its obligations to the American people while it experiences new difficulties (Democracy 2024).

In this chapter, we have introduced the system thinking approach, we have mentioned two examples and in the next section, we will go through a fictional practical example. The main point of this work is not just to inspire people to seek change, but to realize that it can easily fail if we do not take into account many aspects. Very often, people take a stance only on the day they vote for the elections, for then being totally ignored by their own institutions and feeling powerless. We should start recognizing that change is possible, and many social-purpose organizations around the world are proof of this. Instead of feeling a sense of power only on election day (if not even that), people can organize themselves into civil society groups or interact with less formal entities such as NGOs. Rather than losing hope and remaining paralyzed, we can choose to learn from the organizations that are doing it right, even in small ways. We have to take a more holistic view, asking ourselves which are parts of the system which can indirectly undermine our plans. We can start to foster new practices and approaches that distribute agency to people closest to these challenges, opening up new possibilities as we enter an era demanding radical transitions to new ways of organizing our societies and economies. For example, using digital technologies to enhance innovation and reduce inequalities (Vărzaru and Bocean 2024). System thinking can help in this, and the next section is about a fictional, detailed example.

1.4 Boost-Education Project. Fictional Example of System Thinking

In this section, we can reiterate the steps advised to follow (Stroh 2015), with a fictional practical example given by an NGO that wants to improve education in a neighborhood with poor transportation infrastructure.

1. Describe the Issue
   The city of Dreamopolis in the Republic of Utopia is densely populated, yet has very limited transportation infrastructure, which is provided by infrequent and poorly funded bus services. This creates further complications to everybody. On one side, we have people who cannot afford a car to leave their children to school in person; on the other side, those who can afford a car use it, create scenarios where there is one-car-one-person, generating further traffic jams. In any case, the transportation issue ultimately results in low attendance rates, declining educational outcomes, and increased inequality among students who rely on public transportation to commute to school. Let us proceed with the previously defined steps identifying components and relationship as a holistic system.
2. Define the Components
   (i) People: Students, parents, education professionals, school administrators, bus drivers, and municipal authorities.
   (ii) Procedures: School schedules, bus schedules, funding allocation processes, and city planning meetings.
   (iii) Materials: The public spaces of the city, school buses, bus stops, and educational materials (books, digital resources).
   (iv) Data: Bus schedules, travel times, attendance records for the pupils, grades over time for the pupils, and city funding reports.
3. Determine Connections and Relationships:
   (i) Between the Students and the School. More precisely, how the pupils' attendance affects educational outcomes.
   (ii) Between the Parents and the School. More precisely, how the parents can influence student engagement and attendance with their transportation choices.
   (iii) Between School and Municipal Authority. More precisely, how the school interacts with the municipality for funding and feedback, and whether the school informs about attendance and performance the municipal authority.
   (iv) Between the Bus Drivers and Students. More precisely, whether the bus drivers are aware of how the bus services directly impact student attendance.
   Those elements are better visualized in a block diagram, as in Fig. 1.4. In practice, a block diagram is preferable to a Venn diagram when there are several relationships.
4. Create Feedback Loops (i) Attendance-Performance Loop. We expect that increased attendance leads to better performance, which in turn encourages higher attendance.
   (ii) Funding-Quality Loop: Improved bus services require more funding, which results in better transportation quality and higher attendance, justifying further funding. This might also reduce the private cars as a means of transportation and the related traffic jams, and in turn, more users for public buses.
5. KPIs:
   - Student academic performance
   - Student attendance rates
   - Bus punctuality and reliability
   - Funding allocation amounts

6. Examine Behavior Through Time:
   Initial Phase (Months 1–3): In this phase, we monitor the current attendance rates and punctuality of buses. We focus on identifying the initial patterns.
   Mid-Term Phase (Months 4–9): Here, we track changes in academic performance and further changes in attendance rates from the initial situation through the intervention carried out.
   Long-Term Phase (Months 10–12): Then, we assess the overall trends and sustained behavioral changes.
7. Determine Your Leverage Points (i) Bus Scheduling: Bus schedules need to be aligned as closely as possible with the school start and end times, taking into consideration worst-case scenarios given by traffic jams. (ii) Funding Allocation: There is a need to advocate for reallocating city funds to improve bus services, for example, add one more bus run to compensate for delays or to match more school timetables.
   (iii) Parental Engagement: The program involves parents in their children's education and transportation planning.
   (iv) Data Utilization: The pupils' attendance and performance need to be monitored continually to refine transportation and educational strategies.
8. Create Strategies and Interventions
   (i) Improved Bus Schedules: We need to coordinate with schools to ensure buses run at optimal times.
   (ii) Funding Campaigns: There is a need for initiatives to secure additional funding from the city and private donors.
   (iii) Parental Outreach: Develop programs to engage parents, such as workshops and volunteer opportunities.
   (iv) Data-Driven Decision-Making: Establish a data monitoring system to continuously assess and adjust strategies based on KPIs.
9. Put into Practice and Monitor
   (i) Launch Improved Bus Services: The new bus schedule is launched and monitored for punctuality and reliability.
   (ii) Monitor KPIs: We need to regularly review attendance, performance, and transportation data to identify trends and areas for improvement. (iii) Adjust Strategies: We use feedback from monitoring to make necessary adjustments, ensuring the system remains responsive and effective.

With those steps, the intervention to increase the school attendance and performance is achieved by indirectly improving the transportation and taking into consideration the connected actors, such as the municipal authority. This is indeed a fictional example, which nevertheless highlights the typical scenarios that can be encountered and what the steps are to be followed, addressing only the parents to encourage better attendance, or talking only to the bus driver would not have produced effective results. The system or the changes we want to apply are as weak as the weakest part. For example, the policy will fail even if parents and bus drivers are willing to do their part, but the municipality does not take action to reallocate some funds to increase the number of buses. Many interventions and pilot studies fail due to similar circumstances.

1.5 Why Change Is so Hard, Internal Barriers

The reason why changing behavior, economy, or culture is often discussed is because change is hard. It is difficult to identify triggers or causes and it is hard to implement alternative policies that are effective or sustainable. Sometimes, it is nothing related to having an innovative idea, funding, or an established brand. Many people propose useful innovations, but they fail for reasons like the lack of

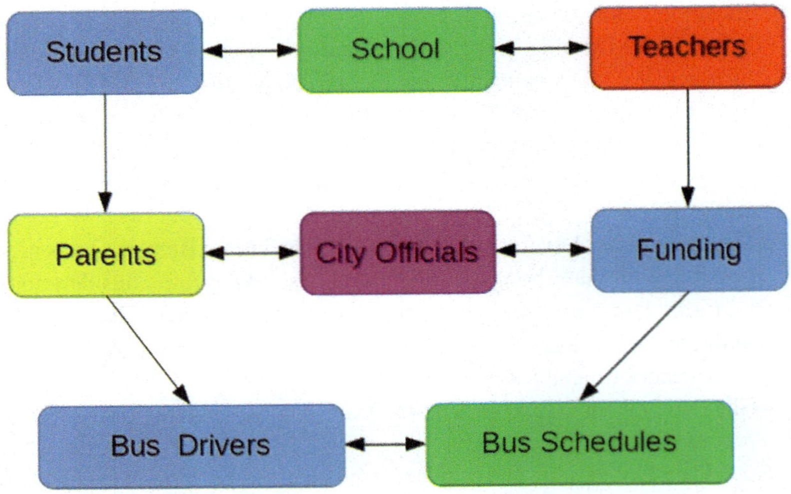

Fig. 1.4 Example of system thinking with different parts

system thinking we discussed previously and other barriers. In the previous sections, we discussed the importance of going deeper, dealing with fundamental beliefs like at the bottom of an iceberg, or taking into consideration all actors in a system, where each of them can have different barriers. We now discuss further how to consider those barriers. We could summarize barriers to change into two major categories. Internal and external circumstances. The external factors are discussed later in this book, when we talk about "interest groups". The internal circumstances can be related to human nature. The analysis of this draws on the work of Sigmund Freud up to contemporary behavioral analysis (Cautilli and Santilli-Connor 2000). In short, the human brain (and nature) is conservative in the energy it spends. It is easier to maintain a habit that has been acquired and it requires a lot of effort to change it voluntarily, even if there are clear advantages. People often rely on existing belief systems to make sense of the world. Many studies in cognitive psychology point out that individuals tend to display confirmation bias, and filter any information or behavior through the lenses that support pre-existing views rather than challenge them (Nickerson 1998). Those limiting beliefs are generally reinforced by social identity and group dynamics. In some contexts, adopting radical changes might be related to undermining cultural, family, national, or professional belonging.

In practice, national or local policies can improve or worsen the circumstances. There are several known examples of this. For example, regarding a successful case can be found in Japan's history. Before the Second World War, Japan's industrial and educational culture was highly hierarchical with limited openness. After the war, a cultural shift related to the influence of the USA led to reforms that reshaped education, land ownership, and industrial policy for the better (Johnson 1925). Knowledge diffusion and collective learning became highly adopted in Japanese culture in general, even forging the term "kaizen", which is now copied by some western cultures. In contrast, for the past 20 years in the USA, despite overwhelming scientific evidence, parts of society have resisted adopting sustainable behaviors due to confirmation bias and lobbying pressures (Dunlap and McCright 2011). Progressive policies are often blocked or reversed (Stokes 2020). This shows how deep beliefs, lobbying, and political polarization can prevent a society from turning knowledge into adaptive change (Klein and Thompson 2025).

As for other hypothetical examples, we can imagine that an educational system based on conformity and memorization can inadvertently inhibit critical thinking and creativity, causing group learning to slow down (Stiglitz and Greenwald 2014). As we said, the opposite is also unfortunately true. Societies that encourage problem-solving, creativity, and critical thinking prepare people to revise their beliefs in

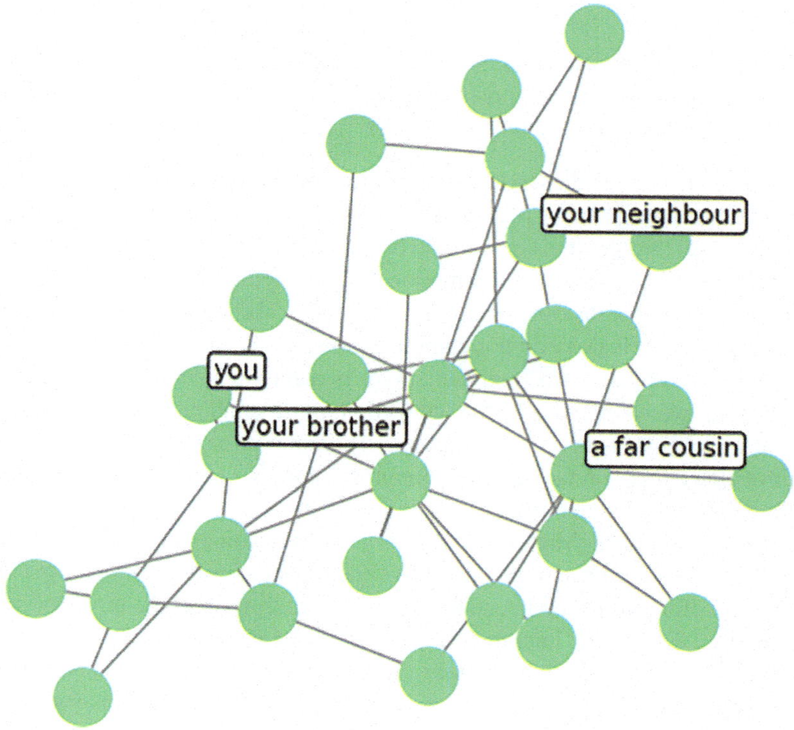

Fig. 1.5 A randomly drawn network where each node is a person, and edges are relationships that allow the exchange or block of ideas

light of new evidence. This is true for policies related to education, but also within other contexts, such as research and development and startup creation. This huge responsibility is entrusted to governments or institutions and we have to trust that they will make the best decision. Alternatively, civil society can start from the bottom to address some issues. From a policymaker perspective, there has been intensive analysis, for example, on how to promote healthy behaviors (Firestone et al. 2017) or even introduce renewable energy (Dietz 2023).

Many behaviors spread through social contacts, like epidemics; a person can influence another one or his/her neighborhood. Complex networks are substantially graphs, and in contagion models, we use graphs where each person is a node and the edges are our relationships or exchanges. Ideas and rumors contagion can be modeled by random walks (Iacopini et al. 2018) or differential equations (Brockmann and Helbing 2013), allowing interactions across the nodes/people as in Fig. 1.5.

More formally, a society can be defined by a graph/network $G = (V, E)$, with:

- V: the set of nodes (individuals, like you, your cousin, and your neighbor.)
- E: the set of edges (connections between individuals).

Each node may adopt an idea based on certain interaction rules, depending on the model. If we take the approach that behavioral adoption by social proof (reinforcement from the neighborhood) (Centola and Macy 2007; Centola 2010), a node adopts an idea only if the fraction of its neighbors who have adopted it exceeds a threshold T.

$$\frac{m_i}{k_i} \geq T,$$

where

- m_i: number of neighbors of node i who have adopted
- k_i: total number of neighbors of node i
- T: adoption threshold (e.g., $T = 0.5$).

Indeed, some studies have studied either through simulations (Centola and Macy 2007) or validation on human data given by relationship traceable with social media (Centola 2010) how ideas are spread or blocked through this type of network. It has been observed that in studies using complex networks, obstacles to change or idea adoption fall into four groups: excitement, legitimacy, credibility, and coordination. For those not familiar with dynamical complex systems, I would like to reassure the reader that these conclusions do not come from magic or randomness. We say something is "complicated" when it has many parts, and something is complex when the many parts that there is an emerging behavior which emerges by the interaction of the small parts, including social and economic behavior (Farmer 2024). This is not a textbook on complex dynamical systems. Therefore, I leave the reader to investigate more on the reported references; here, we focus more on the results, explaining what those four emerging behaviors are:

Coordination highlights the fact that some innovations, such as Facebook or WhatsApp, make sense when a large number of people utilize them concurrently. Changes must be observed being used by others before they may persuade skeptics to accept them; the more individuals who engage with the changes, the better. Gaining trust through social proof is the foundation of credibility, as people are typically hesitant to embrace new ideas unless they observe others using them successfully. Before receiving a vaccination, we wait to find out if it has bizarre adverse effects.

Social acceptance is another factor that determines legitimacy; it verifies that a behavior, such as wearing a certain way or acting in a particular way, complies with cultural standards. Excitement emphasizes that something seen on social media must also resonate in emotional contexts. In order to overcome obstacles and gain acceptance, social proof of an innovation or social aspect is often necessary. People are not effectively influenced to make this kind of social change by news and scientific studies about the environment and the need for solar panels; yet, if you see that all of your neighbors have solar panels installed on their roofs, you will buy one right away. Unfortunately, social evidence holds greater weight than rational arguments and scientific revelations. Expecting social exclusion anxiety (informally called "fear of missing out") appears to help: If someone sees a neighbor with a solar panel, he/she might also want it to not feel inferior to him/her; peer pressure might be more effective than scientific alarming news distribution. Media and social networks can take advantage of this fear by highlighting people or groups that have already adopted eco-friendly technologies. This approach can create a sense of urgency and competition, causing people to make changes more quickly to avoid being left behind. Those effects might not even be planned, as unfortunately, the goal of social media and the press is often simply to maximize engagement regardless of the content. Studies show that social influence is a significant predictor of the adoption of green technology, as people are motivated by the desire to conform to social norms and improve their social status (Bollinger and Gillingham 2012). Moreover, in our society we have people who are more connected to other people than others. In graph theory, we call "degree", the number of edges incident to a specific node. Therefore, a politician, an influencer, or person with many social contacts can be seen as a hub to a high degree, as shown in Fig. 1.6, hub nodes have an impact on social proof as we can imagine.

Beyond social proof and fear of missing out, the adoption of a new, better behavior for society can be addressed by policies complemented by *social marketing*. The idea of social marketing is to integrate marketing concepts with social policies to influence behaviors that benefit individuals and communities for the greater social good (Domegan 2021). For example, it can be used to promote more COVID-19 or HIV testing, or to make health products and services appealing and affordable

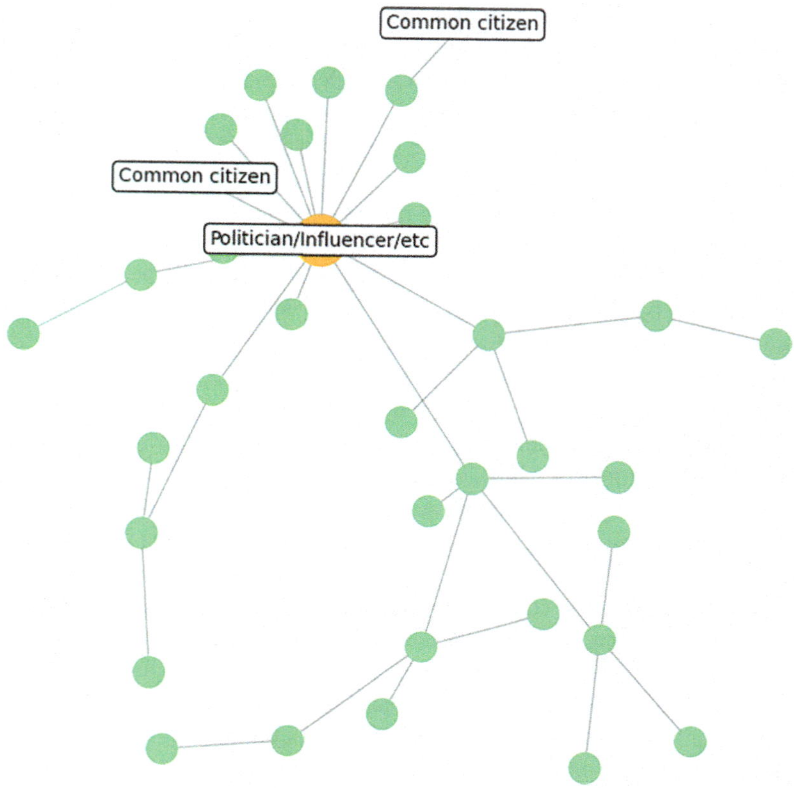

Fig. 1.6 A graph with a highlighted node with high degree. This node represents a hub connecting different other nodes which can be grouped as a cluster

to both health care providers and consumers. The goal is not profit, but improvement of health status (Firestone et al. 2017).

In summary, modeling behavior with complex networks is an entire field of study Gribbin (2005), Estrada (2012), and further discussion of this is beyond the scope of this book. Here, we highlight the methodology and main aspects that have been investigated with complex networks that can represent barriers to changes, and we recommend taking into account social proof as a more effective element than other approaches based on science communication (Dietz 2023).

1.6 25% Is All You Need

Even though for some societal changes coordination of many individuals is required, changes rarely begin with the majority. History is full of solitary outsiders taking the first steps, from Rosa Parks to Martin Luther King, catalyzing major social transformations. Yet, in daily life we tend to agree that large-scale change requires broad consensus. Nevertheless, recent research in social dynamics suggests that transformation can occur once a committed minority reaches a certain threshold, which is surprisingly as low as 25% of a population (Xie et al. 2011; Centola et al. 2018). This challenges relatively the traditional models of social proof and coordination, which we previously discussed, leading to a reasonable trade-off to adopt new behaviors: we do not need outstanding heroes, nor to convince entire populations; a quarter of it will suffice. When approximately a quarter of one's social network adopts a new behavior, people begin to shift their own behavior as well, even in the face of resistance or social risk.

The idea that relatively small but committed agents can drive widespread change is echoed in other domains of research. The seminal Granovetter threshold model of collective behavior laid the foundations for understanding how individual decisions aggregate into collective outcomes (Granovetter 1978). His work showed that even when most people are reluctant to act, a minority with low thresholds for action can initiate a cascade that tips the system. More recently, other studies confirmed the 25% tipping point through computational modeling and social network simulations. They showed that once a critical mass of activists reaches roughly one-quarter of a population, rapid spread of new norms becomes not only possible but likely (Xie et al. 2011; Centola et al. 2018). Again, we can imagine a society or a country like a network living in a specific state; when enough nodes of this network change, we reach a sort of criticality, and the whole network starts to change its state, or, in simpler words, a change has been adopted sufficiently by the society.

In this network-like world, it is not only important how many people support a new norm, but how they are connected. In tightly clustered networks with high reinforcement, social norms are more resilient. Yet, once a critical minority penetrates diverse clusters, the chances of widespread diffusion increase dramatically (Watts 2002).

At the same time, the path to large-scale change is often blocked by psychological inertia. Sometimes we encounter the so-called "bystander effect", where individuals avoid intervening in a situation when others are present, each assuming someone else will take responsibility (Darley and Latané 1968). This has been observed in emergency situations, but also in civic protests. It highlights a cruel paradox: while after passing the 25% threshold a change can be considered ongoing, the more people witness this, the less likely any one person is to act. People might think that the strike or the riot has already been successful. Therefore, why should they risk it on their own? A small group of activists can play a vital role in this situation and should not be discouraged by an apparent group of people not engaging with them. Social movements that counteract the bystander effect by individual appeals, decentralized leadership, or collective accountability are often the ones that reach the tipping point. The lesson is not to be deterred by the presence of spectators or to wait for universal agreement. Social change does not need an entire society. It just needs a sufficient amount of active people, in the right places, to join together. According to the evidence, this number may be as low as one in four people.

1.7 Culture Helps or Complicates Change

Sometimes, resistance to change is not just related to social proof, the presence of a large network of users, it is also related to culture. Or better, depending on the culture, change might require more or less work. Even personal aspects, whether a person prefers to work alone or in a team, are related to culture. This also has an impact on how suspicious or open-minded a person might be toward something new. We generally refer to "culture" as the set of fundamental ideas, customs, and social behavior of a particular group of people or society. Generally, we simplify this "group of people" to the country where they live. Geert Hofstede was a Dutch psychologist who revolutionized how we understand cultures while working at IBM. He identified six key dimensions that shape national values and how we work, think, and innovate (Hofstede 1984). One of the most important dimensions is individualism versus collectivism. Individual cultures like the US or Northern Europe, or the UK people value independence, personal achievement, and new ideas, and this often fuels innovation. In collective cultures—like many parts of Asia, Africa, and Southern Europe—people prioritize group harmony and traditional loyalty. This is great for social bonds, but sometimes it slows down changes and entrepreneurship. Obviously, these are trends perceived at the population level; they do not represent all citizens of a country, who surely have their own unique characters, neither they should be used for profiling or stereotyping people.

Nevertheless, the scores of the cultural dimensions are generally reported at the country level, though in large territories where different regions might have had independent and heterogeneous histories, considering sub-regions might be more appropriate. For example, Italy can be further subdivided into North and South. In southern Italy, for example, tight family relationships and community structures foster strong support, but may resist disruptive ideas (Piumatti et al. 2016). Here, startups and innovation might not have an easy life, since they are generally made by people breaking norms. This pinpoints the fact that even within a country, you can have such a huge difference, and even something valuable, such as strong social bonds, could be limiting innovation.

This has been investigated in other contexts, as "a social trap" (see next chapter), where kin-based societies may linger, inhibiting the transition to a market economy. For example, once a member of a kin group is in a managerial position with power to recruit and promote, the tendency will be to hire and promote people of his/her kin blocking the labor market, as this will be more nepotism than the most productive decision. A moral hazard that, if expanded to the entire society, could limit development and even lead the entire society to a cycle of poverty or economic stagnation (Hoff and Sen 2006; Bowles et al. 2011). The social bond that might have helped a society when it was mostly tribal or kin-based might block further advancement to the next stage of a society where more talent exchange is required.

Combining the ideas together, we could say that the internal barriers to change are related to social proofs, credibility, and coordination. Furthermore, these elements are also influenced by cultural elements that increase or decrease those barriers. Yet, we have considered so far factors that are internal to a group of people or culture, but often changes are reinforced from the top as policies or regulations.

1.8 Death by Regulation, External Barriers

Sometimes, it is surprising that we live in a world with artificial intelligence everywhere, quantum computing, vertical take-off cars, and still some aspects of our lives are based on some inefficient mechanism like filing multiple times reports for medical purposes, or that a series of tormented documents have to be presented to start a specific business. Especially when those paths often differ from country to country to considerable extent without any apparent reason. In theory, regulatory systems exist because a government or an institution introduced a mechanism to protect citizens at some point. However, sometimes those mechanisms appear as the results of specific groups of interest that lobby to some degree with institutions, and they are more a matter of bureaucracy than citizen security. These are the external barriers to innovation and change that we mentioned earlier. In fact, there have been reported cases of startups in Russia and other countries which were experiencing several serious issues as they disrupted some status quo related to some institutions (Bayrasli 2015), or criminal organizations masked by legitimate businesses operating intertwined with local politicians, a system mostly observed in Latin America and Africa, but also present in Italy, Slovakia, and Sweden (Mehlum et al. 2003). While these are extreme cases, and they should not be generalized to entire countries or industries, lobbying is the process by which companies (and other interested groups) try to influence government decisions. Unfortunately, it is more common than people think, and very often this results in limiting innovation rather than protecting citizens (Drutman 2015).

Nevertheless, recent history is made of examples of startups that had to disrupt not only an industry but also the regulatory system and lobbying around their area of operation. This did not happen overnight, and in some cases, expert lobbyists were hired by the startup itself. The iconic example of this is the Uber company. Without patronizing Uber, which, as many other companies in some cases, might have acted in debatable manners, it provides us a clear example. Uber famously involved Bradley Tusk, a former adviser to politicians such as Michael Bloomberg (Tusk 2018). The taxi industry has historically been intertwined with local policies, and proposing a novel service that disrupts this ecosystem did not create a few difficulties that required serious networking and social engineering (Burfield and Harrison 2018). However, this worked in the US and has been scaled in many countries but not all over the world. In Italy, for instance, the local legal system has been largely in favor of the taxi industry. More specifically, Uber drivers do not confirm the provisions of Law 21 of January 15, 1992, and changing this will require a large legal maneuver that even Uber is not able to carry out. Especially, since taxi driving licenses are costly to obtain and they are paid to the state. If there are Uber drivers in Italy, most likely they are regular taxi drivers using the mobile app (Urbinati et al. 2018). In cynical terms: the lobby of the taxi drivers is stronger than the lobby created by Uber.

In general, the lobbying system is given by the following interdependencies: Lawmakers are often related to political units, which depend on donors to run campaigns mostly. Those are often private entities, and it is perfectly legal for them to donate large sums to political units. In turn, those private entities provide financial or otherwise support those lawmakers, helping them advance their respective agendas and gain more power. In successful cases, when the time comes, those private-sector groups would expect to be consulted when new rules affecting their interest come up for discussion; otherwise, in the future, they will not fund the campaigns. It is practically common that private entities (such as large companies or powerful individuals) have therefore some leverage on political decisions (Burfield and Harrison 2018), the renewable energy industry versus established sectors as oil and other form of energy is another example in the US (Stokes 2020; Narum 1992), but also in South Africa's coal lobby resisting a green transition (Baker et al. 2014), or even just big tech companies lobbying for more loose privacy laws for their websites and services (Tarrant and Cowen 2022).

Generally, startups, while defining their business plan, list other companies as competitors. Although this is important, it is not enough. One critical aspect to be taken into account when a social change or startup is launched is to ask "Does someone lose power or make less money because of this solution?" Organizations or startups should identify a private institution, consortium, or individual that would be damaged if our ideas are successful, and those are not necessarily a direct competitor. This is as critical as deploying our idea. This will define a power-map. We need to identify all players and not only our ideal customer persona (Burfield and Harrison 2018). Fair enough, a group of individuals, for example, minority activists, can also mobilize networking and even lobbying (Alemanno 2017). Taking advantage of the same mechanism. Indeed, even if lobbying has always been associated with a negative connotation, the social engineering behavior related to it can be used for a greater good by civil society, social entrepreneurs, and even a small group of private citizens in favor of a more sustainable future, for promoting the rights of a minority or bridging the divide between classes. This can indeed be called "lobbying for change" (Alemanno 2017). If the social welfare of the state is sub-optimal, lobbying for change can help eliminate regulations that hinder innovation and impede the fight against poverty.

In summary, a group of activists, a startup, or an NGO cannot ignore that we live in a larger world. Instead of improving individual parts, we need to understand how doctors, hospitals, finances, and even the communities they serve all interact and influence each other. This approach highlights the ripple effects of decisions. For instance, adding more doctors might seem helpful, but if the system lacks sufficient medicine, it could create a bottleneck. In summary, we really need to focus on the aforementioned system thinking (World Health Organization 2007). Nevertheless, lobbying is not always required; sometimes, following the required certification will suffice.

1.9 Should We Really Change?

So far, we have considered the underlying causes and how we could address them. However, a very important question should also be whether our change is really needed or feasible. If we consider an activist, a startup company, or an institutional officer (either an academic or a policymaker), the attitude and the frame of reference are different, although they share some similarities.

An activist is generally moved by the observation that there is a lack of equity or that a minority does not have the same rights as other groups, and therefore there is a need for action. A company needs to evaluate the product-market fit. That is, if what they want to sell is really wanted by people. An academic or a policymaker starts by worrying statistics about a topic and wants to propose a better solution. In all these cases, apart from the constraints from the systems, we need to prove that our solution with the given costs provides benefits; otherwise, it is better off doing nothing. To give a hypothetical example, we know that prostate cancer can be debilitating, leading to reduced days of work and life in a country. This means fewer days of healthy living for the affected people, less productivity for a country, and also a greater financial burden on the health sector. We have a novel tool which can detect prostate cancer earlier, but it is invasive, as it can introduce additional health complications; plus, screening every year for the all-male population of a country has a higher cost than dealing with the consequences of prostate cancer for the same population. In summary, even if the change is attractive, it might be better if we leave things as they are. We need to quantify and analyze the costs and benefits to make a decision.

Cost-benefit analysis (CBA) is a methodical technique that estimates all costs and benefits related to a certain project or decision to assess the advantages and disadvantages of various options (Hansson 2013). It entails putting a monetary value on the costs and positive effects (benefits) in order to assess if the investment is justified, if the benefits exceed the costs. This method compares net benefits, which are determined by deducting the total expenses from total benefits, to assist decision-makers in determining the relative economic viability of various options. In order to account for the time value of money, the analysis usually entails discounting future costs and benefits to current values. In addition, sensitivity analysis is frequently performed to ensure the resilience of the decision-making process by adjusting for uncertainties and fluctuations in estimated values. This is, in some sense, a formal view of the feedback in the system thinking described previously. Sensitivity analysis can be used to identify how much variation in the input values for a given variable impacts the results. In practice, we look at whether removing one component in our strategy or policy affects the entire system change or not. In health economics, outcomes are typically measured in natural units, such as life years gained, cases of disease prevented, or improvements in health status. In addition, key metrics are used in the financial world. We often talk about *return of investment* (ROI), which is calculated by subtracting the initial cost of the investment from its final value divided by the initial cost of the investment. Nevertheless, in health-economy and similar field it is preferred to look at the incremental cost-effectiveness ratio (ICER) (Marseille et al. 2014). The ICER represents the difference in costs divided by the difference in health effects between two or more interventions; this comparison can also include the comparison to an active policy, which could be the currently used or no action at all. More practically, an ICER is defined by the difference in cost between two possible interventions, divided by the difference in their effect. This can be defined by the following formula:

$$\mathrm{ICER} = \frac{\Delta\mathrm{Cost}}{\Delta\mathrm{Effectiveness}} = \frac{C_1 - C_0}{E_1 - E_0}, \tag{1.1}$$

where C_1 and C_0 are the costs of the new and standard interventions, respectively, and E_1 and E_0 are their respective effectiveness.

There are QALY and DALY associated to all known diseases. To give an example. The disability weight for active tuberculosis, which reflects the severity of health loss, is often referred to as around 0.333, and uncomplicated malaria, which can be treated in a couple of weeks, between 0.01 and 0.05 (Diel and Lampenius 2014). Beyond the wealth of an individual person, this can refer at the population level to the overall incidence, and therefore the loss of productivity of a country if no preventive policy is taken.

Regarding costs, ICER applies a common set of thresholds for all assessments, including those for treatments of ultrarare disorders, to ensure that a uniform range is used. Different thresholds are often used in cost-effectiveness analysis to determine whether an intervention is considered cost-effective. These thresholds represent the willingness to pay for each additional quality-adjusted life year (QALY) gained, or reduced disability-adjusted life year (DALY). For example, a common threshold range is 100,000–150,000 USD per QALY (Schwarzer et al. 2015). However, despite general recommendations, academic health economists and policymakers continue to disagree about whether or how to quantify and incorporate these values into cost-effectiveness analyses, despite some recommendations to adopt different cost-effectiveness thresholds for various treatments and/or conditions (Schaffer et al. 2016; Vanness et al. 2021).

Analyzing various treatments according to their incremental cost-effectiveness ratio and comparing them with different thresholds to determine cost-effectiveness is the cost-effectiveness analysis process of ICER results (Marseille et al. 2014). Looking at Fig. 1.7, we can see the axis representing costs and outcomes (e.g., DALY or QALY). If we consider again hypothetical interventions to reduce prostate cancer. At the intersection of the axis, we can have the current policy to randomly test all males who come to a clinic with some suspicious symptoms. We can have an alternative "terrible solution" as performing a biopsy for all males in a country older than 40 years. This could be considered a terrible solution because the cost of all biopsies could be accessible and histological exams accurate, but it

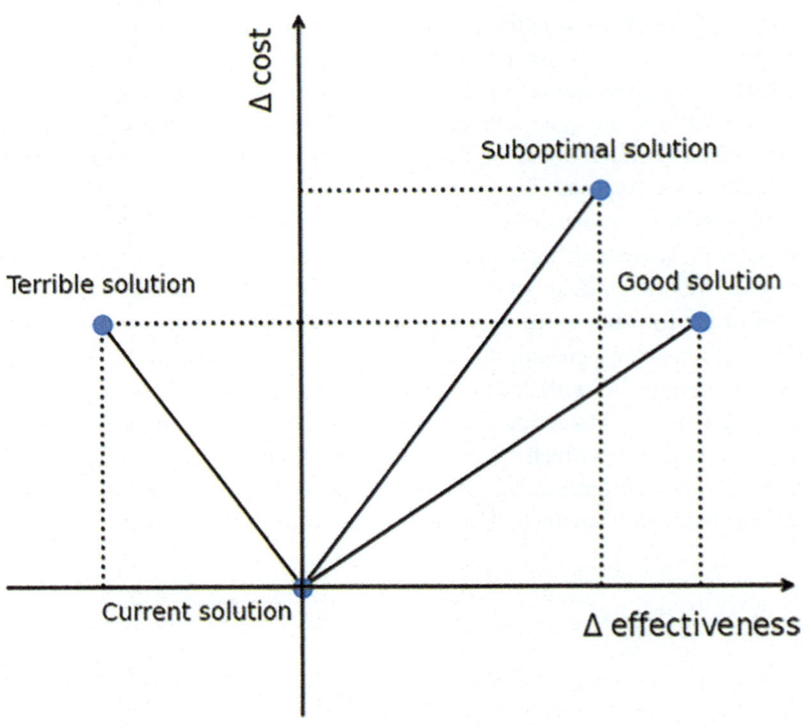

Fig. 1.7 In this hypothetical example, we consider interventions to reduce prostate cancer. We have here a solution that not only is more expensive than the current one but also introduces some harms for health (terrible solution); then we have a solution which introduces some health benefits but costs (suboptimal solution), and a final solution with even more health benefits and cheaper (the so-called "good solution")

will introduce further complications in the subjects tested, which will decrease the value of the policy. And a good-value alternative solution is given by a PCR/CRISPR exam of all males beyond 40 years. This solution will be a bit more expensive than the current one, but catching more cases at risk will increase their lifespan.

Alternative metrics include the Benefit-Cost Ratio (BCR). BCR is another important metric and is defined as the ratio of the present value of benefits to the present value of costs.

$$\mathrm{BCR} = \frac{\sum \frac{B_t}{(1+r)^t}}{\sum \frac{C_t}{(1+r)^t}}, \tag{1.2}$$

where B_t and C_t are the benefits and costs in year t, and r is the discount rate. A BCR greater than 1 indicates that the benefits exceed the costs.

In conclusion, cost-benefit and cost-effectiveness analyses, which employ ICER, provide systematic frameworks that allow the evaluation of the economic viability and impact of projects. These methods consider not only the monetary costs and benefits but also the wider impacts on productivity and health, as evidenced by the assessment of QALYs and DALYs. Those analytical calculations can be employed by activists, entrepreneurs, academics, and lawmakers to evaluate that their strategies are beneficial and rational. This will help them make well-informed judgments that strike a balance between costs and observable good results.

1.10 Multidimensional Definition of Impact

In pursuit of a better world, well-intentioned actions are not enough. The same should be said for ideology and pre-existing power dictating policies. We previously introduced concepts such as DALY and QALY, which are specific for epidemiology and not necessarily applicable to all cases to show impact (Global Impact Investing Network (GIIN) 2023). When we talk about impact, we refer to a significant, positive change that addresses a root cause of a problem, rather than simply alleviating its symptoms, or claiming to have solved the problem without key performance indicators. This is more critical today, as we deal with changes in multidimensional contexts. A technology that increases agricultural yield (economic value) but depletes local water sources (ecological damage) has mixed impact. Imagine that we want to launch an educational app for children, to improve their school attendance, and costs 1 USD. If it has millions of downloads, it might be considered a financial success. But imagine also that it does not improve learning and school outcomes, or even creates attention deficit disorders; this will redefine the financial success as a negligible impact, and therefore the whole project will be considered non-impactful.

In view of having a multifaceted definition of impact, with some aspects more relevant than others, or considered sequentially, we can consider key dimensions such as scale, significance, sustainability, and equity. In more detail, those dimensions can be defined as:

- Scale: How many people or hectares of ecosystem are affected?
- Significance: How profound is the change in each life or system? Does it serve a small minority for a not-so-relevant aspect? Or is it a fundamental improvement in well-being?
- Sustainability: How long can the change last? What about its self-sustainability?

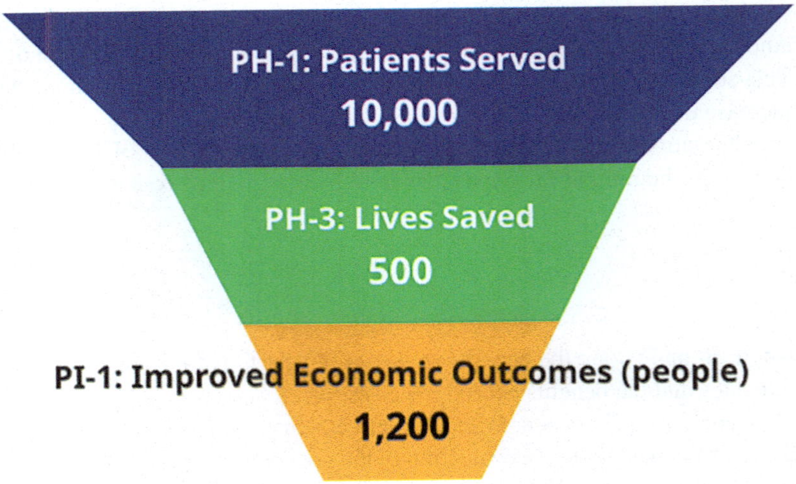

Fig. 1.8 A simplistic theory of change diagram represented as a funnel diagram

- Equity: Who benefits from it? Does the intervention reduce existing inequalities or risk exacerbating them by primarily helping those already better off?

The field of impact management has developed sophisticated frameworks to guide this process, ICER results are only focused on cost and effectiveness, and there are more comprehensive systems. For example, the IRIS+ system is a set of tools and guidance that translate impact intentions into measurable results. The Global Impact Investing Network (GIIN) has proposed it in 2019 (Global Impact Investing Network (GIIN) 2023), to provide a curated set of standardized, comparable core metrics sets to address specific social and environmental challenges, from "Climate Change Mitigation" to "Access to Quality Education". For example, a health-focused social enterprise would not just track "patients served"; using IRIS+, it could measure:

- PH-1: Number of people provided with health services
- PH-3: Number of lives saved (for specific interventions like malaria prevention)
- PI-1: Number of individuals whose economic outcomes improved (e.g., due to fewer sick days)

Those are some of the standard IRIS+ indicators from its catalog. Impact is generally reported through dashboards and scorecards, showing, for example, PH-1 and PH-3 as KPIs, and theory of change diagrams, used to show causal pathways (e.g., patients served → improved health → better livelihoods). An example of a theory of change diagram is depicted in Fig. 1.8 simplistically as a funnel. This allows for comparison between organizations and the aggregation of data to understand the progress of the sector. DALYs and QALYs require detailed epidemiological and clinical data, while the IRIS+ metrics are more comprehensive, measuring social, environmental, and financial outcomes of investments in many fields.

However, quantification alone is insufficient. The challenge of impact valuation arises when we attempt to compare or aggregate across different dimensions. How do "lives saved" compare to "hours of delivered educational content" or "tons of CO2 sequestered"? Despite their flaws, approaches such as social return on investment (SROI) try to put a monetary value on environmental and social benefits so that investors and policymakers can assess the cost-effectiveness of certain actions (Nicholls et al. 2009). For example, an SROI study may show that, through reduced medical expenses and higher productivity, five dollars of social value are produced for every dollar spent on a preventive healthcare program. Although it must be applied openly and with recognition of the presumptions underlying such assessments, this is a potent instrument for lobbying and resource allocation.

Determining impact is ultimately a simple and humble effort. It compels innovators to map their presumptions, clearly state their theory of change, and constantly look for proof of the results they assert. Adopting this rigorous paradigm is the first step for the players in this book to make sure that their work produces not only activity, but also a true, sustainable, and fair transformation, whether they are using artificial intelligence in agriculture or developing new educational models. It is the vital discipline that distinguishes real progress from hope.

1.11 Summary of the Chapter

Technological advances often increase inequality despite their potential to promote equality. The wealth distribution remains unequal globally, and significant poverty persists even in the face of large investments in sectors like tech startups in the Global South. Humanitarian aid has been carried out by many governments and international agencies, but often led to dependency and lacked long-term effectiveness. We now live in a post-humanitarian world aware of this, and we have tools such as cost-benefit analysis and system thinking to design better policies and interventions.

In the unfortunate circumstances that governmental agencies are inefficient, we can hope in the actions of civil society, social and non-social entrepreneurs, and engaged scientists. Regardless of whether a policy is carried out by governmental agencies or other private entities, often ignored aspects in our fast-paced society should be taken into account, especially from a bottom-up point of view:

- Focus on grassroots organizations and ethical businesses.
- Improve infrastructure and create jobs locally.
- Policy recommendations include improving education, reducing loneliness due to technology, and supporting young businesses.
- Social acceptance and proof are essential for behavior change.
- Emotional resonance, seen in movements like Black Lives Matter, helps gain support.
- Social marketing can promote health behaviors and public health initiatives.
- Regulatory systems can hinder innovation, influenced by lobbying.
- Lobbying can be used for positive change by civil society and small groups.

References

Adhikari A, Heller P (2024) Civil society, the state and institutionalizing welfare rights in India. World Dev 182:106687
Akiwumi, P, LDC Insight #3: Digitalization as a driver of structural transformation in African LDCs (United Nations 2023), www.un.org/technologybank/news/digitalization- driver-structural-transformation-african-ldcs, accessed 16 November 2023
Alagna F (2024) Civil society and municipal activism around migration in the EU: A multi-scalar alliance-making. Geopolitics 29(4):1245–1271
Alemanno A (2017) Lobbying for change: find your voice to create a better society. Icon Books
Baker L, Newell P, Phillips J (2014) The political economy of energy transitions: the case of South Africa. New Polit Econ 19(6):791–818
Bayrasli E (2015) From the other side of the world: extraordinary entrepreneurs, unlikely places. Public Affairs
Bollinger B, Gillingham K (2012) Peer effects in the diffusion of solar photovoltaic panels. Mark Sci 31(6):900–912
Bond B, Exley Z (2016) How big organizing can change everything. Chelsea Green Publishing, Rules for Revolutionaries
Bornstein D (2007) How to change the world: social entrepreneurs and the power of new ideas. Oxford University Press
Bowles S, Durlauf SN, Hoff K (2011). Princeton University Press, Poverty traps
Boyd A, Mitchell DO (eds) (2012) Beautiful trouble: a toolbox for revolution. OR Books
Boyd A, Oswald D (2013) Mitchell (ed) Beautiful trouble: a toolbox for revolution. Or Books, pocket edition
Brockmann D, Helbing D (2013) The hidden geometry of complex, network-driven contagion phenomena. Science 342(6164):1337–1342
Brown M, Jacoby (2007) Building powerful community organizations: a personal guide to creating groups that can solve problems and change the world. Long Haul Press
Burfield E, Harrison JD (2018) Regulatory hacking: a playbook for startups. Penguin
Cautilli JD, Santilli-Connor L (2000) Assisting the client/consultee to do what is needed: a functional analysis of resistance and other forms of avoidance. The Behavior Analyst Today 1(3):37–42
Centola D (2010) The spread of behavior in an online social network experiment. Science 329(5996):1194–1197
Centola D, Macy M (2007) Complex contagions and the weakness of long ties. Am J Sociol 113(3):702–734
Centola D, Becker J, Brackbill D, Baronchelli A (2018) Experimental evidence for tipping points in social convention. Science 360(6393):1116–1119
Christensen CM, Ojomo E, D, K (2019) The prosperity paradox: how innovation can lift nations out of poverty. Harper Business
Christensen CM, Ojomo E, D, K (2019) The prosperity paradox: how innovation can lift nations out of poverty. No Title
Andy Crump, Morel CM, Omura S (2001) The control of onchocerciasis. Nature Rev Microbiol 9(7):1–10. Nature Publishing Group, UK, London
Darley JM, Latané B (1968) Bystander intervention in emergencies: diffusion of responsibility. J Pers Soc Psychol 8(4):377–383
Davids N, Waghid Y (2021) Academic activism in Higher Education: a living philosophy for social justice, vol 5. Springer Nature, p 2021
Democracy fund website. https://democracyfund.org/who-we-are/. Accessed July 10th 2024
Diel R, Lampenius N (2014) Cost-effectiveness analysis of interventions for tuberculosis control: DALYs versus QALYs. Pharmacoeconomics 32:617–626
Dietz T (2023) Decisions for sustainability: facts and values. Cambridge University Press
Domegan C (2021) Social marketing and behavioural change in a systems setting. Current Opin Environ Sci Health 23:100275
Drutman L (2015) The business of America is lobbying: how corporations became politicized and politics became more corporate. Oxford University Press
Dunlap RE, McCright AM (2011) Organized climate change denial. The Oxford handbook of climate change and society 1:144–160
Easterly W (2014) The tyranny of experts: Economists, dictators, and the forgotten rights of the poor. Basic Books
Eliazar I, Cohen MH (2014) On social inequality: Analyzing the rich-poor disparity. XXPhys A 401:148–158
Estrada E (2012) The structure of complex networks: theory and applications. American Chemical Society
Farmer J, D (2024) Making sense of chaos: a better economics for a better world. Yale University Press
Feinleib D (2012) Poor product-market fit: pivot your way to a successful launch. And How Yours Can Succeed. Apress, Berkeley, CA, Why Startups Fail, pp 3–13
Firestone R, Rowe CJ, Modi SN, Sievers D (2017) The effectiveness of social marketing in global health: a systematic review. Health Policy Plan 32(1):110–124
Flores W, Samuel J (2019) Grassroots organisations and the sustainable development goals: no one left behind? BMJ 365

Frangoul H et al (2024) Exagamglogene autotemcel for severe sickle cell disease. New England J Med 390(18):1649–1662
Gibson A (2017) This is an uprising: how nonviolent revolt is shaping the twenty-first century. Fellowship 81(1–6):21
Global Impact Investing Network (GIIN) (2023). IRIS+ Core metrics sets. Retrieved from https://iris.thegiin.org/standards/iris-plus/
Goldin I (2016) The pursuit of development: Economic growth, social change and ideas. Oxford University Press
Granovetter M (1978) Threshold models of collective behavior. Am J Sociol 83(6):1420–1443
Gribbin J (2005) Deep simplicity: bringing order to chaos and complexity. Random House
Hansson SO (2013) Cost-benefit analysis. International encyclopedia of ethics, pp 1–9
Hoff K, Sen A (2006) The kin system as a poverty trap. Poverty traps, pp 95–115
Hofstede G (1984) Culture's consequences: international differences in work-related values, vol 5. Sage
Hopkins R (2011) The transition companion. Green Books, Totnes, UK
Iacopini I, Milojević S, Latora V (2018) Network dynamics of innovation processes. Phys Rev Lett 120(4):048301
Johnson C (1982) MITI and the Japanese miracle: the growth of industrial policy, 1925–1975. Stanford University Press
Kamaludin MF, Xavier JA, Amin M (2024) Social entrepreneurship and sustainability: a conceptual framework. J Soc Entrepreneurship 15(1):26–49
Kauffman LA (2017) Direct action: protest and the reinvention of American radicalism. Verso Books
Klein E, Thompson D (2025) Abundance. Simon and Schuster
Loeb P (2004) Rogat perseverance and hope in troubled times. The impossible will take a little while. Basic books
Lyew DA, Perkins DD, Sohn J-IE (2021) Foreign aid, grassroots activism, and the strength of applied community studies in aid-receiving countries: the case of community psychology. Psychosoc Interv 30(1):1–11
Marseille E et al (2014) Thresholds for the cost-effectiveness of interventions: alternative approaches. Bull World Health Organ 93:118–124
Marseille E, Larson B, Kazi DS, Kahn JG, Rosen S (2014) Thresholds for the cost-effectiveness of interventions: alternative approaches. Bull World Health Organ 93:118–124
Maru V (2010) Allies unknown: social accountability and legal empowerment. Health Hum Rights 12(1):83–93
Mcleod C, Gonzales A, King J, Hui J, Israni A (2024) What is Community?: Informing the design of a community building platform for low-income black and Latino residents
Mehlum H, Moene K, Torvik R (2003) Predator or prey?: parasitic enterprises in economic development. Eur Econ Rev 47(2):275–294
Moyo D (2009) Dead aid: why aid is not working and how there is a better way for Africa. Macmillan
Narum D (1992) A troublesome legacy: The Reagan Administration's conservation and renewable energy policy. Energy Policy 20(1):40–53
Nicholls J, Lawlor E, Neitzert E, Goodspeed T (2009) A guide to social return on investment. The Cabinet Office, Office of the Third Sector, London
Nickerson RS (1998) Confirmation bias: a ubiquitous phenomenon in many guises. Rev Gen Psychol 2(2):175–220
Nogales R, Oldiges C (2024) Multidimensional poverty and conflict events in Nigeria over time. Int Polit Sci Rev 45(1):53–80
Piumatti G, Garro M, Pipitone L, Di Vita AM, Rabaglietti E (2016) North/South differences among Italian emerging adults regarding criteria deemed important for adulthood and life satisfaction. Eur J Psychol 12(2):271
Qin Y (2023) Grassroots governance and social development: theoretical and comparative legal aspects. Humanities Soc Sci Commun 10(1):1–9
Rana P (2024) Civil society activism and government partnerships in India. MIT Press
Rayner C, Bonnici F (2021) The systems work of social change: How to harness connection, context, and power to cultivate deep and enduring change. Oxford University Press
Robinson JA, Acemoglu D (2012) Why nations fail: The origins of power, prosperity and poverty. Profile, London, pp 45–47
Sachs JD (2006) The end of poverty: economic possibilities for our time. Penguin
Schaffer K, Cubi-Molla S, Devlin P, Towse N, A (2016) Shaping the research agenda to estimate relevant cost-effectiveness thresholds for health technology assessment decision making: report for ABPI. Office of Health Economics Consulting
Schwarzer R et al (2015) Systematic overview of cost-effectiveness thresholds in ten countries across four continents. J Comparative Effect Res 4(5):485–504
Shaw R (1996) The activist's handbook: a primer for the 1990s and beyond. University of California Press
Smith J, Johnson A, Rodriguez M, Gupta S, Chenoweth E, Stephan M, Mendelsohn Forman S, Forman R, (2019) Grassroots techniques used by activists in developing countries. J Activism Stud 15(2), 45–62. MLA: Smith J, et al (2019) Grassroots techniques used by activists in developing countries. J Activism Stud 15(2):45–62
Starhawk (2011) The empowerment manual: a guide for collaborative groups. New Society Publishers
Stiglitz JE, Greenwald BC (2014) Creating a learning society: a new approach to growth, development, and social progress. Columbia University Press

Stokes L, C (2020) Short circuiting policy: interest groups and the battle over clean energy and climate policy in the American states. Oxford University Press
Strogatz SH (2018) Nonlinear dynamics and chaos: with applications to physics, biology, chemistry, and engineering. CRC Press
Stroh D, Peter (2015) Systems thinking for social change: a practical guide to solving complex problems, avoiding unintended consequences, and achieving lasting results. Chelsea Green Publishing
Tarrant A, Cowen T (2022) Big tech lobbying in the EU. Polit Quart 93(2):218–226
The Trapese Collective (2007) Do it yourself: a handbook for changing our world. Pluto Press
Tusk B (2018) The fixer: my adventures saving startups from death by politics. Penguin
Urbinati A, Chiaroni D, Chiesa V, Franzò S, Frattini F (2018) An exploratory analysis on the contextual factors that influence disruptive innovation: the case of Uber. Int J Innov Technol Manag 15(03):1850024
Vanness DJ, Lomas J, Ahn H (2021) A health opportunity cost threshold for cost-effectiveness analysis in the United States. Ann Intern Med 174(1):25–32
Vărzaru AA, Bocean CG (2024) Digital transformation and innovation: the influence of digital technologies on turnover from innovation activities and types of innovation. Systems 12(9):359
Waghid Y, Davids N (2020) Educational Philosophy and authentic learning. Lexington Books, Teachers matter
Watts DJ (2002) A simple model of global cascades on random networks. Proc Natl Acad Sci 99(9):5766–5771
Xie J, Sreenivasan S, Barabási G, Szymanski B (2011) Social consensus through the influence of committed minorities. Phys Rev E 84(1):011130
World Bank Open Data, https://data.worldbank.org
Everybody's business-strengthening health systems to improve health outcomes: WHO's framework for action. World Health Organization (2007)
Zhou Y, Liu Y (2022) The geography of poverty: review and research prospects. J Rural Stud 93:408–416. https://doi.org/10.1016/j.jrurstud.2019.01.008

2 How to Change Poverty

2.1 Old and New Inequalities

The first Sustainable Development Goal (SDG) is the "No Poverty Goal", which aims at eradicating poverty in all its forms everywhere by 2030. However, poverty is a hard concept to grasp. We do have thresholds that vary country by country and define a minimum level of income, which is deemed to define a person below or above the poverty line (Ravallion 2008). This definition is more of a measured effect. In a broader view, societies have social stratification, which reinforces inequalities and other social differences, which are, in turn, related to poverty and other social traps. Hierarchies are everywhere in our society. From an intern of an institution compared to a minister, or a grassroots employee compared to a CEO of a company. There have been differences that have existed in our society for a long time, and are called social stratification. They not only exist within a society, they also exist between countries. In fact, Branko Milanović introduced the expression of *two dimensions of inequality or stratification* (Milanovic 2016). Within-country inequality, which is the gap between rich and poor inside a single country, and between-country inequality, which is the gap in average incomes across nations. At the moment of writing this book, the between-country inequality has become the dominant form. The income potential of a person depends hugely on the country of birth. Think of the unfair advantage of being born in Switzerland compared to Swaziland (Eswatini). However, the trend seems to reduce this gap between countries, and there is concern that given the hectic pace of AI, within-country inequality will increase and the stratifications will become more extreme. On the rooftop of the Museum of Contemporary Art of Rome (Italy), also known as MACRO, there is murals of the artist Ozomo (Gionata Gesi). It is depicted in Fig. 2.1 and entitled "voi volate piu' di molti passeri" (you fly farther than many sparrows), provocative depicting the bleak scenario of social stratifications, with money itself on top, and at the same time giving hope to people who "can fly" despite being the bottom of the pyramid.

In this chapter, we will revise what social stratifications are, why they exist according to the literature, and what we can do to reduce their negative impacts. Social stratifications are hierarchical arrangements of individuals and groups (including entire countries as a group) based on factors such as wealth, power, and social status. We can have wealth stratifications within a society, for example, the Indian caste systems or the medieval feudal system, but those hierarchies exist even among countries. It is self-evident that in our society we have an upper class, a middle class, a working class, and lower class, with other potential further stratifications. Among countries, we have the old school and politically incorrect way of classifying nations as first, second, and third world countries. The "Third-world countries" are sometimes even referred to as "developing", which is an even weirder definition, because every country

© The Author(s), under exclusive license to Springer Nature Switzerland AG 2026

A. Crimi, *Innovate for Impact*, Sustainable Development Goals Series,
https://doi.org/10.1007/978-3-032-21563-5_2

Fig. 2.1 The social stratifications depicted in "Voi volate più di molti passeri" (you fly farther than many sparrows) by Ozmo (Gionata Gesi), MACRO rooftop, Rome, Italy. Picture of the author

is developing. The classification of First, Second and Third World drives back to the Cold War when policymakers classified the Western bloc as the First world, the Soviet Union as a Second World and all the rest of the planet was put together as the Third World (Cox 1987), this classification was reflecting the split between capitalist and communist ideology, and those who are outside the fight between them.

Following the conclusion of the Cold War, the expression "Second World countries" slowly faded away. But instead the denominations of "First World" and "Third World" remained in use. The First world used to refer to rich Western countries, and here I call them "Global North". The Third world used to refer to countries that we consider "poor", which is kind of inaccurate because generally we tend to see the Global South as the Third World, including countries like Singapore and South Africa, which are actually kind of rich.

A slightly better stratification is given by sorting countries into groups based on their gross domestic product (GDP), and we say high-income countries, middle-income countries, and low-income countries per capita. This is a biased indicator as we consider the total level of productivity, which even if it is averaged pro-capita, it does not take into account that the total GDP can come from a small number of people and the rest of the inhabitants live in poverty. To compensate for the oversimplifications introduced by the GPD neglecting inequalities, we complement the GDP score with other indicators, such as the Gini index. We will return to this topic in the following chapters.

Yet, this does not explain why we have stratification country-wise, and even less within a country, because for much of the history of humankind, the human beings were more or less all poor. We were all "third world countries". At an individual level, some people have been able to collect more wealth and use technology to their advantage. The first men who understood how to use spears and create more organized social networks had more chances compared to those who did not. Fast-pace this for thousands of years and you have the answers about today. At the country level, there have been some events that created inequalities that did not align all countries at the same level. If, for a second, we forget the criticism of bad governments, which we discussed previously in the literature, we will find two theories: "the modernization theory" and "the dependence theory". Modernization theory comes from the structural-functional school. The same that claims that there are inequalities in our societies because we need them to function (Davis and Moore 1945). Individuals need to fulfill a role, and given their role, they take higher responsibility and therefore are rewarded with higher wages. We need a boss in a company, we need someone as a middle-level manager, and we need someone to do just not-so-relevant work for a small salary. An idea which sounds correct, if it were not for the fact that some ideologies interfere with what is a valuable contribution to a society (Tumin 1953). In fact, in most societies, we have scientists and health workers—who undoubtedly provide great value to society—paid way less than certain actors and football players. In this view, the generalization at the country level sees inequality as a function of technological and cultural differences, and the development is portrayed as a linear path that all nations could theoretically follow. It is more of a willingness issue, whether "a country is lazy or not". This theory assumes that all nations can acquire the necessary forms of economic, cultural, and social capital as they were universally available. Modernization theory considers some historical events behind why the West has been faster in this kind of linear path: The discovery of the Americas, which allowed the exchange of new goods, and the industrial revolution, which started in the United Kingdom with all the steam engines, mass production and all the things initially benefiting only the elite. Industrialization eventually raised the general living standards for more or less everybody. A society that adopted this shift accumulated institutional and technological capital, reinforcing their dominant position locally but also around the world. Essentially, the modernization theory says that any country can follow this path of modernization, with or without the industrial revolution. It is more a matter of whether they are lazy or not. This linear path has been deeply described by the American economist Walter Rostow, who defined four stages of development: The *traditional society* where we are all just families, the *takeoff* when there is some innovation and trades between tribes or nations, the *technological maturity* when we have a certain level of education scaling the economical effect, and finally the *mass consumption* which is literally what we meant with Industrial Revolution, Information Revolution, etc. Indeed, this model masks all the possible historical and political circumstances that might hamper or accelerate development. Moreover, it depicts low-income countries as lazy for not following this path. In reality, things are a lot more complex.

The other theory most common in the literature is the dependence theory. The dependence theory is like the other side of the coin of modernization theory. It states that some countries are richer because they have exploited other countries, and foreign aid is just a very recent structural adjustment.

Indeed, this is perhaps another extreme point of view based on victimism, or victim mentality. It has been shown that sometimes, to have more economic margin, we introduce some levels of inequality, which can be seen as exploitation: outsourcing production in a country with lower wages, automating a process, etc. However, explaining all social stratifications as the effect of exploitation is somewhat extreme. The dependence theory points to the fact that colonization is the fault of everything. It is true that colonialism left some serious scars in history. If you visit Ghana or Nigeria, you can still see the forts where people were put as slaves, in horrible dungeons, and then brought to America as tools, not humans. They were passing the "doors of no return", leaving the African harbors to never come back.

However, colonialism does not explain why some countries are still stuck in the low-income group, and others have changed their status. We have countries that have been colonies, like Singapore, or even the US itself was a colony, which have been flourishing financially, economically, and politically (Abshire 2011). So, the truth is probably that both theories are over-simplistic and ignore the impact of the government's policies and other kinds of inequality that may have appeared.

There have been countless theories and policies aiming at the redistribution of wealth, and the rest of the book is about some of them. Even if poverty is defined as people living with an income below a threshold. We cannot simply give more money to the poor. We must address the underlying causes. One of the major criticisms to welfare policy is that people are motivated to integrate themselves into society and just take advantage of the policies (Rahman and Pingali 2024).

Historically, we are used to saying that education is the great equalizer. It neutralizes inequality and fixes all inequalities that have been introduced by either modernization or dependency. A person with higher education can obtain a better wage job climbing the social ladder, and a country with many educated people will have more trades and technological innovations. In practice, education reduces the difference in stratification between and within countries.

However, this is not always true. It is a socially accepted lie of our previous generations: "Obtain a degree, be a good person, and you will find the job that will raise you financially". In practice, some people come from a rich background, and their success will be given not only by the support they receive while studying, but also by the family network effect while finding a high-level position after getting the degree. Or another example is that more than one third of all Ivy League university students are the son or daughter of an alumnus of one Ivy League university (Castilla and Poskanzer 2022). To some extent, it is true that education is the *major equalizer*, but often elitist factors come into play. This unfair advantage might be transferred to new equalizer tools as well. There is the general view that artificial intelligence (AI) and large language models hold the promise of fixing everything. They are the great panacea. They are the new promise as a super-education to boost productivity and knowledge, also in underdog social groups of a country, and ultimately also in middle- and low-income countries.

Likewise, for education, AI systems can introduce elitist tricks. Chatbots can be powerful access to knowledge more than any encyclopedia. It is, substantially, education on steroids. We will discuss better how to fight those tricks in the next chapter, but let's start introducing the idea of *biased training*: AI models are generally trained and are based on local data, and this can deepen inequalities, benefiting groups from existing hierarchies. Moreover, there is also the risk that AI may devalue traditional and marginalized cultural forms, prioritizing dominant norms embedded in data. For example, if you ask specific questions, maybe the answers to those questions will be the results of AI training from text from a specific background or in a specific geographic location. If you train an AI model in this way, it might not generalize to everyone. And finally, technology has always been in the hands of the elite, at least at the beginning. Therefore, they might arrange things in a way to improve their own productivity, but not necessarily to reduce inequality; but actually they might even increase inequality.

In short, while AI has the potential to support efforts to create greater social equity, it cannot solve inequality on its own. It must be intentionally designed to be inclusive and more integrated in a broader societal way in different countries, different statuses, and also to redistribute all forms of capital, economic, cultural, and social. Without this AI will be more like a minor reinforcement of previous inequalities rather than dismantling them. We will navigate more on this topic in the last part of the book. Before discussing future traps, it is time to revise further the old and current traps.

2.2 Poverty and Other Traps

Poverty is the condition of barely meeting basic needs such as food, shelter, and clothing. Since the 1960s, we have been hearing expressions like poverty traps and poverty cycles (Rosenberg 1960). To understand why we refer to poverty as a cycle, you should imagine someone hearing so little who is not able to save nothing, barely cover his or her basic needs, not in a condition to move socially and, therefore, looping over a cycle of minimum income, expenses, no income, and from back to the beginning. The general image could be a homeless person, but it could also be someone who has a low-income job and spends all money to survive; this is also why we refer to this condition as a trap. These are self-sustaining mechanisms that prevent individuals or countries from escaping poverty. These traps/cycles are characterized by a complex interplay of factors such as poor access to education, healthcare, and infrastructure, which further hinder economic growth and perpetuate poverty. One of the most passionate advocates for the use of this concept was Jeffrey Sachs, who argued that this self-reinforcing cycle is prevalent in sub-Saharan Africa and Southeast Asia due to malnutrition and endemic diseases such as malaria (Sachs 2006). In short, to maximize our income, we need to be in a condition to have sufficient energy and good health, and we can fix poverty by funding programs to improve health, or provide initial aid to leave the poverty trap. It was the first humanitarian wave when we believed that sending inconsiderably aid to low-income countries would have fixed everything, because some of this aid would have provided enough food, shelter, and health tools, allowing people to escape the poverty trap. History proved us wrong, and this simplistic solution instead introduced another trap: "the social welfare trap" (Easterly 2014; Moyo 2009), where a country or a group of people do not improve their status because they are dependent on donations or welfare programs.

In the literature, Paul Collier (Collier 2008) expanded the general poverty trap to the other four poverty traps: the conflict trap, the natural resource trap, the landlocked trap, and the poor governance trap. In case of conflicts, civil or international wars destroy infrastructure, displace populations, and scare off investment. Countries caught in conflict often relapse into war, creating a vicious cycle of poverty and instability (Ghani 2009). This is the worst and the best condition, and we sometimes label those countries as "failed states". The worst, because there is not much to do, everything becomes cumbersome and under martial rules. The best is that once the war has ended, we might have plenty of opportunity to create blooming economies, assuming that we do not reintroduce the circumstances that have led to the conflict. However, some states have been in conflict for decades, reducing hopes of improvements. The natural resource trap can be referred to as lack of resources or the opposite. Lack of resources puts people in disadvantaged conditions, while too many resources often fuel power struggles rather than development, as, instead of having a wealth redistribution, a country can be a victim of vicious cycles of corruption and exploitation by foreign evil investors (Sachs and Warner

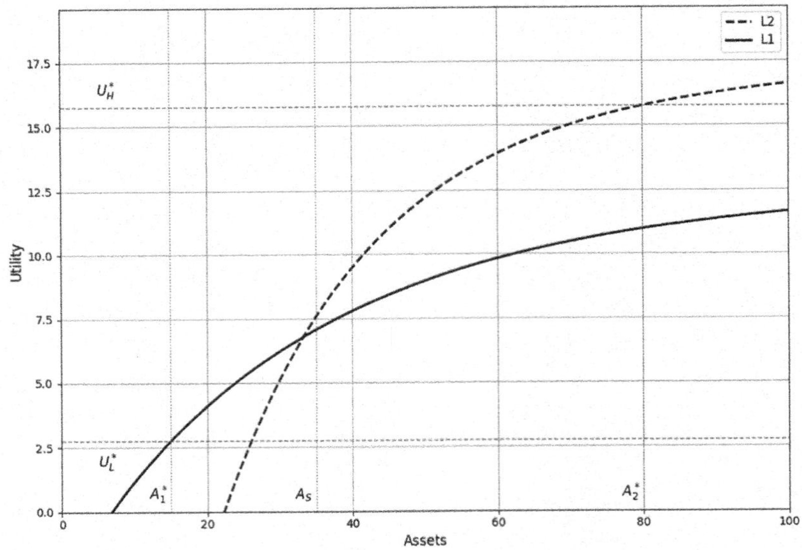

Fig. 2.2 Curves representing 2 cases with different relationships between assets and utility. Here, L2 represents more advantageous circumstances with a greater possibility of escaping the poverty trap than L1

2001). Similarly, being landlocked with no access to the sea has been argued as limiting growth since the Industrial Revolution or even earlier. Those two points have been strongly criticized as some countries, like Switzerland, have few resources and are landlocked, but have a very high GDP. Lastly, the poor governance trap. A trap that is broadly accepted: Poor governance, weak institutions, and misuse national and international funding, undermine development. Corruption, mismanagement, and lack of public trust in government reduce investment, stifle entrepreneurship, and prevent effective public services, keeping countries stuck in poverty (Robinson and Acemoglu 2012). Summarizing "Why Nations Fail", some countries do not have an inclusive economy, and even if there are democracy and established institutions, those do not favor growth and innovation, keeping some people in poverty or inequality (Robinson and Acemoglu 2012). We discussed in the previous chapter that some of the work to address this can be done bottom-up style, by entrepreneurs and civil society addressing the issues that their government is not solving.

About 40 years after the concept of traps was introduced, we had the first graphical representations, highlighting graphically how income can evolve with time and might allow people and country to either improve their status or keep them where they are. For instance, as shown in Fig. 2.2. Carter and Barrett (2006) illustrated how poverty traps arise from nonlinear relationships between assets and utility. Where a country, a person, or a household at some point given the assets should produce more utility, if it does not it stays poor. The points of the lines $L1$ and $L2$ represent two stable equilibria. Households/Country with low assets tend to fall toward $L1$, a poverty trap, while those above a critical threshold move toward $L2$, a prosperous equilibrium. Those evolutions are theoretical, since they imagine a country/household which, even if would increase its assets, does not produce enough increase in income to move socially. The utility thresholds U_L^* and U_H^* mark the poverty lines based on income and assets. Households below U_L^* are income poor, while those below U_H^* lack sufficient assets to accumulate sustainably. On the asset axis, A_1^* and A_2^* are tipping points. Below A_1^*, households spiral downward into poverty. Above A_2^*, they accumulate assets and approach prosperity. A_S is a survival threshold; below it, asset levels decline, while above it, households may at least maintain their position. This depiction means that sometimes the current income/GDP is not necessary to push a person or country out of poverty, as the income is lost to cover survival expenses (the L1 curve), while people having a higher financial boost can succeed. These kinds of view advocate for the use of foreign aid and welfare programs,

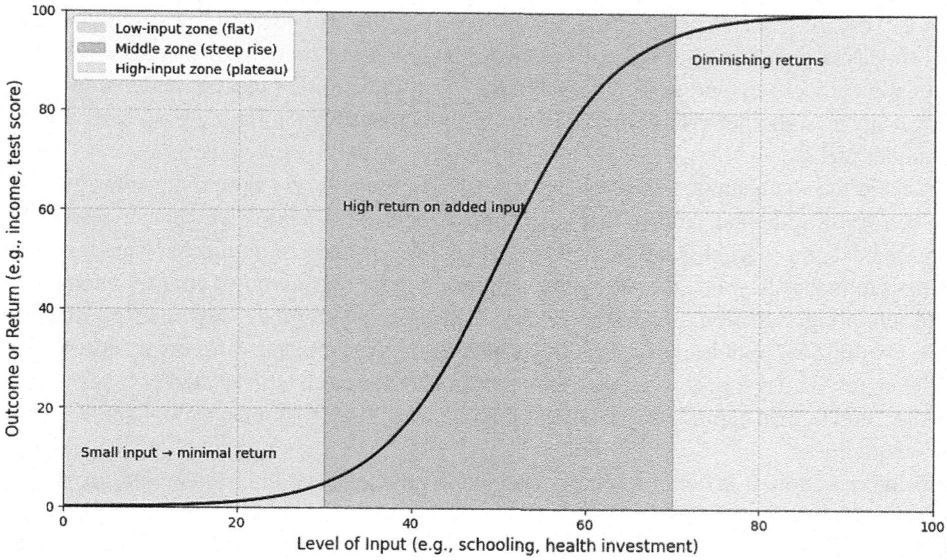

Fig. 2.3 Hypothetical household asset dynamics. This graph should not be read from left to right, as a person, a country or household can remain in the same point indefinitely

such as universal basic income or plans to reduce malaria (Sachs 2006). Later, poverty traps were graphically modeled with the now well-known S-shaped (Adato et al. 2013; Banerjee and Duflo 2007) as depicted in Fig. 2.3, as a way to relate the relationship of income today versus income tomorrow. In this representation, the S-shaped curve (or sigmoidal curve) shows how the impact of an intervention (like a financial support, or educational program or health treatment) changes non-linearly as the input increases. You can also imagine someone having a small bakery selling few pieces of bread, receiving a micro-loan that can be used to buy a second oven and hire a helper, and then selling more bread. Or a country providing vaccine and supplements for free allowing people to work and earn more. On the X-axis: Level of input (e.g., amount of fertilizer, years of schooling, and money spent); on the Y-axis: Outcome or return (e.g., crop yield, test scores, health outcomes, income). The space where the curve lies has three key zones: the low-input zone (flat). With small changes that have almost no effect, again, the case that someone has a little income sufficient enough to cover basic needs as food and shelter, and no possibility of saving, or giving a child one vitamin pill might not improve their nutrition measurably enough. The Middle zone, where returns increase rapidly with more input, for example someone now has enough energy to work because there are no more malaria outbreaks, or is able to save a little each day. The latter is the plateau, where we have diminishing returns with little improvements despite the efforts, namely there is change if we provide further vitamin supplements. The traps occur where someone is stuck in the first zone. The S-shaped curve should not be seen as automatically moving from left to right, a person or country can stay in one point or zone forever. They are also hypothetical. They answer questions like "what would happen if someone received a loan and launched a successful business with microcredit?"

Formally, the curve in Fig. 2.3 models the possible case/scenario of a household/country assets over a function of previous-period assets, for example, income today A_t or at time t, and the day before A_{t-1}:

$$A_t = f(A_{t-1}). \tag{2.1}$$

In the case of escape from the poverty trap, a person or a country will always have A_t growing compared to A_{t-1}. However, someone could go back to the initial low-input zone for many reasons. For instance, if poor health and consequent medical bills hinder work. Equation 2.1 can be modeled in many ways. From local linear smoother (Naschold 2012) to high-degree polynomial regression model (Giesbert and Schindler 2012).

Apart from the mathematics and how we model it in general, we should consider that a poverty trap is a self-reinforcing mechanism that keeps people poor. In this book we neglect mechanisms that are controversial as geography and being landlocked. We focus more on mechanisms that are related to bad institutional policy, health, and human capital. A poor household or country cannot guarantee adequate schooling, nutrition, or healthcare care, and subsequently they stay poor, cycling forever in this. Bad institutional policies have been dealt with in the first chapter, where we addressed them as societal changes. The rest of this chapter will continue to discuss health related policies with specific case studies, and human capital. In growth models, we often refer to human capital and ways to reduce income inequalities.

To avoid confusion, it is better to clarify that some policies have indeed allowed people to escape poverty traps. However, they were the result of a favorable system, and we should realize that we cannot simply provide assistance to let people escape the poverty trap (Solar 1995). For instance, we should follow those 5 points related to analysis of misuse of funding or avoiding the creation of dependency is critical:

1. **Build Local Capacity**
   Invest in institutions, governance structures, and human capital to make systems self-sustaining. The aid should support *institutional reform*, not replace it (Robinson and Acemoglu 2012).
2. **Monitoring & Evaluation (M&E)**
   To determine what works and make adjustments. While doing this, we possibly use rigorous evaluation methods, such as randomized controlled trials (Banerjee and Duflo 2007), where we run a policy or intervention in a controlled manner randomly assigning a participant to a group undergoing a policy, or not, to determine the effectiveness of such a policy.
3. **Community Involvement**
   Encourage local participation so that local communities are stakeholders, not just recipients (see previous chapter).
4. **Time-bound or Exit Strategies**
   Design welfare programs with *built-in exit plans* (Deaton 2024).
5. **Promote Economic Opportunities**
   Focus on *livelihoods, microfinance, infrastructure, and education* to allow people to earn a living and become independent (see the rest of this chapter and the following).

2.3 Running Projects in the Global South

Getting ethical approval for research, or registering a business can be difficult tasks everywhere. In the Global South, there are further issues to consider. The habits, traditions, and age-old practices of former local communities, including chiefs, may still be followed in rural areas. Without following local laws, it might not be feasible to carry out clinical research or sell goods in a nearby clinic. The primary authority is the local stakeholders, often even exceeding the governmental authorities (Chigwata 2016). There have been reports of health projects that went wrong as they did not have the proper trust of local stakeholders (Jegede 2007; Singh and Mills 2005).

To run a business, make social changes, or conduct your clinical trial, it is necessary to first interact with the chief of the community. You can move on after receiving the approval of the local stakeholders.

Chiefs will occasionally be so excited about the prospect of something new in their town that they will call a community meeting to present you and the project you are starting. Instead of portraying you as a white man who comes to impose your business or research question, and take advantage of people, it fosters a structure of cooperation. Despite all formal clearances, a research project or business activity might be stopped or problems may arise if stakeholders in the local rural areas are not adequately introduced. This is obvious for someone from this local background. If someone is from outside the local community of interest, this represents an extra step. However, this extra step must be taken into account and incorporated into the budget and schedule. If there is a plan to conduct a clinical trial, operate a business, or conduct research in these fields, projects or businesses can be delayed or even shut down if local customs are not followed (Nyika 2010).

In the literature, we can find numerous examples of projects that have effectively engaged local stakeholders, and here the devil is in the details. Those examples provide valuable insights and lessons learned for future projects for all academics or policymakers interested. Interestingly, some of those involve not only typical community members, but in some cases exceptionally even herbalists and figures who are traditionally against science have been involved.

The *Community-Led Total Sanitation* (CLTS) initiative is a community-based approach to encourage communities to use sanitation practices and improve hygiene. It was initially introduced in Bangladesh, where the local government was also rewarding participating communities with a certificate of "open defecation free" community (Galvin 2015). Following its success, it was repeated in various rural areas in Sub-Saharan Africa (Kamal et al. 2015). The goal of this strategy is to allow local communities to work together to address sanitation problems, leading to a long-lasting behavioral change. It is not a push policy from the above; it is more empowerment, long-term impact enabled by local stakeholders (e.g., village chiefs) collaborating with educators, formal and informal health professionals.

In fact, over the years, there has been a subtle but noticeable advance in water, sanitation, and hygiene (WASH) interventions, and CLTS has been shown to be the most effective approach to addressing the sanitation crisis on a scale. However, the complexity of the issues facing the WASH sector and CLTS in particular has become evident as a result of the emphasis of the SDGs on universal coverage and reaching the poorest and most vulnerable people. The SDGs push us to consider who the existing efforts to expand access to sanitation are not reaching. A goal that the CLTS approach seemed to have reached thanks to local integration rather than forcing.

After sanitation, one of the current hot topics is agriculture due to the changes in temperatures due to global warming. Similarly to sanitation, there have been some projects with the goal of introducing sustainable agriculture practices into rural communities. Even before current concerns about temperature increases, the *Participatory Rural Appraisal* (PRA) technique was introduced by a combination of international development practitioners and local NGOs. It was a widely used approach in projects centered on agriculture and the management of natural resources in rural regions (Chambers 1994). Basically, to help local farmers from rural areas in the Global South engage with each other and other relevant stakeholders in decision-making processes. Introduced also mainly in Bangladesh and Sub-Saharan Africa, PRAs promote a cooperative and inclusive approach as active focus groups, which exchange knowledge, ensuring that local rural actors have their point of view respected.

In addition, several projects in rural Africa use herbalists, also called "traditional healers", to gain community trust and improve healthcare delivery, rather than fighting the herbalist approach. The integration of traditional herbalists into scientific research projects has emerged as a promising strategy to improve community engagement and trust in rural Africa. Herbalists are often highly respected figures from rural communities who practice pseudoscience as medicine, often comparing themselves with traditional scientists or medical doctors. Although this may seem counterintuitive, herbalists often clash with traditional science. They can be involved in scientific projects to take advantage of the trust they have in local communities, or to gather information on how patients are used to be treated.

In fact, a study conducted jointly by Hunan University in China and the University of Pretoria in South Africa on the prevention of spread during the COVID-19 pandemic in Africa highlighted the crucial role traditional healers play in rural health care. Rather than fighting with the herbalist, taking advantage of their trust might be a resource to carry out healthcare interventions (Cordeiro-Rodrigues and Metz 2021). Other studies indicated that during pregnancy, women use many herbs, such as ginger, thyme, chamomile, green tea, and echinacea leaves consistently. A study reported anecdotally the sentence *"We are nothing without herbs"* said by local pregnant women (Peprah et al. 2019). These observations lead to the conclusion that modern medical care mu1st be combined with traditional herbal medicine from the perspective of social adoption, to meet the unique needs of rural African communities. This obviously does not refer to physiological improvements or respecting cultural traditions, but to the overall effectiveness and accessibility of healthcare services.

There has been a general decrease in maternal mortality worldwide (von Salmuth et al. 2021) in the last decade. Despite this, there is still room for improvement, especially in low- and middle-income countries. In Ghana in 2023, the maternal mortality ratio (MMR) is 234 deaths per 100,000 live births (World Health Organization 2025). This is about half of the neighboring countries currently, showing outstanding improvements. These are also recent improvements. In fact, in 2013 the national MMR was 336 deaths per 100,000 live births (World Health Organization 2025), with only 54% of women attending the minimum number of four prenatal visits (Moyer et al. 2012).

Despite the improvement in recent years, it can still be quite difficult to find prenatal care providers in rural areas. A modern healthcare provider may be more than 15 km away for expectant mothers. Although there are still some exceptions that we mentioned earlier, most Ghanaians are educated and prefer traditional medicine to herbalists.

In 2013, ETH-Zurich (the Technical University of Switzerland in Zurich) funded a cooperation project in Ghana called *DocmeUP*, specifically a prenatal care study using biomedical equipment and telemedicine, which in 2013 was still in its infancy. The project was carried out indefinitely with the support in Ghana of the African Institute for Mathematics Science (more about the institute in the next chapter). In addition to establishing a cooperation between ETH-Zurich and the institute in Ghana, the objective of the project was to increase prenatal care for women in rural areas and offer reasonably affordable telemedicine solutions. The project was also a research project that lasted from 2014 to 2016 (Amoah et al. 2016).

The project consisted of training women (called community health workers) living in local communities so that they could keep track of pregnant women in their community through a mobile phone app and, when necessary, remind them to go to their prenatal visits. In cases where women were not in a position to do so, ultrasounds would be acquired in the rural community. In practice, the app given to community health workers also created a calendar for trained technicians who could visit rural areas with portable ultrasound machines, sending scans to gynecologists in urban areas who could alert them to take more action when danger to mother or fetus was detected. In its pilot version, the project was covered by a research grant, while potential scaling was aimed at being entrusted to the government and sponsors.

The project received ethical approval from the local institutional review board (Noguchi Memorial Institute for Medical Research in Accra) to run this project. Despite having all official documents in possession, an introduction was necessary to the local chief of each community where the pilot was carried out to explain the rationale and steps of the process and get their approval.

Generally, the chiefs were interested in listening to my ideas and the project and, after traditional interactions, honored to give access to their communities. In some cases, news related to the running projects was shared in the public assembly. In other cases, there were local radio stations or town criers that would spread the noise that something new was happening in the area (Abdulai et al. 2023). In Fig. 2.4, we can see one of the meetings with the chiefs of one of the villages involved, where the chiefs

Fig. 2.4 Dr. Crimi during a training of the Docmeup project explaining to some chosen women of a rural community and the Chiefs of the village the technological part of the project

were so enthusiastic that immediately invited potential community health workers. Chiefs are typically well educated and proficient in English, but interactions typically take place in the native tongue, and even if the chief speaks English, an interpreter is still needed. This is anecdotal evidence worth sharing. In certain situations, the interpreter may serve as an advisor, talking with the chief about any matters that look questionable, not only translating. It is also a way of respect, as a guest must not address the chief directly.

2.4 Inequalities and Investing in Human Capital

We do not need to focus only on people living in extreme poverty, such as the homeless in large cities. It is equally important to focus on the broader spectrum of inequalities, both within and between countries, as they significantly impact sustainable development. There is relative poverty, or stagnation that keep some people lagging behind compared to the rest of a country or other countries. We can still reduce child mortality or the impact of malaria and lead healthier, safer, and more enjoyable lives. After all, even in countries that are considered high-income because on average there is a high GDP per capita, many inequalities exist.

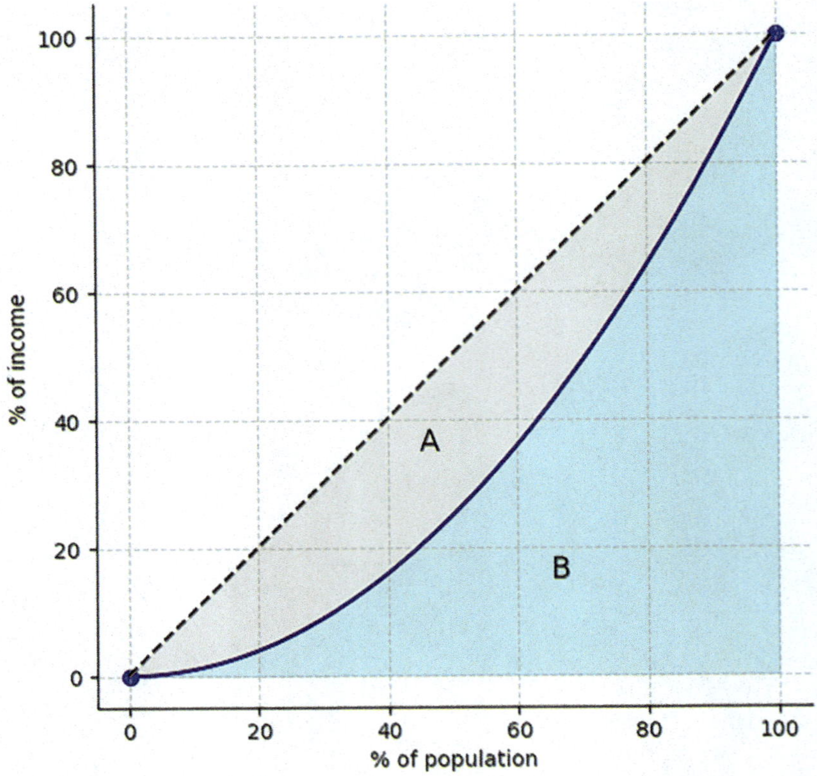

Fig. 2.5 A graphical representation of the income dispersion in a country with a Gini index. If the A area disappears we would have a perfectly income-distributed society. The more the A area is spread, the more the B area is skewed, pointing out that few people have the majority of the nationwide value created through the production of goods and services

In this, the GDP is a biased indicator as it boils everything down to a nationwide number without taking into account oligarchies. The Gini index measures the statistical dispersion, representing the income or wealth distribution of a nation or social group. It quantifies the inequality among values of a frequency distribution, with a Gini coefficient of 0 meaning perfect equality and 1 meaning perfect inequality. More in details, the Gini coefficient expressed via the Lorenz curve:

$$G = 1 - 2\int_0^1 L(p)\,dp, \tag{2.2}$$

where $L(p)$ denotes the Lorenz curve, representing the cumulative income share as a function of the population percentile. If we want to visualize it, we can use the representation in Fig. 2.5, there the index can also be summarized by the ratio $G = A/(A + B)$.

Yet, the Gini index is summary-only, and it cannot tell why inequality exists (Cowell 2011). Mixture models are a more powerful statistical framework, which can clarify the complex nature of inequality and provide pathways toward more effective poverty reduction strategies. This is not a mere mathematical exercise to achieve better precision. The ultimate goal is to also have a better understanding which policy for investing human capital will be more adequate. Modern institutional investments can comprise many programs: from early childhood development programs, which focus on nutrition, stimulation, to education technology (EdTech), which is transforming how learning happens, espe-

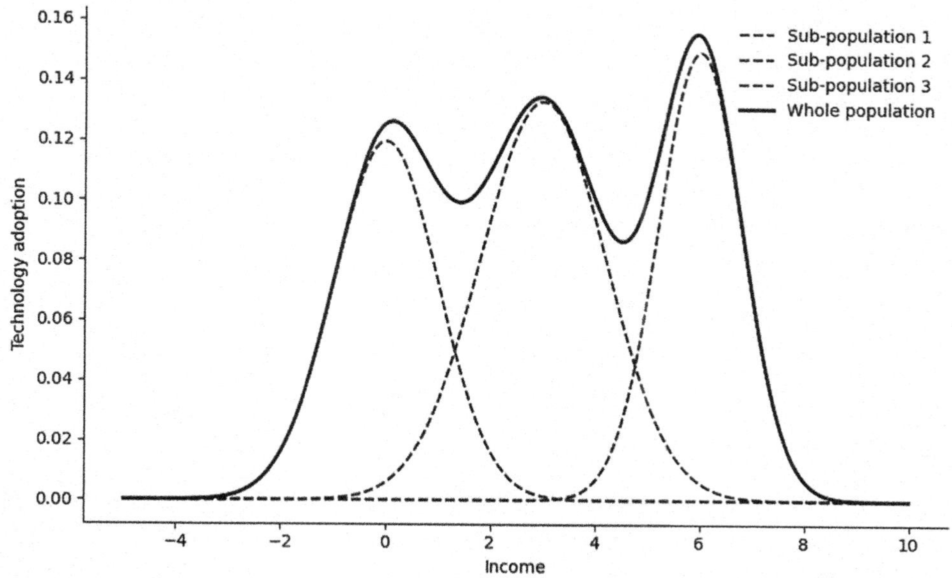

Fig. 2.6 A fictional quantification of three populations, each of them being represented as a Gaussian distribution and how they can result in a mixture

cially in remote or underserved regions. Alongside this, there's renewed emphasis on technical and vocational training for adult to ensure that education aligns with the demands of the labor market. Last but not the least, governments are prioritizing health coverage also for adults especially elderly, including preventive care and maternal health services, and entrepreneurship.

The conventional approach to studying and treating inequality would treat income distributions as homogeneous phenomena, obscuring the underlying heterogeneity that characterizes real-world economies, or apply indistinctively one of the aforementioned programs. We could imagine a population as shown in Fig. 2.6, highlighting that subgroups exist, and we consider the individual elements of the mixture not a fit-for-all solution. In this fictional drawing $K = 3$ so we have only 3 sub-populations.

However, a country is given by multiple, distinct groups with different income-generating processes, market access, and structural constraints (Stiglitz 2012, 2015).

A mixture model assumes that the observed income data come from a population composed of several distinct sub-populations, each with its own income-generating characteristics. We mentioned earlier that society is given by social stratifications. Instead of seeing a society as a sum lump, assuming that a policy or a prediction fits everyone, this approach recognizes that the overall income distribution is a weighted combination of distributions from different socioeconomic groups. Making a general assumption about technology adoption, work retention, income growth while we have a mixture of sub-populations can have detrimental effects. Mathematically, this can be expressed as follows:

$$f(y) = \sum_{k=1}^{K} \pi_k f_k(y|\theta_k), \tag{2.3}$$

where $f(y)$ represents the overall income distribution, π_k is the proportion of the population in the group k, and $f_k(y|\theta_k)$ describes the income distribution for a specific group. Each component in the mixture model can represent distinct economic realities: stable middle-class workers with log-normal income distributions reflecting human capital returns, precarious gig economy participants with high-variance exponential distributions, capital owners with Pareto-distributed incomes reflecting superstar effects, or systematically excluded populations with truncated low-income distributions. If you remember, at the beginning of this chapter, we introduced the concept of social stratification. Since society is generally organized into groups that have a lower or higher average income. We can imagine one of those sub-populations represented by each of these k sub-distributions. Now, it is intuitive to see society as a mixture of them, though we should treat them independently.

For example, the previous equation to decompose the Gini index as

$$G = \sum_{k=1}^{K} \pi_k^2 G_k + \sum_{k=1}^{K} \sum_{j \neq k} \pi_k \pi_j \frac{|\mu_k - \mu_j|}{2\bar{y}}, \tag{2.4}$$

where G_k represents the inequality within the group for the component k, μ_k is the mean income of the group k and $\bar{y}$ is the total mean income.

This decomposition demonstrates whether inequality is generated primarily by inequalities in opportunities in various socioeconomic classes or by variances within relatively homogeneous groupings. The main causes of inequality may be market segmentation and structural obstacles if mixture model research shows that the majority of disparity results from disparities between groups rather than within them. On the other hand, if group inequality predominates, this may suggest that personal traits and chance elements are more important.

This distinction is crucial for policy design. High between-group inequality suggests that targeted interventions addressing specific barriers faced by different groups may be most effective. High within-group inequality might call for broader policies that affect individual capabilities and opportunities across all groups. Piketty's analysis of wealth concentration (Piketty 2014) demonstrates how mixture models can reveal the distinct dynamics of capital accumulation among different social classes.

The mixture model framework has been widely investigated by Stiglitz and his colleagues (Stiglitz 2012, 2015), providing empirical tools to identify population segments that exist within a society, to define what proportion of the population belongs to each group, and to show how income-generating processes differ among groups. This ultimately allows us to quantify social mobility and identify the factors that enable or prevent transitions between economic groups.

We can imagine that for groups characterized by low human capital and limited access to the labor market, policies could focus on education, training, and removing other barriers to employment. For groups facing credit constraints, microfinance or guaranteed loan programs might be most effective. Failing to properly segment the target of a policy intervention might result in people remaining in their relative poverty status, and inequality might even increase. This has led to the seminal expression and book title "The Price of Inequality" (Stiglitz 2012).

Countries with similar GDP or overall inequality levels might have very different underlying structures, which require different policy approaches. International comparisons using mixture models can reveal best practices and successful policy interventions.

For example, to measure human capital investment returns, mixture models can guide education policy by identifying components with the highest returns to education:

$$R_k = \frac{\partial \ln(\mu_k)}{\partial E_k}, \tag{2.5}$$

where R_k is the return to education in component k and E_k is the average level of education. This enables targeted educational investments that maximize social returns.

Technology has historically been in the hands of rich early adopters, at least at the early stage. Therefore, technology-driven inequality is not uniformly experienced, and this goes from steam engines to AI large language models. It has often been suggested that finite mixture models could capture these dynamics by assigning different probability distributions to the income trajectories or employment risk of each group. Although not fully investigated with mixture models, Korinek and Stiglitz introduced the idea of discussing the nonneutrality of technology, challenging the neoclassical idea that it automatically benefits all (Korinek and Stiglitz 2018). Paving the way to the need for further investigation of the impact of AI and novel technologies, segmented across populations and not assumed equal for entire populations.

2.5 Models Measuring AI Growth and Poverty

We have already discussed that separating populations into latent subgroups based on technological impact might be a good idea, especially now that we are experiencing the AI renaissance. Undeniably, automation has always been focused on productivity. However, productivity is not directly proportional to the benefit of a large group of people, including workers. In a liberal society, if certain roles are minimized or disappear, the employees are "relocated" to other jobs or instructed to higher roles, e.g., a mechanic twisting nobs, can be re-trained and re-employed in the supervisor of the software twisting nobs. This is true until replacement innovation and new employment are in synchrony. If innovation surpasses everything and is focused exclusively on productivity, this might not be the case. A possible analysis we can conduct in this context is related to simulations measuring and predicting inequality and automation adoption.

Simulations have been used in different fields of science for decades, from the spread of disease to heat conductivity in materials, including the spread of innovation, as we discussed in the previous chapter. Simulation models have also been designed to estimate growth, explaining the dynamics of economic expansion, but also incorporate novel approaches to measuring inequality. In the last section of the book, we will examine with practical examples how the accelerating race in AI can positively affect low-income countries, thereby influencing poverty levels. However, given the current hype and interest in AI for productivity, there is the risk that AI will also increase inequality. In the context of the development economy, Acemoglu and Restrepo (2020) examined the impact of industrial robots on employment and wages in the US labor markets between 1990 and 2007. The authors investigated how the adoption of industrial robots affects employment and wages in local labor markets in the United States. They examine both the direct displacement effect of robots on employment and the potential compensating mechanisms. Acemoglu and Restrepo developed a model that simulates the case of robots that can replace human labor in specific tasks, creating a displacement effect. However, this can be counterbalanced by various compensating adjustments through productivity effects, capital accumulation, and the creation of new tasks that favor human labor. The key variable is the "exposure to robots" *ETR* for each commuting zone, defined as

$$ETR = \sum_{i \in I} \frac{L_{ci0}}{L_{c0}} \times \Delta R_i, \tag{2.6}$$

where

- L_{ci0}/L_{c0} is the initial employment share of industry i in commuting zone c.
- ΔR_i is the increase in robot usage in industry i in the US.

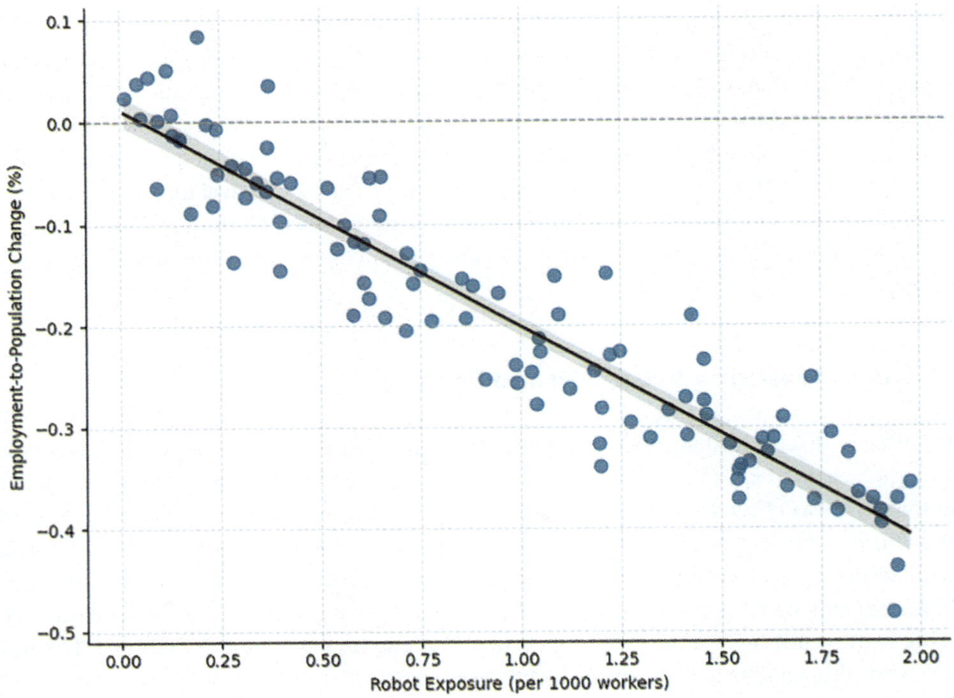

Fig. 2.7 Scatter-plot depicting the time evolution according to the simulation of robot-explosion as in Acemoglu and Restrepo (2020)

Running these models on trained data and future prediction led to the conclusion that one more robot per thousand workers reduces the employment-to-population ratio by approximately 0.2% points and wages by 0. 42%, suggesting that the displacement effect of robots outweighs the productivity effect in the time period studied, as depicted in Fig. 2.7. In conclusion, workers with less than a college degree, especially those in manufacturing, manual, physical labor, assembly, and related occupations, are disproportionately affected when there is a lack of appropriate policies in place.

The findings have significant implications for policy, suggesting that the rapid adoption of automation technologies can exacerbate inequality and create localized employment challenges. These effects are not inevitable technological consequences, but depend on the institutional and policy environment. Even in medieval times, which are rarely considered times of innovation, we had sort of policies in act to reallocate people. During the middle age, we had the introduction of watermills, windmills, and the magnetic compass. Just to mention a few. The guild system, churches, and monasteries were training centers. Innovations like the windmill or the watermill created a demand for millwrights, who trained assistants informally (Lucas 2006). However, there is a reason why we remember medieval times as bleak, and the reason is that even with the retraining of people, innovations did not translate into improved living standards for the majority (Acemoglu and Johnson 2023).

Therefore, it is worth focusing on both retraining policies and profit sharing, taxation, and social safety nets. Workers with less than a college education will be the hardest hit, and men will be more affected than women due to their higher representation in these vulnerable occupations. Currently, in Sub-Saharan countries we have observed negligible impact related to increase in automation (Parschau and Hauge 2020), but while those countries will increase their adoption, we can imagine they will be also hit hard.

The fear of techno-feudalism is not a mere paranoia. Without appropriate policy interventions, the continued adoption of AI, robots, and automation technologies could lead to higher unemployment and wage inequality. The power is currently in the hands of a few tech giants, which might be the new kings. It is crucial that countries implement retraining programs aimed at workers displaced by automation and regulatory policies to avoid unlimited power to the new kings (Varoufakis 2024).

2.6 The Robot Tax

The simulation models discussed in the previous section articulate a critical economic warning: the capital-driven logic of automation risks displacing labor and depressing wages unless addressed by safety nets and reallocation programs (Acemoglu and Restrepo 2020). Although this idea points to potential compensatory mechanisms such as new tasks and productivity gains, history cautions that such benefits are neither automatic nor equitably shared. The policy conversation, therefore, must broaden from a singular focus on *retraining* the displaced worker to encompass strategies for *redistributing* the wealth automation creates and interrogating the *physical substrate* upon which this new economy is built.

Retraining programs are a necessary but insufficient response to systemic displacement. They place the full burden of adaptation on the individual and often fail to match the velocity of change. Structural policies that transform economic relationships are required to complement them. We mentioned safety nets a few times, and we can also discuss reduction of working hours or universal basic income (UBI) policies. The 4-day workweek policy reduces the standard working week (usually to 32 h) without cutting pay, aiming to improve the balance between work and home, productivity and mental health (Lewis et al. 2023). UBI is a policy in which every adult receives a regular unconditional cash payment from the state to guaranty basic economic security, regardless of employment status (Hasdell 2020). Yet, one question will remain: Where can we find the funding necessary to implement safety nets or those potentially useful policies without borrowing from other financial resources such as for healthcare and education? Considering that the source of concerns is the automation, it might also be the solution in the form of the so called robot tax.

The concept of a robot tax, or more accurately an automation impact levy, addresses a core market failure. When a firm automates, it privatizes the savings from a reduced wage bill while socializing the costs of unemployment and community decline. A tax on displacement aims to slow the pace of automation to a socially manageable rate and generate revenue to fund transition policies like UBI or other welfare programs. Experimental evidence supports its mechanistic function, showing that such a tax can reduce the probability of worker substitution (Cabrales et al. 2020). However, significant design and philosophical critiques challenge its viability. Defining the taxable unit as "the robot" or "the AI algorithm", is fraught, as automation is often a process of software integration, not discrete hardware purchase. Prominent tax scholars argue that a new, targeted robot tax is less effective than reforming broader capital taxation systems, suggesting that its political appeal may stem from behavioral biases more than sound fiscal policy (Oberson 2017).

Apart criticisms related to the excessive "socialism" in this policy, the robot tax debate exposes a broader governance problem: the absence of standardized metrics to quantify automation-induced displacement. An effective policy would require firm-level reporting of labor substitution, productivity gains, and capital deepening attributable to automation. Without such accounting frameworks, taxation risks being blunt or easily arbitrated, undermining both efficiency and legitimacy (Hoette et al. 2024). Nevertheless, at a deeper level, the robot tax debate reflects a renegotiation of the social contract in automated economies. If productivity increasingly derives from capital rather than labor, continued reliance on labor-based taxation becomes normatively unstable. The question is not only how to fund welfare, but how to redefine contribution and entitlement in a post-labor growth model (Stiefenhofer 2025). Even if the robot tax sounds like a great idea, its practical deployment is not straightforward.

2.7 Talking to New Generations About Decoupling While Innovating

According to the Malthusian growth model depicted in Fig. 2.8, the human population probably grows exponentially, while the resources it uses are available or regenerate linearly. This ultimately leads to a point where there are less available resources, inequality is introduced, and well-being is compromised (Malthus 1826).

This is a pessimistic view which not only points out the catastrophic circumstances where inequality will increase over time, but also a view where well-being of the human race is detrimental to the system where it lives. A paradox in which we improve and threaten ourselves at the same time. Regardless of this pessimistic view, there is general agreement that our current lifestyle and growth models impact our environment, with negative effects especially for people with low financial status, since global warming lowers agricultural yield, causes more frequent extreme weather events such as flooding and heat spikes, and favors epidemics in areas with an already weak healthcare system (Skoufias et al. 2011).

Therefore, beyond the limited scope of conventional growth paradigms, the issue of wealth creation in the Global South via technology and artificial intelligence needs to be rethought. Instead of mindlessly pursuing economic development as determined just by GDP, it is crucial to introduce new generations to the concepts of decoupling. In ecological context, we refer to "decoupling" as an economy that would be able to grow without corresponding increases in environmental pressure. There are several schools that discuss how this decoupling will happen. In its extreme form: "Degrowth", as a conscious downscaling of material throughput. Other times referred to as "Sustainomy" (Isarabhakdee 2025) or well-being-growth decoupling (Okpoti et al. 2024). Briefly, scholars are divided into those who believe

Fig. 2.8 Graphical representation of the Malthusian growth model. Population grows exponentially while resources increase or regenerate only linearly. The dark gray area marks the onset of scarcity-driven inequalities

that we can still maintain well-being even for a growing population, and those who believe that all policies and innovation will be insufficient to compensate for the overall expansion of economic output, and the only choice is to reduce growth (Hickel et al. 2022). Green growth is substantially imagined as a trajectory, where society at an early stage inevitably exploits resources in an inconsiderate manner, and then after a tipping point, they evolve their technology so that well-being is still maximized while minimizing the impact on the environment. Technology and policy win in turning pollution into a continuous sustainable growth, obviously if we take serious actions. Talking about degrowth to low-income countries is a superchallenge, as their governments have reduced funding, still fighting corruption, recovering from civil wars or epidemics that disappeared less than ten years ago.

Understanding which scenario is the most likely is beyond the purpose of this book, and the reader is referred to contemporary reviews (Okpoti et al. 2024). We can discuss here how to present this scenario to the Global South, especially considering AI. Nevertheless, decoupling can be represented graphically as in Fig. 2.9 where two elements increase at the same rate and one decrease. Something has to decrease, either is our throughput/GDP, our well-being, or the sustainability.

Among the creative views on this topic, there are some ideas related to inequality around the world that behave like waves (Milanovic 2016) or self-regulating complex systems (Farmer 2024). Waves in the sense that countries oscillate from high inequality to low inequality and back. We move evolving technologically and socially, but at the same time we grow in population (as the exponential Malthusian growth), creating scarcity, and once we are too many, people cannot afford to have children, reducing the population and environmental impact, and bringing us back to abundance. Basically, the decrease in

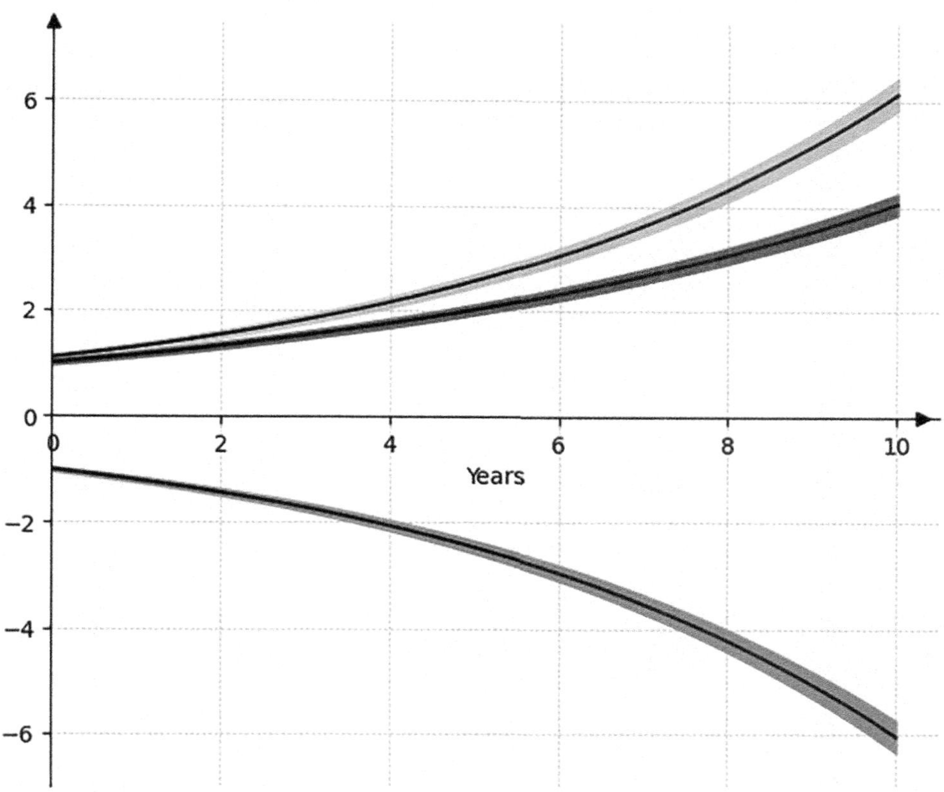

Fig. 2.9 Three variables plotted over time: GDP, well-being, and impact, depending on the scenario, one variable must decline while the other two rise. Time will tell us whether the divergent curve is GDP, well-being, or sustainability

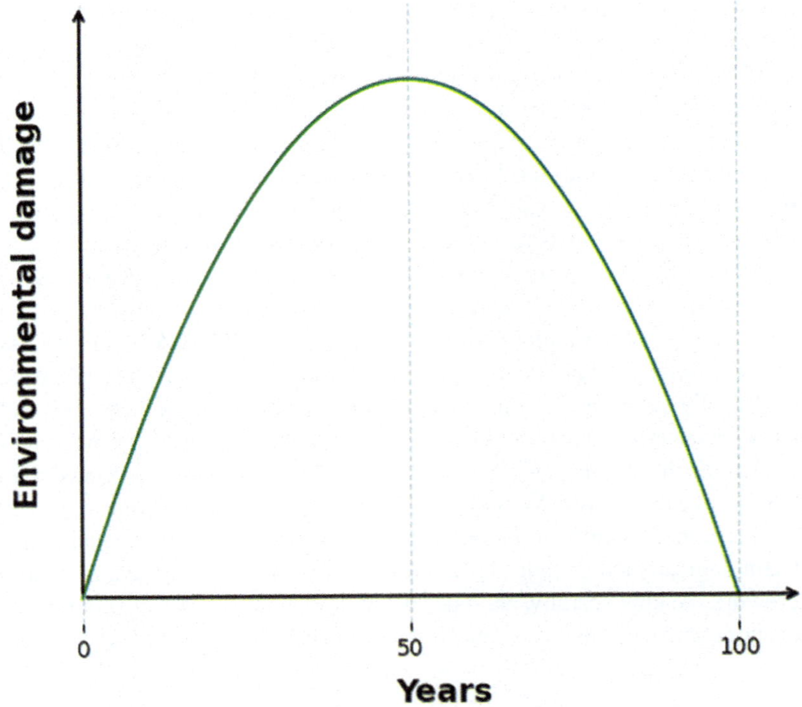

Fig. 2.10 This figure depicts the Kuznetz curve, where we start from a point of low technological advancement and low environmental impact. Technology at some point creates a lot of environmental impact, but slowly becomes more sustainable. The represented years are just indicative and not based on any estimate

birth rates that advanced countries are experiencing is the result of self-regulation. It is a sort of implicit degrowth. While this is happening, low-income countries advance, reducing the difference, and slowly also entering this game of waves abundance-scarcity, equality-inequality, growth-degrowth. This is a social phenomenon widely observed in bacteria cultures (Madigan et al. 1997), where bacteria increase their population in culture, up to the point which is unsustainable and ultimately leads to a decrease of population. Hopefully, humans are more organized and conscious than bacteria, and maybe technology advancement will save us all as the Green Growth mindset foretells, and we do not need to sacrifice our birth rate. We could imagine that technological advancement proceeded as an upside-down U shape shown in Fig. 2.10. We start with low environmental impact, low technology, and economic growth, and progress to a point of high technological advancement, scarcity, and high environmental impact, but then slowly our society improves and we have less scarcity and less environmental impact (Kuznets 1955).

AI in particular has the potential to revolutionize economies and civilizations by opening up new avenues for innovation, production, education, and problem solving. We have already mentioned that this technological advancement has the potential to increase current disparities, inequalities, and environmental issues if it is not critically addressed. Not least of all, the energy consumption that is needed to create and update AI models. Integrating AI-driven innovation with social ideals that place a high priority on shared wealth, society, and ecological balance is a very difficult task.

Young people in the Global South see technology as a way to regain agency and self-determination rather than only as a tool for financial gain or consumer convenience. Even later in this book, we talk about these technologies to "decolonize". While we proceed with development and social change, the decoupling from the economy, increasing GDP, and quality of life has to happen from pollution and non-sustainable technologies. It is a double challenge for low-income countries, if just one of them was not cumbersome enough, but there is little choice.

A key component of this vision is social innovation, as we discussed in the first chapter. Social innovation encourages grassroots cooperative projects that address urgent social and environmental concerns by redefining value beyond market measurements. Crucially, by prioritizing sufficiency, local resilience, and solidarity over wealth, they exemplify the values of growth. After all, according to recent estimates, all continents and sub-continents in the world South have the potential to become solar powerhouses, closing the world's energy access gap (International Energy Agency (IEA) 2021). Young innovators who are encouraged to participate in such projects develop a mindset that strikes a balance between their passion for technology and their social and environmental responsibilities.

At the policy level, given the growing demands, policies should also protect against the environmental costs of AI, such as energy-intensive computing, by promoting low-impact alternatives and principles of circular economy. We do not know whether the decoupling will be more Well-being-GDP-oriented rather than GDP-impact-oriented. We should nevertheless develop and adopt more efficient technologies that can reduce resource consumption and pollution. This is already happening with electric cars and saving lights, which even if they still have carbon footprints, they are definitely lower compared to older technologies (Hawkins et al. 2012).

In the end, the discussion with younger generations is about developing a conception of prosperity that goes beyond material excess. Even contexts like the Global South, which are seeing technological improvements now, need to align with paradigms aligned to sustainability (Wilson and Milanez 2021). If we think that innovation such as mobile phones has leapfrogged the economic and environmental challenges given by the landline phone infrastructure. We could be a bit optimistic. It is crucial to establish areas for experimentation, education, and cooperation where new technologies enhance group capabilities rather than deepen divisions. The wisdom and values required to manage technology for the benefit of society will be passed on to the following generations in this way, in addition to the tools and knowledge. All these are probably nice words, and in practice, this is the fusion of demanding constraints which can be hardly be satisfied. The take-home message in the end is that while innovating, we need to focus on being sustainable focusing on KPI related to sustainability rather than just GDP, attempting to satisfy all those constraints, and educating new generations to think like this.

2.8 Redirecting Economics

We can summarize the main policies of the past in Table 2.1. Those can give us valuable lessons that we can adapt to the new trends of automation and AI. Hence, given all elements related to inequality, we need to recognize the dual challenge of technological disruption and persistent social stratification, hypothetical policy interventions should include:

- **Progressive Redistribution:** Social programs can be financed by enacting tax laws that take a cut of the exceptional returns of AI investments. Obviously, those tax systems are progressive, with higher tax rates for those with higher income or more wealth.
- **Inclusive Education and Training:** It is crucial to improve the competencies of labor to be engaged in an AI-driven economy. This requires significant investment in ongoing education and training.
- **Support for Innovation Diffusion:** We should focus on policies that ensure the diffusion of AI benefits at different levels of the society, such as subsidies for small and medium companies adopting AI, vocational educational plans for people with only basic education, can help mitigate concentration effects.
- **Strengthening Social Safety Nets:** By strengthening social protection mechanisms, vulnerable groups can be protected from the shocks of rapid technological advancement. If necessary, those

Table 2.1 Past approaches to fighting poverty across education, healthcare, and other social changes

Domain	Past approaches	Impact	Limitations
Education	• Universal primary education (e.g., UNESCO 2015) • Conditional cash transfers (e.g., Bolsa Família Soares et al. 2010, Progresa Skoufias 2005) • Vocational and skills training (McKenzie 2017)	• Increased school enrollment • Improved literacy and future earnings • Better labor market participation	• Quality gaps in teaching • Weak alignment with job market • Gender and rural-urban disparities
Healthcare	• Universal health coverage (e.g., Thailand's UHC Tangcharoensathien et al. 2018) • Maternal/child health programs (Campbell and Graham 2006) • Community health workers (Perry et al. 2014)	• Reduced mortality rates • Increased productivity • Improved quality of life	• Poor infrastructure • High out-of-pocket costs • Rural-urban access gaps
Other social changes & • Microfinance programs (e.g., Grameen Bank Yunus 1998) • Women's empowerment initiatives especially in the countries still lagging behind (Kabeer 2012)	• Expanded access to credit and jobs • Greater participation in economic activities	• Risk of debt traps • Backlash to affirmative action • Persistent social stigma	

nets should be provided by companies if they continue to grow more than the economy of certain countries.

In other words, to adapt to the shifting capital-labor balance given by the stifling innovation and obsession of stakeholders in reducing costs, nations may think about enacting robot taxes or other measures to ensure that the benefits of automation are distributed more widely. While the topic is still controversial, most people argue that this will allow us to create the buffer money to be used for safety nets and other subsidies. Some people have already talked about "Googlization" (Suleyman 2025), where many products are turned into services in the hands of a few large companies.

These wage subsidies or other types of income support may be required during transitional times to enhance unemployment benefits and ensure that displaced workers can continue to live comfortably. Combining both previous ideas of the "re-instatement effect" (Acemoglu and Restrepo 2020) and mixture models (Stiglitz 2015), new jobs may be facilitated by policies that support human labor rather than replace it, targeting interventions to specific segment of the population to prevent a widening of inequality.

Following Schumpeter's theory (Langroodi 2021), many economists argue that the destruction of old jobs and industries is a necessary part of creating new, more productive opportunities. In fact, with the dot-com economy we had many new opportunities, and as we said even medieval times had created new job opportunities. But our main discussion is that this is not automatically translated into higher standards of living. Hence, government intervention, even if it could slow this beneficial process of economic evolution, is necessary.

Creating wealth and reducing poverty effectively requires effective policies, integrating local customs, and using innovative and ethical business practices. The possibility that we are convergent in another medieval age full of innovations but low standards of living for certain people is real. Given the still existing income differences, collaboration between the Global North and South can still foster meaningful social changes in those contexts. Something like optimistic green growth where it is accepted that some threat to the environment is unacceptable with the pledge that we will fix with appropriate technologies and policy.

Like the Environmental Kuznets Curve, the inverted U-curve where the relationship between economic growth and inequality in the long run posits that environmental impacts tend to increase sharply with industrialization but that after a certain turning point they start to decrease (Kuznets 1955).

The next chapters will cover more practical and technological aspects related to the theoretical frameworks introduced in this chapter.

2.9 Summary of the Chapter

The persistence of global poverty reveals fundamental tensions between economic theories and on-the-ground realities. There is a large literature framing those realities as traps or cycles which force people to remain in their low status. These manifest not only through income deprivation but through intersecting barriers in health, education, and governance. Key poverty traps include:

- Health-nutrition barriers preventing human capital accumulation.
- Conflict dynamics destroying physical and institutional capital.
- Resource curses creating perverse economic incentives.
- Governance failures perpetuating exclusionary systems.

There have also been debates about whether those traps really exist and how much they are still impacting given the advancement of technology and society. Nevertheless, contemporary development economics has moved beyond simple GDP metrics to model poverty's cyclical nature. While we have always thought of education as the great equalizer, AI is appearing as the education on steroids, and therefore there are great expectations mixed with many fears of becoming uncontainable. Successful interventions like Ghana's prenatal telemedicine program demonstrate that technological solutions only succeed when integrated with traditional authority structures. Community health workers using mobile diagnostics achieved impact precisely because they worked through village chiefs and respected local hierarchies.

Emerging technologies present both promise and danger in the reduction of poverty. Thanks to new technology we generally experience increase of quality of life. Although AI could democratize access to education and financial services, research on the relation of automation to the job market warns of about polarization effects that may exacerbate inequality without deliberate policy safeguards. Compensatory mechanisms to ensure inclusive progress:

- Constant reallocation and reintegration programs for workers, especially for grassroots workers.
- Safety nets to protect workers during the reallocation process.

Ultimately, sustainable poverty reduction requires moving beyond either/or both frameworks. Neither pure market approaches nor top-down redistribution suffice alone. The most effective strategies combine targeted human capital investments with institutional reforms that transform the rules of economic participation—creating not just temporary escapes from poverty, but permanent pathways to prosperity.

References

Abdulai M, Ibrahim H, Anas AL (2023) The role of indigenous communication systems for rural development in the Tolon District of Ghana. Res Globalization 6:100128

Abshire J (2011) The history of Singapore. Bloomsbury Publishing USA

Acemoglu D, Restrepo P (2020) Robots and jobs: evidence from US labor markets. J Polit Econ 128(6):2188–2244

Acemoglu D, Johnson S (2023) Power and progress: our thousand-year struggle over technology and prosperity. Hachette

Adato M, Carter MR, May J (2013) Exploring poverty traps and social exclusion in South Africa using qualitative and quantitative data, pp 60–81 Understanding and reducing persistent poverty in Africa. Routledge

Akiwumi, P, LDC Insight #3: Digitalization as a driver of structural transformation in African LDCs (United Nations 2023). www.un.org/technologybank/news/digitalization-driver-structural-transformation-african-ldcs, Accessed 16 November 2023

Amoah B, Anto EA, Osei PK, Pieterson K, Crimi A (2016) Boosting antenatal care attendance and number of hospital deliveries among pregnant women in rural communities: a community initiative in Ghana based on mobile phones applications and portable ultrasound scans. BMC Pregnancy Childbirth 16:1–10

Banerjee AV, Duflo E (2007) The economic lives of the poor. J Econ Perspect 21(1):141–167

Cabrales A, Hernández P, Sánchez A (2020) Robots, labor markets, and universal basic income. Human Soc Sci Commun 7(1):1–8

Campbell OM, Graham WJ (2006) Strategies for reducing maternal mortality: getting on with what works. The Lancet 368(9543):1284–1299

Carter MR, Barrett CB (2006) The economics of poverty traps and persistent poverty: an asset-based approach. J Dev Stud 42(2):178–199

Castilla EJ, Poskanzer EJ (2022) Through the front door: why do organizations (still) prefer legacy applicants? Am Soc Rev 87(5):782–826

Chambers R (1994) Participatory rural appraisal (PRA): analysis of experience. World Dev 22(9):1253–1268

Chigwata T (2016) The role of traditional leaders in Zimbabwe: are they still relevant? Law Democracy Dev 20(1):69–90

Collier P (2008) The bottom billion: why the poorest countries are failing and what can be done about it. Oxford University Press, USA

Cordeiro-Rodrigues L, Metz T (2021) Afro-communitarianism and the role of traditional African healers in the COVID-19 pandemic. Public Health Ethics 14(1):59–71

Cowell FA (2011) Measuring inequality. Oxford University Press

Cox RW (1987) Production, power, and world order: social forces in the making of history. Columbia University Press

Davis K, Moore WE (1945) The idea of social stratification. Am Soc Rev 10(2):242–249

Deaton A (2024) The great escape: health, wealth, and the origins of inequality. pp 1–384

Easterly W (2014) The tyranny of experts: Economists, dictators, and the forgotten rights of the poor. Basic Books

Eliazar I, Cohen MH (2014) On social inequality: analyzing the rich-poor disparity. XXPhys A 401:148–158

Farmer JD (2024) Making sense of chaos: a better economics for a better world. Yale University Press

Galvin M (2015) Talking shit: is community-led total sanitation a radical and revolutionary approach to sanitation? Wiley Interdiscip Rev Water 2(1):9–20

Ghani A, Lockhart C (2009) A framework for rebuilding a fractured world. Oxford University Press, Fixing failed states

Giesbert L, Schindler K (2012) Assets, shocks, and poverty traps in rural Mozambique. World Dev 40(8):1594–1609

Hasdell R (2020) What we know about universal basic income. A cross-synthesis, Standfor Basic Income Lab

Hawkins TR, Gausen OM, Strømman AH (2012) Environmental impacts of hybrid and electric vehicles-a review. Int J Life Cycle Assess 17(8):997–1014

Hickel J, Kallis G, Jackson T, O'Neill DW, Schor JB, Steinberger JK, Victor PA, Ürge-Vorsatz D (2022) Degrowth can work-here's how science can help. Nature 612(7940):400–403

Hoette K, Theodorakopoulos A, Koutroumpis P (2024) Automation and taxation. Oxf Econ Pap 76(4):945–969

International Energy Agency (IEA) (2021) Africa energy outlook 2022. Paris: IEA. https://www.iea.org/reports/africa-energy-outlook-2022

Isarabhakdee P (2025) Achieving sustainable growth requires rethinking the economy (Sustainomy). Time. Accessed from April 7, 2025. https://time.com/7275422/sustainable-economic-growth-sustainomy/

Jegede AS (2007) What led to the Nigerian boycott of the polio vaccination campaign? PLoS Med

Jerome A, Singh EJ, Mills (2005) The abandoned trials of pre-exposure prophylaxis for HIV: what went wrong? PLoS Med

Kabeer N (2012) Women's economic empowerment and inclusive growth: labour markets and enterprise development.SIG Working Paper 2012/1

Kamal S, Shaheed A, Majumder MAA (2015) Community-led total sanitation and its impacts: a literature review. Environ Dev Sustain 17(6):1343–1360

Korinek A, Stiglitz JE (2018) Artificial intelligence and its implications for income distribution and unemployment. University of Chicago Press, An agenda. The economics of artificial intelligence, pp 349–390
Kuznets S (1955) Economic Growth and Income Inequality. Am Econ Rev 45(1):1–28
Langroodi FE (2021) Schumpeter's theory of economic development: a study of the creative destruction and entrepreneurship effects on the economic growth. J Insurance and Financial Manag 4(3):65–81
Lewis K (2023) The results are. The UK's four-day week plot, vol 26. Autonomy
Lucas A (2006) Wind, water, work: ancient and medieval milling technology. Brill
Madigan MT, Martinko JM, Parker J (1997) Brock biology of microorganisms, vol 11. Prentice hall, Upper Saddle River, NJ
Malthus TR (1826) An essay on the principle of population: a view of its past and present effects on human happiness; with an inquiry into our prospects respecting the future removal or mitigation of the evils which it occasions, 6th edn. John Murray, London
McKenzie D (2017) How effective are active labor market policies in developing countries? A critical review of recent evidence. The World Bank Research Observer 31(2):159–198
Milanovic B (2016) Global inequality: a new approach for the age of globalization. Harvard University Press
Moyer CA, Aborigo RA, Logonia G, Affah G, Rominski S, Adongo PB, Williams J, Hodgson A, Engmann C (2012) Clean delivery practices in rural northern Ghana: a qualitative study of community and provider knowledge, attitudes, and beliefs. BMC Pregnancy Childbirth 12:50
Moyo D (2009) Dead aid: why aid is not working and how there is a better way for Africa. Macmillan
Naschold F (2012) The poor stay poor: household asset poverty traps in rural semi-arid India. World Dev 40(10):2033–2043
Nyika A (2010) Engaging diverse communities participating in clinical trials: case examples from across. Africa Malaria J
Oberson X (2017) Taxing robots? From the emergence of an electronic ability to pay to a tax on robots or the use of robots. World Tax J 247
Okpoti C, Oswald Y, Vogel J, Malik A, Steinberger JK (2024) Unsustainable prosperity? Decoupling wellbeing, economic growth, and greenhouse gas emissions over the past 150 years. World Dev 175:106610. https://doi.org/10.1016/j.worlddev.2024.106610
Parschau C, Hauge J (2020) Is automation stealing manufacturing jobs? Evidence from South Africa's apparel industry. Geoforum 115:120–131
Peprah P, Agyemang-Duah W, Arthur-Holmes F, Budu HI, Abalo EM, Okwei R, Nyonyo J (2019) 'We are nothing without herbs': a story of herbal remedies use during pregnancy in rural Ghana. BMC Complement Altern Med 19(1):65
Perry H et al (2014) Community health workers at the dawn of a new era: 1. Introduction: tension, uncertainty, and opportunity. Health Res Policy Syst 12(1):1
Piketty T (2014) Capital in the twenty-first century. Harvard University Press
Rahman A, Pingali P (2024) Anti-poverty transfers: policy successions with little success. The future of India's social safety nets: focus, form, and scope. Springer International Publishing, pp 95–131
Ravallion M (2008) Poverty lines. The new Palgrave dictionary of economics, 2nd edn. Palgrave Macmillan
Robinson JA, Acemoglu D (2012) Why nations fail: the origins of power, prosperity and poverty. Profile, London, pp 45–47
Rosenberg N (1960) Capital formation in underdeveloped countries. Am Econ Rev 50(4):706–715
Sachs JD (2006) The end of poverty: economic possibilities for our time. Penguin
Sachs JD, Warner AM (2001) The curse of natural resources. Eur Econ Rev 45(4–6):827–838
Skoufias E (2005) PROGRESA and its impacts on the welfare of rural households in Mexico. IFPRI Research Report
Skoufias E, Rabassa M, Olivieri S (2011) The poverty impacts of climate change: a review of the evidence. Policy Research Working Papers
Soares FV, Ribas RP, Osório RG (2010) Evaluating the impact of Brazil's Bolsa Família: cash transfer programs in comparative perspective. Lat Am Res Rev 45(2):173–190
Solar PM (1995) Poor relief and English economic development before the industrial revolution 1. Econ Hist Rev 48(1):1–22
Stiefenhofer P (2025) Artificial general intelligence and the social contract: a dynamic political economy model. J Econ Anal 4(3):142–183
Stiglitz JE (2012) The price of inequality: how today's divided society endangers our future. Norton & Company, W. W
Stiglitz JE (2015) The great divide: unequal societies and what we can do about them. Norton & Company, W. W
Suleyman M (2025) The coming wave: AI, power, and our future. Random House
Tangcharoensathien V et al (2018) Health systems development in Thailand: a solid platform for UHC. The Lancet 391(10126):1205–1213
Tumin MM (1953) Some principles of stratification: a critical analysis. Am Soc Rev 18(4):387–394
UNESCO (2015) Education for All 2000–2015: Achievements and challenges. UNESCO Publishing

Varoufakis Y (2024) Technofeudalism: what killed capitalism. Melville House

von Salmuth V, Brennan E, Kerac M, McGrath M, Frison S, Lelijveld N (2021) Maternal-focused interventions to improve infant growth and nutritional status in low-middle income countries: a systematic review of reviews. PLoS ONE 16(8):e0256188

Wilson DC, Milanez B (2021) Decoupling: a key discourse in environmental policy, but what does it mean for sustainable consumption? J Clean Prod 295:126361

World Bank Open Data. https://data.worldbank.org. <!– Missing/Wrong Year –>

World Health Organization (2025) Trends in maternal mortality 2000 to 2023: estimates by WHO. UNICEF, UNFPA, World Bank Group and UNDESA/Population Division

Yunus M (1998) Banker to the poor: the story of the Grameen Bank. Penguin Books India

Zhou Y, Liu Y (2022) The geography of poverty: review and research prospects. J Rural Stud 93:408–416. https://doi.org/10.1016/j.jrurstud.2019.01.008

3 Educational Impact

Education is the great equalizer, and many policies have been applied for a long time (Snilstveit et al. 2015). Those are of critical importance for both the Global North and the Global South, as inequality exists even in the richest countries. In this chapter, we do not review policies related to education but examine more opportunities for creating better collaboration for non-local people who want to start cooperation with learning and empowering initiatives. The relationship between education and economic growth has been studied extensively (Bah and Brada 2009). There have been many confirmations that the quality of education (especially primary/secondary) is a significant growth factor in many countries (Goczek et al. 2021). However, even if education increases the skills, knowledge, and productivity of the workforce, increments are not linear. For example, a 10% increase in education per worker could increase GDP by 4–5% in neoclassical models (Dickens and Sawhill 2006), and more specifically growth in Sub-Saharan countries is more proportional to investments in education when political stability, corruption control, and other factors are in place (Abu and Abdullahi 2010). Nevertheless, there is a significant body of research and debate linking infant protection and education and the development of a country. As countries see a decrease in child mortality correlated with faster growth (Fogel 1994), with potential causal relationships that can be summarized in the diagram in Fig. 3.1. The idea is that infants are the future of a country, and we should nurture them, by taking care of their health and nutrition, then of their education which will create higher human capital, and ultimately an increased labor force and productivity. An ideal productive society is a society where education and continuous learning are prioritized (Stiglitz and Greenwald 2014). In summary, we cannot hide the social impact of education, and in this chapter, we focus on this, especially in the perspective of a Global North reader interested in the Global South and in contributing with educational exchanges.

3.1 Rural Communities and Progressive Universities

In the previous sections, a series of general aspects related to change and system thinking have been presented. Instead, in this and the following sections, we delve into aspects related to human capital investment, especially for the Global South: education and other relevant trainings. Global South literally refers to vibrant cultures like Sub-Saharan Africa, Southeast India or rural Latin America, or literally the southern hemisphere ,which is often disadvantaged from the point of view of innovation and financial revenues for most of the population of those countries. Those places full of breathtaking

© The Author(s), under exclusive license to Springer Nature Switzerland AG 2026

A. Crimi, *Innovate for Impact*, Sustainable Development Goals Series,
https://doi.org/10.1007/978-3-032-21563-5_3

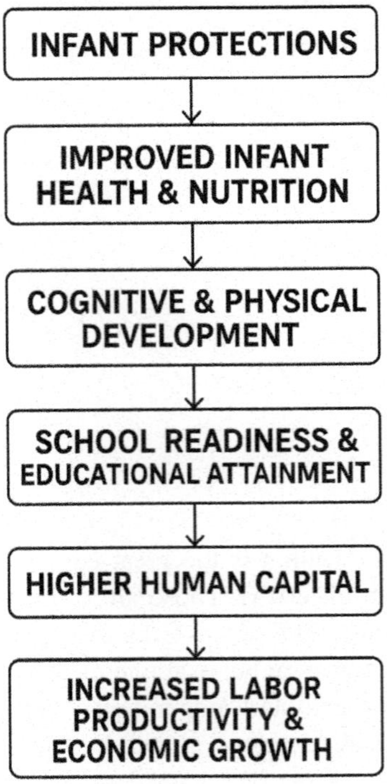

Fig. 3.1 Simplistic causal relationship in favor of the infant protection and education linked to faster economic growth

landscapes and immense potential offer academics a unique opportunity to share knowledge and contribute to the continent's burgeoning educational landscape. However, the transition from a Western university to the Global South can present a series of challenges for foreign professors.

We can start from the most obvious: the resource disparity. Coming from well-equipped institutions, American or European professors might find themselves grappling with limited classroom resources, outdated technology, even overcrowded lecture halls, or circumstances between the idyllic and suboptimal, as shown in Fig. 3.2. Then, it takes imagination and adaptability to modify instructional strategies employed with pupils who have all the conveniences of home to these limitations. It could be necessary to switch from standard lectures to more interactive techniques, such as case studies or group discussions. Beyond logistical difficulties, there are also cultural differences in learning styles from an academic perspective. Western classrooms typically emphasize critical thinking and independent learning. Global South students, on the other hand, may be more used to teacher-centered learning, where it is still considered inappropriate to interrupt someone to ask a question. Ironically, I would call this teaching style "the transfer from the notes of the lecturer to the notes of the students" without real human interaction. This should be particularly avoided, with some cultural sensitivity and the readiness to modify teaching strategies to foster critical thinking, and active participation is necessary to close this gap. An anecdotal example is the lack of interactions and total awkward silence if students are prompted by statements like "any questions?" anecdotal differences pioneered even by Feynman (2010) 60 years ago, which unfortunately persist (where students were amazed by a more interactive style and talk to the lecturer rather than just listen and take notes).

For example, problem-based learning (PBL) is an educational approach that has the potential to equip learners. The general idea is that learners have a better grasp of the content if first they are exposed to the difficulties and challenges related to a topic and then learn the theories associated with the topic and their solutions. An upside-down approach to motivate more and have a better understanding, and in contrast to passive lectures where a lecture is limited to the process of memorizing information

Fig. 3.2 A poetic view of a blackboard on a balcony at the African Institute for Mathematical Science (Biriwa, Ghana). This, at the same time gives an idyllic impression of studying in nature, and points out the need of relocating outside a classroom, maybe because air-conditioning is not working

based on repetition of what the lecturer said (Allen et al. 2011). Although PBL has been used in higher education institutions in the Global North for some time, its adoption in Africa has been limited. This is because PBL can be complex with various information, discussions, projects, and approaches to draw from, and an appropriate structure of challenges articulated to teach. Given the different environment in the West, this requires a considerable redesign of the curriculum. Difficulties that can be more pronounced in the case of medical or other higher education (Solano et al. 2023). Contextualizing this within South Africa, in the literature, we can find cases for developing a curriculum structure that is oriented toward the country's development needs (Malan 2014), or definitions of educational curricula that help sustainable solutions for their communities in East Africa (Aalto PBL East Africa design 2024).

Beyond PBL, limited resources pose further challenges. African universities and colleges often face resource limitations in terms of infrastructure, equipment, and instructional materials compared to their counterparts in Europe or America. In 2015, I met students from Uganda who told me that they learned to program in C++ writing on sheets of paper without ever compiling their code in a computer, and I was amazed. Although, I believe, we are not at this level of discrepancy anymore, this anecdotally points out that the quality of instruction and learning opportunities in the Global South may suffer as a result of this shortage of resources. The efficiency of African professors' instruction may be impacted by their inability to obtain up-to-date research materials, sophisticated lab apparatus, and even reliable Internet connectivity (Moshtari and Safarpour 2024). The high rates of brilliant people migrating to other nations in quest of better training and research possibilities are another important effect of underdeveloped higher education institutions in low-income nations. Even some First World European countries are not immune to brain-drain disease. However, in the Global South this is more pronounced, only hindered by VISA requirements. In fact, African universities also struggle to retain highly skilled professors and researchers. This also includes qualified academic staff who migrate and leave understaffed local educational institutes (Moshtari and Safarpour 2024).

Special mention is given to those realities that push low-cost education focused on advanced topics such as biotechnology. Today, we have several movements of do-it-yourself biology, and several resources are available online. Some even hazardous movements gained momentum during the COVID-19 pandemic. We will go into more detail in the next chapter on biotech, but it is worth introducing the idea.

Many scientists had the initial insight to develop a more sustainable strategy to combat these diseases in the areas where they are most prevalent by empowering local researchers. In biotech polymerase chain reaction (PCR) is still widely used for testing and other fundamental steps in research. Although professional tools are considerably expensive (5000–10000 USD) relative to low-income countries, the reaction could be conducted with frugal components, making it possible to achieve high-level results in low-resource settings (Harris 1998). There have also been computers like Raspberry PI that are reduced to the pocket size and can be used both for programming in low-resource settings and to understand how to build a computer. If you can build your own computer with affordable pieces, you understand how it works. We will re-iterate on frugal innovations and accessible biotechnology in the next chapters. It is worthwhile to consider frugal innovation even for teaching and academic research in general.

In conclusion, teaching in the Global South has certain difficulties. Brain drain, disparities in academic standards, lack of infrastructure or equipment, and inadequate finance are the main problems universities and lecturers face. The Global North and South need to start working together to bridge the gap in the southern hemisphere. Mutuality in partnerships is the most interesting path, moving from an aid-focused model to collaborations with shared benefits where both the Global North and the Global South can learn (Mudaly and Chirikure 2023). This has already been highlighted by several case studies, for example, in a partnership between Norwegian and Ethiopian universities (Hanada 2021), although more cooperation is still needed.

3.2 Digital Divide and Inclusivity: Challenges and Solutions

Internet and cellular access have been extremely beneficial to low-income countries, especially those without landline infrastructure. Nonetheless, the global north and the global south differ greatly in terms of connectedness. This keeps drawing attention to the intricate variations in the way some groups have access to digital opportunities and resources. The construction of infrastructure is essential to closing the digital divide. Universities and research institutes require expensive devices for many disciplines, but knowledge and access to cloud computing is the basic need to address. This involves developing programs to ensure that everyone has access to reliable and reasonably priced Internet services, improving network infrastructure, and increasing broadband connectivity. Increasing connectivity to under-served places, such as isolated and rural communities with limited access, is essential because they still exist (Lythreatis et al. 2022).

In order to provide people and communities with the resources they need to thrive in the digital world, digital literacy must be promoted in tandem with infrastructure development (Vassilakopoulou and Hustad 2023). Important digital skills such as using Internet resources, assessing the reliability of information, with and without foundational models, and protecting personal data can be taught and trained in both official and informal digital literacy programs. People of all ages should have the opportunity to improve their digital skills. Even a street vendor from a rural area can benefit from basic internet and computing literacy and training can be performed in community centers, schools, and church associations even in rural areas. Finally, in order to effectively solve the issues caused by the digital divide, cooperation between numerous stakeholders is crucial. To share resources, governments, non-governmental groups, the commercial sector, and civil society organizations must collaborate.

Most African universities cannot afford institutional journal fees, or they are forced to resort to pirate networks where academic papers are freely available by a paywall (Björk 2017). From the point of view of research, HINARI (Health Inter-Network Access to Research Initiative) was supposed to reduce the divide. It was launched by the World Health Organization (WHO) to provide access to thousands of biomedical and health literature journals to non-profit institutions in low- and middle-income countries. It offers access to content from major publishers, greatly helping healthcare professionals, researchers, and policymakers in these regions (Katikireddi 2004). In practice, many papers that are typically behind paywalls become accessible to eligible institutions in low-income countries. An acceptable solution, while the entire scientific system will move toward open-access. This is an improvement, but it is far from being widely accepted and used by all publishers and in all universities in the Global South. The situation is even more cumbersome for publishing papers. While there has been a rapid shift pushing people to publish papers as open-access, and therefore removing the paywall for the reader. Many publishers still charge high fees (currently about 3000 USD) to publish, even to African authors (Mekonnen et al. 2022). There is a growing number of journals that allow one to publish in a hybrid manner. Namely, when authors cannot pay for the open-access fee, they can still publish the version of their paper in a "behind-paywall" manner, or full waiver if they can prove that they are from a low-income country. However, those are still few. A 2023 study analyzing article processing charge (APC) policies in most large open-access publishers found that 68.8% of journals offer fee waivers for authors in low- and middle-income countries, including many in Africa, although many articles were often excluded in the presence of co-authors from middle or high-income countries (Lawson 2015), or other cases of universities which despite the lack of funding were nevertheless classified as from middle-income countries and therefore excluded from the waiving process, victims of a threshold. Too rich to be labeled as low-income, and too poor to afford fees, which are still corresponding to one year salary of a PhD student in that country. We hope that the numbers improve with time.

3.3 African Institute for Mathematical Sciences (AIMS)

The African Institute for Mathematical Sciences (AIMS) is a prominent education and research institute in Sub-Saharan Africa, and at the time of writing this book is the most progressive place for education I have ever witnessed. It is a pan-African network of affiliated institutes throughout the continent, including institutes in Senegal, Ghana, Cameroon, and Rwanda, although the first center is located in Muizenberg, South Africa, not far from Cape Town. The Tanzanian center existed for a few years and was then closed due to lack of funding. The institute was established in September 2003 and is a growing hub for mathematical sciences, AI, education, and research in Africa. The original idea was to promote fundamental mathematics, as it was expected to have a larger impact on society, inspired by the idea to find the next Einstein among talented young students in Africa. This is a provocative idea that aims to empower local people, especially in believing in their true potential. The networks shifted slowly its focus toward AI and other applied math fields including also epidemiology and meteorology.

AIMS is the first network of centers of excellence at the international level for innovative education and research in mathematical sciences fostering a pan-African spirit. It was founded by The Next Einstein initiative (2024), a South African professor educated in the United Kingdom, together with other British and South African academics. The Center has made many significant contributions to the field of mathematics and related fields, including computer science.

The goal of AIMS is to develop and assist the upcoming generation of African mathematical scientists by equipping them with the know-how and abilities needed to address challenging problems in a variety of domains. With a special emphasis on giving African students the opportunity to pursue higher degrees in the discipline, the institute provides postgraduate training programs in mathematical sciences. Even if not explicitly said, the goal is also to create future leaders for the continent, showing them how to build international networks and be inspired to commit to changes in their own community.

AIMS has had a profound impact on the African continent, fostering collaboration and knowledge exchange between researchers, educators, and students from different African countries. By promoting excellence in mathematical sciences, AIMS contributes to the development of a highly skilled workforce that can address pressing challenges in areas such as healthcare, finance, and technology. In fact, most of the students graduating from one of the centers are then helped in the follow-up to find further research positions in Africa or around the world. Furthermore, some of them return to be lecturers at AIMS again closing the loop. In addition, the institute also plays a crucial role in bridging the gender gap in science, technology, engineering, and mathematics (STEM) fields by actively encouraging the participation of women in its programs and initiatives.

Since its launch, the institutes have also hosted many well-known lectures coming from around the world to conduct workshops and intense lecture cycles, from Carlo Rovelli, to Yann LeCun, Cédric Villani, etc. I have been visiting the center in Ghana for 9 years, and during the COVID-19 pandemic I conducted a course remotely for the center in South Africa.

The idea is also to provide a full immersion environment for students. In fact, the centers are often located in structures that previously occupied relatively isolated hotels by the beach, such as the one in Fig. 3.3. In a way that students are always immersed in a 24-hour environment where they can focus on science. It is not unusual to wander around the institute after 10 pm, and see students having tea with snacks while discussing partial differential equations on the blackboard. Lecturers often come from all over the world specifically for courses, workshops, or thesis supervision, and they are also living in a full immersion environment. In contrast to the pedagogical styles of some universities, which are highly conservative and limit interaction, the center reinforces the adoption of the aforementioned problem-based learning. The recruitment of visiting lecturers and thesis supervisors is running continuously in all centers. In summary, AIMS is a pioneering institution dedicated to promoting excellence in mathematics education, and teaching there for many years has been one of the most enriching experiences of my life. The AIMS model paved the way for other institutes that are now more prone to international exchanges within and outside the continent.

3.4 Entrepreneurial Education

As was mentioned at the beginning of the chapter, social entrepreneurship or just entrepreneurship, as long as done ethically and respects the law, can have a huge impact, especially in low-income countries. Sometimes, these impacts are even more sustainable than foreign aid policies (Christensen et al. 2019). If the main weapon against poverty relies on people capable of creating business opportunities on their own, developing an entrepreneurial mindset to promote self-reliance is the first step in breaking the cycle of poverty.

With this view in mind, it is clear that there is a need to increase entrepreneurial education to reduce poverty for all, which is still the SDG 1. Governments in the Global South should also play a crucial role in expanding entrepreneurial education through vocational training programs and youth business camps, recognizing the importance of fostering an entrepreneurial mindset among their young population. When this lacks, we can push this through the third sector, as discussed in Chap. 1. NGOs could play a pivotal role in carrying out this objective. With numerous training programs, organizations, and institutions that focus on giving young people entrepreneurial skills and information, entrepreneurial education has accelerated across the Global South in recent years. One notable initiative is the School Enterprise Challenge, implemented by Teach a Man to Fish, which supports young entrepreneurs around the world (School Enterprise Challenge 2024). This program is more for small-cap revenue

Fig. 3.3 The building of AIMS Ghana from outside (top), and the view of the beach from it (bottom). Pictures taken in 2018. It can be reported anecdotally that both lecturers and students often go/went to the beach after some lectures

and related to local capacity building, while traditional startup incubators and accelerators are popping up all over the Global South, backed by local and international venture capital companies. Organizations like the Network for Teaching Entrepreneurship (NFTE) are empowering partners and school districts in the Global South to integrate entrepreneurial education across curricula and equip students with the necessary skills and connections to thrive as entrepreneurs (Network for Teaching Entrepreneurship 2024). These programs seek to equip students with the necessary skills that are valued globally and to handle their money proactively. Another group that provides entrepreneurship courses in the Global South is JA Africa, which aims to equip young people to start their own businesses and thrive in a global economy (Entrepreneurship Education 2024).

In addition, entrepreneurial education is actively promoted by universities in the Global South, some even having a technology transfer office or relationship with commercial companies. Due to their commitment to promoting an entrepreneurial culture and offering pertinent educational opportunities, numerous institutions, including those in Indonesia, have been recognized as entrepreneurial universities (Maritz et al. 2022). In the Global South, these universities are essential for fostering and assisting the upcoming generation of business owners.

A study of 52 universities in Latin America found that entrepreneurial orientation, incubators, and market efficiency at the university level significantly influenced the creation of new companies, Brazil being among the top countries for pushing this (Yovera et al. 2025). A positive outcome has also been seen in Africa, with South Africa creating most of the startups and patents. However, the numbers still point to an ecosystem in its early stages. A 2023 study reported only 25 patent applications per million population in 2020, compared to about 641 per million in upper-middle-income economies (Urban and Seely 2023).

With numerous training programs, companies, and institutions devoted to giving young people entrepreneurial skills and information, entrepreneurial education is a rapidly expanding field in the global South. Governments and organizations such as NFTE and JA Africa are supporting initiatives like the School Enterprise Challenge, youth business camps, and vocational training programs that aim to enable young people to become prosperous entrepreneurs. In fact, similar programs are popping up every day in all low-income countries, sometimes even supported by other companies that want to attract new talent. The Global South's ecosystems are also aggressively advancing entrepreneurship education and cultivating an entrepreneurial culture on campus. By fostering the next generation of creative and influential businesspeople, this collaborative endeavor seeks to establish a flourishing entrepreneurial environment in the Global South. Despite promising news, such as for the digital divide in academia, university spin-offs are rare due to limited tech transfer support, weak business models, and a lack of startup financing.

3.5 Academic Financial Stability

According to various indices, for example, the number of published articles or patents, universities, and research-based companies in the Global South perform poorly compared to their counterparts in Europe and the United States (World bank 2024). This discrepancy in performance can be attributed to several factors, including the lack of financial stability in the projects. Due to the initial paucity of funding, pilot programs frequently start, but never end, or yield noticeable results (Unesco report Education 2024). Investigating the potential to secure funding, create self-sustainable spin-offs companies, and encourage greater sustainability in African educational initiatives is essential to solving this problem. Partnerships and collaborations between nations in other regions (North-South) and within the continent (South-South) can accomplish this (Unesco report Education 2024). Using these opportunities, African educational institutions can overcome financial challenges and improve their overall performance and impact. Although, realistically, we are still all aware that there is an unfair advantage by the Global North. Nevertheless, the promises of AI, due to their lower entry barriers compared to other technologies, might spark new hopes.

Financial stability plays a crucial role in the performance and outcomes of educational institutions in Africa. The lack of follow-up or visible output in pilot projects due to initial funding constraints greatly hampers the development and progress of these institutions. The lack of sufficient funding for pilot projects is one of the main problems African educational institutions face. Many projects are started, but they never finish or yield any noticeable results due to a lack of funding. The project is frequently abandoned due to this initial lack of funds, leaving it unfinished and ineffective.

The impact of financial stability on educational institutions in Africa is multi-fold. In the first place, it affects the ability of these institutions to attract and retain qualified teachers and staff. Insufficient funds make it difficult to provide competitive salaries and benefits, resulting in a high turnover rate and a decrease in the quality of education offered. We mentioned earlier that the Global South still experiences a considerable brain drain.

The resources available to improve the facilities and infrastructure of these organizations are limited by financial instability. With the surge of AI, we would be tempted to believe that this should decrease, as many services will be provided digitally simply connecting to a cloud computing system, reducing costs of expensive instruments. However, this view is not shared by Global South scientists. In fact, they first see problems related to data security and trust (Sabi et al. 2018). While it is clear that for traditional machine learning the use of cloud computing can lead to reduced costs and increased productivity, for the training of large language models, the cost might still be inaccessible to universities with reduced funding.

In addition, the development of curriculum and the application of creative teaching strategies are heavily dependent on financial stability. The investigation and acceptance of novel strategies, tools, and instructional resources is made possible by adequate funding. We mentioned earlier that culture plays an important role in terms of adoption and change. Most of the Sub-Saharan countries do not rank very high in the dimensions related to acceptance of novel approaches. Therefore, further investments are expected to carry out the successful programs. Without them, educational institutions' capacity to change and grow is constrained, which results in antiquated and stagnant teaching methods.

It is crucial to look at different options of financial help in order to handle these issues. Still there is a plethora of available grants: from philanthropic foundations, non-governmental groups, international organizations, or even funds of mixed nature. Partnerships and cooperation between institutions in the north and south could also offer opportunities to build capacity, share knowledge, and receive financial support.

Furthermore, the establishment of spin-offs and entrepreneurial initiatives can contribute to the financial stability of educational institutions. By creating income-generating projects or ventures, these institutions can generate funds to support their educational programs and initiatives.

The rest of this section will list some of the most popular granting agencies that can support academic institutions, research centers, and research-based companies in the Global South, some general and others more focused on new possibilities related to AI.

The *Bill and Melinda Gates Foundation* is currently the most widely known foundation that supports projects in health and also the development of AI in healthcare in Africa; each of their initiatives is called *Grand Challenges*. Those initiatives are focused on specific issues to produce impact (Grand Challenges n.d.).

Chan Zuckerberg Initiative (CZI), like the Bill and Melinda Gates Foundation, has a series of projects and calls addressing different issues. For instance, the imaging program seeks to spearhead the creation of a new suite of imaging technologies that can be used to observe biological processes at the level of tissues, cells, and proteins across spatial scales. In addition, the program will establish robust frameworks for the quantification, analysis, and sharing of imaging data, as well as methods and tools (Chan Zuckerberg initiative 2024).

The *Lacuna Fund* is a program that aims to fill in the gaps in the available data sets from the Global South, that are essential for research and social benefit, which are mostly linked to AI and machine learning projects with different topics each year. Lacuna offers financial support for the development, maintenance, and growth of datasets in low- and middle-income environments, especially in fields such as linguistics, agriculture, health, and climate. To enable more equitable and efficient solutions to global concerns, the Lacuna Fund aims to democratize access to high-quality data and guarantees that databases reflect various people and environments. Their focus is on health, agriculture, climate, and natural language processing (Lacuna Fund 2024).

The Artificial Intelligence for Development in Africa (AI4D Africa) program was initiated in 2020 by the Swedish government's SIDA and the International Development Research Center (IDRC) of Canada. The goal of this 4-year project was to use $20 million Canadian dollars to enable Africans in all regions to develop and employ AI to live longer, happier, and more environmentally friendly lives, as well as research on climate action innovation within Africa (AI4D 2024). The initiative encourages excellence in applied research and the application of AI technology to address development issues and improve the quality of life for those who are impoverished. Several of the projects supported by this program are related to developing Responsible AI for Global Health. Innovation Center on Artificial Intelligence for Sexual, Reproductive and Maternal Health in Africa. This AI4D program has now grown with combined investments from the United Kingdom Foreign, Commonwealth and Development office, the Bill and Melinda Gates Foundation, USAID, and others (Combining forces for a new phase of AI for development: Africa and beyond 2024).

Lastly, also big tech companies like Alibaba, Amazon, Intel, IBM, and Google are significantly increasing the creation of partnerships or even offices in the global south. There is a consolidated understanding of the importance of IT in general and AI, even for low-income countries. For example, Alphabet has launched the Google African initiative in the Google office in Accra (Ghana), which is also partnering with AIMS Ghana. IBM laboratory in Kenya and South Africa supports research groups that have formed to address local health problems for local needs.

All these initiatives point out that for future funding, a partnership with existing big tech could be a possibility to mitigate risks, and grants are also emerging for the global south. However, a series of barriers still exist, and these will be discussed in the next chapter.

3.6 Scaling Impact in the Global South

A topic related to financing is the scaling of a project. In fact, it is common for funding agencies to often finance a pilot study or intervention, and after the publication of a paper or a report to authority things die or go back to their original status. Instead, scaling projects in the global south aim to make social change persistent or integrated in a larger society beyond small pilot initiatives.

In fact, SDG 17 seeks to strengthen global partnerships, particularly between the Global North and South, in research and development (Luetkemeier et al. 2024). This goal highlights the importance of collaboration and cooperation in scaling projects in the Global South, possibly representing also opportunities for the Global North. Even though, some reports showed that sometimes Northern stakeholders involved in the process, led to power imbalances, communication breakdowns, unclear accountability, and marginalized Southern actors, producing counterintuitive damages (Kotze and Dymitrow 2022).

Scaling a successful project is already a challenge on its own. This happens because scaling the size of an intervention becomes more complex to handle, and because new unseen factors come into play. The main challenge is the need to think holistically about the ecosystem both locally and at a broader level to achieve scale, we need very large system thinking. For a project to be successful, it needs to understand its ideal customer persona or end user, which is tightly anchored to a single cultural context. Assuming this was successful, how can we bring the same service or product to a larger area or a completely different country? Scaling up rarely means replicating the exact same product. And adaptation to the new or larger context has to be taken into account. For example, for a project that involves farmers in a different region and/or livelihood, a need assessment is required to understand the agricultural strategies of the government in the different region or country, which can even speak another language (Tran et al. 2020). These translations are obviously not without pain and can present several challenges that are amplified by innovations in the humanitarian sector (Kuckertz et al. 2023). Despite these difficulties, there have been success stories of scaling projects in the Global South. There have been grassroots organizations that have successfully scaled up their development impact over the course of a decade (Guerrero et al. 2023).

The National Rural Living Mission (NRLM) (now known as Deendayal Antyodaya Yojana) is a well-known poverty reduction program conducted by the Ministry of Rural Development in India, to improve the income and economic empowerment of poor women by organizing through self-employment and skilled wage employment opportunities launched in 2011 (Mishra 2017). However, although the launch was national in ambition, implementation followed a phased, block-by-block roll out strategy. This approach recognized that rural contexts vary greatly in India, and the local capacity to form and nurture self-help groups also differed. To manage this complexity, NRLM introduced the concept of "intensive blocks", specific blocks within districts chosen to receive focused attention and resources to serve as demonstration zones for mission methodologies and institutional innovations (Ghosh and Pattanayak 2014).

Practically, the national strategy for the program was established by trial and error in ten states with high rates of poverty. In contrast, there are many scales of projects that have been carried out by other programs without deep consideration. Generally, programs are conducted first in one region as a pilot and then blindly repeated with more funding, which can be a risky assumption. Today, in 2025, 83 million women have been served by NRLM and it is the largest livelihood initiative in the world. The success of the program is credited to grassroots innovations and years of testing prior to national expansion. The path of NRLM serves as a reminder of the value of creativity, adaptability, and state-level ownership in creating long-lasting federal initiatives (Rangaprasad et al. 2015).

The success of scaling up the NRLM mission in India could be attributed to several key factors:

- Grassroots Innovations: The foundation of NRLM was built on decades of grassroots innovations by civil society and community-based organizations. These early experiments with self-help groups provided a proof of concept that organizing women could lead to significant socioeconomic benefits (the Integrated Rural Development Program, Training of Rural Youth for Self-Employment and others were unsuccessful program, previously launched, often misaligned with local economic needs).
- Incremental Adaptation and Experimentation: The self-help model was extensively tested and adapted in different districts, without assuming that what worked in one district would work in the next. Different models were experimented with and tailored to local contexts before being scaled up. This iterative process allowed the approach to be refined to fit the diverse realities in different states.
- Data-driven monitoring: The project prioritized the use of digital platforms that allowed real-time tracking of self-help group formation, fund flows, credit links, and performance classification.

This and other success stories provide valuable insight and lessons on how to approach scaling projects, pointing out that it is not so straightforward, but it is possible.

3.7 Social Change and Leadership

The concept of leadership is probably one of the most discussed. Leaders focus on providing the vision, providing direction and inspiring people to reach common goals, managers focus more on executing the vision set by leaders, by organizing resources, managing tasks, and assuring that the day-to-day operations align with the strategic goals of a company or organization. Both leadership and management are dependent on the combination of vision and interaction with people. Although leadership relies more on influence and less on formal authority; they inspire people to follow them, for example, the figure of Mahatma Gandhi lives in his iconic speeches. Managers instead use their positional authority to accomplish tasks, for example the figure of a CEO or group director. Indeed, Mahatma Gandhi passed away many years ago, and some people still follow his lines. The moment a CEO leaves his/her job, almost no employee will listen to him/her anymore. Sometimes people occupy a role between and as people occupying a managerial role can still have personalized vision, things are not black and white. There are several ways that a leader can inspire others to achieve social change. Moreover, a general difference between being a manager and a leader is that the latter is more prone to challenging the status quo and proposing novel solutions that can lead to social change. We generally picture in our mind as a leader Gandhi, Martin Luther King, Rosa Parks, Nelson Mandela, etc. Leaders must be willing to push boundaries and generally put themselves in a vulnerable position. Apart the idea of taking initiative in general, a core element is to be willing to confront entrenched power structures and social norms that perpetuate injustice and inequality and work to create new systems and institutions that promote greater equity and inclusion (see the networking/lobby barriers mentioned in the previous chapters).

The starting element is usually to define a compelling vision. A clear compelling vision has to be defined to point out a better future. This vision should be grounded on a deep understanding of the issues and challenges facing a community or society. A solution needs to be outlined, even in the future. This solution also has to be clearly defined to be understood by others. One should not romanticize a vision defined by a hero from a cinematic representation. A vision can simply be defined by a mathematics student attending an AIMS course, learning new tools and ideas from foreign lecturers, and coming up with an idea for his community.

Leadership is not just about having a vision but also about building strong relationships. There is a thin line between networking and lobbying, but we have already mentioned that as long as it is to make a vision of positive change a reality, it can be acceptable (Alemanno 2017). The translation to the real world would nevertheless require funding, or the capacity to cover costs through stakeholders or sister organizations.

Interpersonal skills are also necessary, not just to communicate a vision. As we described in the previous sections, people are prone to maintain their ideals and habits. They might complain about a social issue without taking action. Effective leadership strategies to deal with pessimism and promote a positive mindset in individuals who do not believe that a situation can change can be crucial to driving change and promoting a productive work environment. To address this challenge, leaders can employ several tools and approaches.

An effective tool is to find ways to reduce the "fear factor" for pessimists. Working with them to create contingency plans for the most likely factors, leaders can help pessimistic individuals feel more prepared and less fearful (Maccoby et al. 2004).

Raising the understanding of pessimistic people, rationalizing their thinking as an effect is another crucial step. Leaders can promote introspection and personal development by helping them identify the detrimental consequences of their pessimism. Open dialogues, coaching sessions or workshops centered on awareness and mentality development can accomplish this (Bunjak and Černe 2018).

In conclusion, leaders play a crucial role in fostering positivity and driving change in the face of negativity. Implement effective leadership strategies, such as reducing the fear factor. Those elements can be taught to young people and normal people thanks to civil society, universities, and inexpensive government programs. Those programs should focus on an unexpected demographic from women with a family, retired, or young university students. As AIMS mentioned in their vision "the next Einstein will be African and probably found among unexpected young students".

Taking the point of view of leadership from the Global South should not be difficult. After all, the end of colonialism was started by Ghanaian leaders such as Nkrumah et al. (1963). Nkruma after 12 years abroad pursuing higher education and developing his political philosophy, he organized with other diasporic pan-Africanists, returned to the Gold Coast to begin his political career as an advocate of national independence of what we call today Ghana. Despite cultural differences, promoting leadership in the Global South is not as different as in high-income countries. At a practical level, clarify the importance of communication and resistance to risk and change in people. Lastly, even if leadership should be a trait of any age, especially in youth: encouraging the political participation of young people ensures that the leadership landscape is dynamic and representative of all age groups, as shaping personalities at younger age should be easier and less prone to barriers to change.

3.8 Summary of the Chapter

The educational landscape of the Global South presents both profound challenges and transformative opportunities. Despite the advancement in many low-income countries, resource disparities still exist although not so visible. Classrooms are often overcrowded, limited research funding is available to local scientists, teaching approaches are outdated. Yet, many institutions are popping up to revert the trend. The African Institute for Mathematical Sciences, Rise-MICCAI (2025), Deep Learning Indaba (2017) are the currently most popular, which demonstrate how contextual adaptation and pedagogical creativity can overcome material constraints, proving that excellence emerges not from resources alone but from culturally grounded educational vision.

The digital divide persists at many levels, mostly pointing to infrastructure limitations and cultural exclusion. Transformations are needed, but they also need to go beyond the more technology available. An improvement in the overall ecosystem is required. For example, putting more emphasis on local solutions, supporting local leadership, and taking advantage on what we can take as cooperation from the Global South (not exploitation):

- South-South collaboration networks that share best practices.
- Hybrid pedagogical models blending PBL with local learning traditions.
- Open science infrastructures that bypass predatory publishing.

Like it or not, consumption indirectly creates advancements in our society. Therefore, entrepreneurial education emerges as a critical multiplier effect, with vocational programs and university spin-offs demonstrating how human capital development can break cycles of aid dependency. Successful scaling models like India's NRLM reveal that sustainable impact requires iterative adaptation rather than replication—a lesson applicable from classroom innovations to national policy reforms.

Ultimately, educational transformation in the Global South depends on leadership that combines visionary pragmatism with deep cultural literacy. The educators, researchers, and community organizers driving change exemplify how technical competence must be paired with the ability to build coalitions across sectors, and nurture the next generation of problem-solvers. For example, the African Institute for Mathematical Science is not just a place where people do math, it is a place where people are thought to be leaders in their own community, and they can brainstorm on how to apply technical knowledge into daily business.

References

Aalto PBL East Africa design. https://aaltoglobalimpact.org/pbl-east-africa/. Accessed 19 Jun 2024

Abu N, Abdullahi U (2010) The role of education in economic growth: a comparative study of Nigeria and China. J Econ Int Financ 2(6):107–115

AI4D program. https://africa.ai4d.ai/. Accessed 4 Aug 2024

Alemanno A (2017) Lobbying for change: find your voice to create a better society. Icon Books

Allen DE, Donham RS, Bernhardt SA (2011) Problem-based learning. New Dir Teach Learn 2011(128):21–29

Bah EHM, Brada JC (2009) Total factor productivity growth, human capital and structural change in a developing economy. J Dev Stud 45(5):752–774

Björk B-C (2017) Open access to scientific articles: a review of benefits and challenges. Intern Emerg Med 12:247–253

Bunjak A, Černe M (2018) The role of leader-follower defensive pessimism (in) congruence in fostering perceptions of followers' isolation. Econ Bus Rev 20(1):5

Chan Zuckerberg initiative website. https://chanzuckerberg.com/science/programs-resources/imaging/. Accessed 4 Aug 2024

Christensen CM, Ojomo E, Dillon K (2019) The prosperity paradox: how innovation can lift nations out of poverty. Harper Business

Combining forces for a new phase of AI for development: Africa and beyond. https://idrc-crdi.ca/en/news/combining-forces-new-phase-ai-development-africa-and-beyond. Accessed 4 Aug 2024

Deep Learning Indaba (2017) Deep learning indaba: strengthening African machine learning. In: Annual meeting of the African machine learning community, various locations, first held

Dickens WT, Sawhill IV (2006) Economic growth. In: The concise encyclopedia of economics, vol 2, pp 126–128

Entrepreneurship Education website. https://ja-africa.org/entrepreneurship-programs/. Accessed 1 Aug 2024

Feynman RP (2010) Surely you're joking, Mr. Feynman!": adventures of a curious character. WW Norton Company

Fogel RW (1994) Economic growth, population theory, and physiology: the bearing of long-term processes on the making of economic policy

Ghosh J, Pattanayak S (2014) Scaling-up of self-help groups in India: a case study of NRLM. J Rural Dev 33(2):145–160

Goczek Ł, Witkowska E, Witkowski B (2021) How does education quality affect economic growth? Sustainability 13(11):6437

Grand Challenges website. https://gcgh.grandchallenges.org/. Accessed 4 Aug

Guerrero I, Gokhale S, Fahsbender J (2023) Scaling up development impact. Bowker

Hanada S (2021) Higher education partnerships between the Global North and Global South: mutuality, rather than aid. J Comp & Int High Educ 13(5):135–144

Harris E (1998) A low-cost approach to PCR: appropriate transfer of biomolecular techniques. Oxford University Press

Katikireddi SV (2004) HINARI: bridging the global information divide. BMJ 328(7449):1190–1193

Kotze S, Dymitrow M (2022) North-South research collaborations: an empirical evaluation against principles of trans-boundary research. Dev Policy Rev 40(2):e12555

Kuckertz A et al (2023) Scaling the right answers-Creating and maintaining hope through social entrepreneurship in light of humanitarian crises. J Bus Ventur Insights 19:e00356

Lacuna Fund website. https://lacunafund.org/. Accessed 4 Aug 2024

Lawson S (2015) Fee waivers for open access journals. Publications 3(3):155–167

Luetkemeier R (2024) Lessons learned from a North-South science partnership for sustainable development. In: Sustainability of Southern African ecosystems under global change: science for management and policy interventions. Springer International Publishing, pp 903–931

Lythreatis S, Singh SK, El-Kassar A-N (2022) The digital divide: a review and future research agenda. Technol Forecast Soc Chang 175:121359

Maccoby M, Gittell JH, Ledeen M (2004) Leadership and the fear factor. MIT Sloan Manag Rev 45(2):14

Malan SB, Ndlovu M (2014) Introducing problem-based learning (PBL) into a foundation programme to develop self-directed learning skills. S Afr J Educ 34(1)

Maritz A et al (2022) The emergence of entrepreneurship education programs in Indonesian higher education institutions. Entrep Educ 5(3):289–317

Mekonnen A, Downs C, Effiom EO, Kibaja M, Lawes MJ, Omeja P, Ratsoavina FM et al (2022) Can I afford to publish? A dilemma for African scholars. Ecol Lett 25(4):711–715

Mishra A (2017) Policy design of national rural livelihood mission (NRLM)-a critical assessment. Int J Manag Dev Stud 6(8):54–60

Moshtari M, Safarpour A (2024) Challenges and strategies for the internationalization of higher education in low-income East African countries. High Educ 87(1):89–109

Mudaly R, Chirikure T (2023) STEM education in the Global North and Global South: competition, conformity, and convenient collaborations. Frontiers in education 8:1144399 Frontiers Media SA

Network for Teaching Entrepreneurship Website. https://nfte.com/. Accessed 1 Aug 2024

Nkrumah K, Arrigoni R, Napolitano G (1963) Africa must unite. Heinemann, London

Rangaprasad M, Sahu P, Krishnan C (2015) Self-help groups as institutions of social change: lessons from NRLM. Econ & Polit Wkly 50(8):61–68

RISE-MICCAI (Reinforcing Inclusiveness & Diversity and Empowering MICCAI in Low-to-Middle Income Countries) (2025) About RISE-MICCAI. In: Proceedings of the medical image computing and computer assisted intervention (MICCAI) society

Sabi HM et al (2018) A cross-country model of contextual factors impacting cloud computing adoption at universities in sub-Saharan Africa. Inf Syst Front 20(6):1381–1404

School Enterprise Challenge Website. https://www.schoolenterprisechallenge.org. Accessed 1 Aug 2024

Snilstveit B, Stevenson J, Phillips D, Vojtkova M, Gallagher E, Schmidt T, Eyers J (2015) Interventions for improving learning outcomes and access to education in low-and middle-income countries: a systematic review. Campbell Syst Rev 11(1):1–177

Solano J, Gutierrez MZ, Pinel-Guzmán E, Henriquez G 2023) Barriers and solutions to successful problem-based learning delivery in developing countries-a literature review. Cureus 15(8)

Stiglitz JE, Greenwald BC (2014) Creating a learning society: a new approach to growth, development, and social progress. Columbia University Press

The Next Einstein initiative website. https://nexteinstein.org/about-us-our-story/. Accessed 1 Aug 2024

Tran QQ, Swaans CP, Simelton E, Imbach P, Pham T, Clausen P, Barlis A (2020) Scaling climate services for agriculture in the Global South: an assessment of practitioners' needs

Unesco report Education in Africa. https://uis.unesco.org/en/topic/education-africa. Accessed 1 Aug 2024

Urban B, Seely D (2023) Academic spin-offs in an African emerging market context. Int J Entrep Innov 14657503231213308

Vassilakopoulou P, Hustad E (2023) Bridging digital divides: a literature review and research agenda for information systems research. Inf Syst Front 25(3):955–969

World bank report. https://pubdocs.worldbank.org/en/764421611934520379/One-Africa-TE-and-Covid-updated.pdf. Accessed 1 Aug 2024

Yovera R, Raquel V et al (2025) Academic entrepreneurship evolution: a systematic review of university incubators and startup development (2018–2024). Sustainability 17(12):5365

4 Innovation at the Time of AI and Environmental Crisis

4.1 Decreasing or Increasing Inequality

In pursuit of alleviating poverty, the global community has long focused on alleviating symptoms rather than addressing root causes. We have introduced all kinds of innovation, from food aid, immunization, infrastructure grants, offering immediate relief. Those interventions often failed to ignite long-term transformation. We are definitely observing a decrease in global poverty, and countries on average are converging in standard of living. But we are still observing a sort of persistence of poverty, and relative inequalities seem even to be increasing, despite decades of well-intentioned development interventions. At the same time, societies are evolving, at least from the point of view of available technologies. We cannot arrest progress. This led us to the more realistic observation that innovation, particularly innovation that creates markets, is a more reliable engine of prosperity than aid (Christensen et al. 2019).

With current trends, innovation is strongly related to AI, but also opens up further concerns related to inequality and environmental issues (Strubell et al. 2019). AI is often framed as a force of job displacement, data extraction, and ethical concern, particularly in developing economies that are net consumers of western tech products. Concerns which are realistic as often technology is in the hands of elitist entrepreneurs which are focused on productivity, and not on general well-being. How do we merge those two diametral views: we need innovation in low-income countries to create jobs and well-being, but we have to avoid that elitist productivity increases inequality.

Original feudalism emerged in western Europe around 476 AD, after the fall of Rome, causing the rise of small kingdoms and territories (Reynolds 1994). Without a centralized Roman Empire, people were left under the constant attack of Vikings, Magyars, and Saracens.

Local landowners, who had weapons and men, offered protection to nearby peasants. Those powerful landowners created new hierarchical structures: They granted a fief (usually land) to a vassal. A vassal was a direct servant of a lord and swore loyalty and military service to the lord. The peasants worked the land managed by a vassal in exchange for protection and the right to live there. The peasants were living and producing but did not own anything. This was a deeply unequal and unfair system, in which the majority people (peasants) lived in high inequality compared to the other classes. Feudalism died slowly as new monarchs and new centralized power emerged, together with large peasant revolts happening demanding systemic change.

Neoliberalism has pushed capitalism into a sort of modern feudalism. Where big-tech companies have large financial assets based on privatization, deregulation, and corporate dominance. Similarly to the feudal lords, big tech firms have accumulated enormous economic and informational power,

© The Author(s), under exclusive license to Springer Nature Switzerland AG 2026

A. Crimi, *Innovate for Impact*, Sustainable Development Goals Series,
https://doi.org/10.1007/978-3-032-21563-5_4

they are almost monopolies or bipoly. Current online commerce depends deeply on Google ranking, a product or service to be seen has to advertise on social media platforms such as Facebook, X/Twitter, Instagram, etc. Those big giants also provide information through their large language models. People are like peasants using the platforms for free, but actually producing their content for free. There is the illusion of freedom, but instead it is more a cloud-feudalism (Varoufakis 2024). Users generate value for free for corporations that hold power over data, and become day after day more powerful and rich.

If we reframe our views through the lens of market-creating innovation, AI has untapped potential to catalyze prosperity, not only automation, to reduce the workforce. The question is not whether AI will replace human labor in these regions, but whether it will be leveraged to solve problems of non-consumption at scale. The paradox becomes sharper: AI, a technology viewed as exclusive and elitist, can paradoxically be the tool that opens new markets for the world's poor.

One of the main issues for the health care system in Africa and Latin America is the small number of clinical specialists available (Alemayehu et al. 2018). This can definitely be the blooming field for all AI-driven diagnostic tools we have created in the last years. We could interpret radiographs or detect skin conditions by using smartphones, for example (Maatouk and Lucero-Prisno 2025). In this way, AI has the potential to democratize capabilities that were previously confined to academic institutions or urban hospitals, thus establishing new markets. However, this result is not a given. Real needs must be identified by local entrepreneurs, investors must fund low-key but highly impactful projects, and policy frameworks must promote innovation without overly restricting it. Regulations are also what we need, but not if they limit innovation. A possible solution could be to actually use an AI tool that analyzes legislation, finding the ideal trade-off between lassair-fair and regulation to allow innovation, especially in low-income countries; we will talk more about this in the next sections (Zheng et al. 2022).

The challenge is then one of mindset and structure. Thanks to creative capacity building, we have managed to pilot, and even scale to some degree, community-based water purification systems or solar microgrids. Those can now be augmented with AI to optimize distribution, predict shortages, or personalize services, data science is a powerful ally. The crucial factor is whether local entrepreneurs have the strategic vision to create markets where none previously existed, in addition to having the necessary funds and technical know-how. Instead of being developed locally, innovation is often imported as a completed good. This, more than any algorithmic limitation, is the true bottleneck.

There is also a deeper ethical dimension. If the future of AI is to be shaped by those with the most computing power and training data, the trajectory of innovation will skew toward affluent consumers and problems of convenience. However, the center of gravity might change if entrepreneurs are aware of their impact on society, especially in low-income countries. This acknowledges that inclusive innovation ecosystems, those that encourage local problem solving, are more durable and egalitarian over the long term, rather than being naive. AI's ability to grow quickly makes it a two-edged sword that can either increase effect or exacerbate inequity. Whether we apply the concepts of market-creating innovation to the nexus of poverty and technology will determine the course we take. The old feudalism was broken because of the rise of centralized powers and related legislation. Cloud-feudalism has been contained by governments and their regulation supporting the global wealth, not the interest of large companies. We need to decolonize the tools used by those large companies and give it to the people.

In an age increasingly defined by technological acceleration, the greatest innovations may emerge not from Silicon Valley, but from the places we least expect, if only we are wise enough to invest in them, as the "Next-Einstein" at AIMS. In this and the following chapter we discuss how to make it happen, to achieve reduction of inequality not increase of it.

4.2 Decolonizing Technology and Knowledge Systems

Technology, technology, and technology. Once I was on a stroll on Labadi beach (Ghana), and among some tourist traps for white tourists, I saw a guy sticking a mobile phone in a sort of wooden tube. The structure of the tube was able to amplify the sounds of the mobile phone as speakers, without electricity and without electronics. That was not just a toy, it was design thinking at its highest power and, compared to expensive speakers, also very sustainable. From a need and cheap scraps of available material that guy created something that to me looked very brilliant, and that many people in high-income countries will buy as well. Any reader has probably seen some similar techs, such as washing machines running on bicycles, ovens made by mirrors using the sun, or just simplified versions of devices that were serving their purpose nonetheless. Technology is a central force in the shaping of economies, education, governance, and culture. In most of this book, especially this chapter, we discussed a lot about the digital divide and the knowledge gap between the North and the Global South. What if the starting point was wrong? What if instead of trying to catch up with the Global North, one should reinvent solutions which are already suitable for a specific local context? If we keep copying the Global North, it will always be a Red Queen race, because the Global North is not sitting still with the same innovations, but it obviously keeps improving current innovations or introducing novel ones. This is not as simple as it seems. There is a need to actively develop practices, policies, and infrastructures that place local needs, customs, and resources as a priority, and it is necessary to decolonize technology and knowledge systems. Without mentioning that local people might not even realize their potential and still see their low-cost innovation as duct tape technology, or things coming from a MacGyver movie (Macgyver 1985). The first stage is to support existing community-led innovation ecosystems in middle- or low-income countries. Local institutions should support and encourage projects that employ locally available resources and skills to produce context-specific technology instead of importing high-tech solutions from the Global North. Open Source Appropriate Technology (OSAT) and frugal innovation are two models that allow communities to find innovative, cost-effective, and sustainable solutions to challenges (Radjou et al. 2012). Frugal innovation or frugal engineering is the process of reducing the complexity and cost of a good and its production. This usually refers to taking away features that are not necessary for a durable product, such as a phone or car, to sell it for a more affordable price, or with modifications that make the item more comfortable for the local populations. It has been applied successfully several times, even for high-tech products from General Electric 800 USD EKG for low-income countries (Nesta 2024), to the Foldscope: an affordable origami microscope assembled from a sheet of paper and a lens (Roberts 2014). However, the risk is that the focus remains on "selling to the poor" and not scaling and advancing technologically reducing the digital divide. Nevertheless, it is a promising move to decolonize technology making it stems from the Global South directly. A possible approach could be to start with a frugal innovation and then evolve it technologically and even scale the sales abroad.

Therefore, a complementary "hardware stack" for sustainable development must be championed. Open-source hardware initiatives, inspired by the success of open-source software, aim to democratize the design of physical devices, from agricultural sensors to medical equipment, reducing costs and allowing local adaptation. This is closely allied with the right-to-repair movement, which fights planned obsolescence by securing legal and practical access to tools, parts, and schematics. This extends product life-cycles, reduces electronic waste, and promotes local repair economies. Ultimately, supporting local and distributed manufacturing through maker-spaces, manufacturing laboratories, and policies that encourage small-batch production can build resilience. It shortens supply chains, reduces the carbon footprint of transport, and allows communities to produce tools tailored to immediate contextual needs, from custom farming implements to water quality monitors.

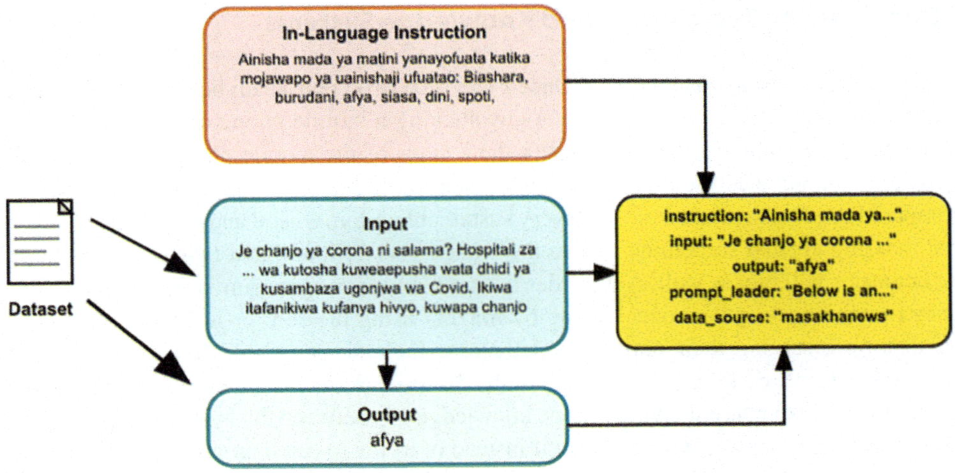

Fig. 4.1 An example of how the instruction dataset was created (Swahili sample), adapted from Tonja et al. (2024)

Another critical step is to prioritize language and cultural relevance in digital tools. The dominance of English, French, or Spanish language, plus western cultural assumptions in digital interfaces limits accessibility and erases identity. Broader participation and cultural continuity are ensured by investing in technology that supports local languages, voice assistants, AI models, and translation apps. There is an increasing body of work that specifically targets Asian and African contexts, focusing on the unique local languages and cultural landscapes of the continents and the need for contextualized solutions, although many research and development programs have a global scope (Pratt et al. 2024). Projects like Masakhane ("We build together" in isiZulu) (Masakhane 2024) and Lanfrica have been at the forefront of the creation of open, community-driven databases and translation models for languages (Lanfrica 2024) such as Swahili, Yoruba, Hausa, Amharic, and many more. African languages are now part of the multilingual training corpus of programs like Samaaj and Bloom (by BigScience). Organizations such as Google and Meta also created models and data sets, Language Left Behind, with the express goal of enhancing NLP capabilities in low-resource languages in Africa. These developments are essential to maintain linguistic diversity, improve accessibility, and enable culturally appropriate AI applications across the continent (Buzaaba et al. 2025; Tonja et al. 2024). Luckily, the approach is taken seriously and two benchmark datasets are even referred to to evaluate large language models in African languages: "AfriMMLU" and "AfriXNLI" (Adelani et al. 2024). Developing LLMs on wide-spoken or minority languages is not impossible. Nevertheless, even if we use just transfer learning or fine tuning of pre-existing models, to match instructions and replies in the target language is tedious and laborious work, which can be summarized as shown in Fig. 4.1.

Decolonizing technology is a shift in perspectives and methods, rather than a singular fix. It calls for a change from technology as a product into a process, which is cooperative, integrated into the community, and sensitive to many realities. The main challenge is not the willingness of developers and policymakers, but the limits of low-income countries, which we have already mentioned in the previous sections.

4.3 The Promise of AI Against Poverty

AI has come to light as a potential solution to some of the most important problems humanity is currently experiencing. Among these difficulties, poverty continues to be a complicated and persistent problem that affects billions of people around the world. Even if conventional methods of reducing poverty have made great progress, incorporating AI into these initiatives presents a game-changing opportunity to accelerate development and reach the most disadvantaged groups. This book advocates that we cannot address poverty directly, but we should intervene in the underlying causes, such as specific diseases, malnutrition, education, etc. All of those underlying causes can be quantified and predicted by the data. In short, if you can predict poverty, you can fight it better. Machine learning algorithms are particularly suited to address the complex nature of poverty due to their ability to process huge volumes of data, spot trends, predict, classify, and produce useful insights. We can reduce poverty by quantifying it and predicting it, allowing for further forecasting of economic trends to optimal allocation of resources. For instance, governments and non-governmental organizations can more precisely target interventions by using machine learning algorithms to identify areas with the highest levels of poverty based on satellite imagery. Furthermore, by integrating AI with citizen science, researchers and policy makers can develop more inclusive and context-specific solutions (Fraisl et al. 2024).

For those who are not familiar with machine learning, a typical machine learning algorithm is a binary or multiclass classifier, where, given a series of features (e.g., sex, age, income, marital status, degree, or living city), we could, for example, predict the capacity of repaying a loan. We will literally receive the label: either able or not able if we present those values for a specific person. Underneath, there are algorithms that "trained" to respond to specific features similar to those we are presenting in the exam. Most common approaches are called support vector machine, discriminant analysis, perceptron, random forest, etc. (Hart et al. 2001). Another typical scenario is the forecast of time series. For example, with the popular autoregressive integrated moving average (ARIMA) or time-specific neural networks such as long- and short-term memory (LSTM) (Siami-Namini et al. 2018). People have been trying for decades to predict the stock market or sales forecast with those tools with relatively acceptable results, but we could use them as well to help people in need.

For example, locals might use smartphones to collect data on crop yields, water availability, and other related topics in rural areas where data is limited. Those data can subsequently be incorporated into AI models, and produce insights that guide agricultural operations and maybe offer geographic insights, helping people carrying out programs or policies.

Other examples related to the healthcare system can be given, as given the disproportion of rural versus urban clinics (Samuel et al. 2021), we can predict the need for healthcare delivery and other infrastructure emergencies.

Hence, prediction is only the beginning. AI may be used to map poverty and its causes, as well as to forecast poverty. This involves modeling the effects of future distress on populations that are currently at risk, such as pandemics, droughts, inflation spikes, or migratory flows. Given the spatio-temporal patterns related to these events, geographic information systems (GISs) can come in handy for this process. A GIS is a computer system that analyzes and displays geographically referenced information. This system can be integrated with AI models that target crop production, climate models, and food price indices, allowing food insecurity and income loss to be forecast weeks or months in advance. As a result, AI becomes a tool for predictive governance, enabling participants to move from reactively delivering relief to actively promoting resilience at a specific geographic level.

For example, by evaluating agricultural data and forecasting crop yields, AI-powered systems such as FarmDrive in Kenya Biallas and O'Neill (2020) are helping small farmers to obtain funding. These platforms provide financial opportunities for farmers by lowering the risk for lenders, allowing them to make investments in improved equipment, seeds, and fertilizer. Farmdrive is indeed a GIS that integrates satellite imagery and other geospatial data and analyzes farm conditions, soil health, and crop yields.

Going beyond this, we can imagine large language models trained to give low-income country residents tailored guidance on everything from healthcare to education. Many times, poverty is viewed as a static state that can be measured using national development indices, income criteria, and household surveys. However, poverty is actually a dynamic and geographically diverse reality. Changes in reaction to market forces, policy changes, climate events, and shocks. Before deprivation becomes ingrained, it is necessary to comprehend where it arises, how it changes, and which communities are the most at risk in order to combat it successfully. This is both the potential and the difficulty of using artificial intelligence to forecast poverty.

Data from a meticulously collected census and home survey is the foundation of traditional techniques for calculating poverty. Although statistically sound, these methods are slow, costly, and frequently outdated by the time they are examined. These kinds of statistics are only collected every five to 10 years in many low-income countries. As a result, there is a risky knowledge gap between the current state of poverty and the treatments sought. This temporal shift undermines even the most well-intentioned initiatives in charity or social protection.

Among other projects, in India, researchers have identified homeless communities that had previously been missed by official surveys by using machine learning to examine satellite pictures. Having a GIS for this, policymakers have been able to expand social welfare services to people in need and distribute resources more efficiently thanks to these data. In a study focused on two South Asian countries (Nepal and Bangladesh) and Namibia, call detail records, anonymized mobile phone metadata, have been used to estimate income levels, mobility patterns, and vulnerability to disasters or being locked below the local poverty lines with surprising precision. The granularity of such predictions allows governments and NGOs to anticipate a need, rather than simply respond to it (Steele et al. 2021).

In summary, we could link these predictive models and GISs to policy making, obtaining tailored effects, and we go more in details on this in the next section, as it is indeed possible to more effectively target conditional cash transfers, implement public works projects in areas expected to see job shocks, and expand school food programs in districts expected to see a decrease in revenue. All possible solutions which have been already implemented and can be further scaled.

4.4 The AI Economist for Ideal Policies

The mixture models for policy design which we have previously introduced highlight the need to mathematically estimate subsections of population when we construct policies. Yet, the question is how do we define the numerical policy parameters? For example, specific marginal tax rates for each income bracket. Given the novel advancement in reinforcement learning (Sutton and Barto 1988), we can do more than this by designing algorithms that are not based on simulation but rather on data science.

Reinforcement learning is a type of machine learning approach in which an agent learns to make decisions by interacting with an environment to maximize a reward. The typical example is a robot in a house that receives a prize if it cleans a house properly. It mimics the trial-and-error approach of humans when they want to reach a goal and experiment with many things. Multi-agent reinforcement learning (MARL) is practically reinforcement learning, but instead on a single agent, we consider many agents learning how to act in an environment at the same time. In our specific case, our goal is to adapt to dynamic socioeconomic conditions. Agents can also be connected by graph network as in Chap. 1, but here we do not simulate a spreading, we follow more a machine learning approach.

It might sound odd that someone starting to throw darts randomly ends up learning complex theories (or the ideal parameters related to them), but given enough time and computational power, it is exactly what it does.

In 2022 Zheng and colleagues introduced the AI economist for taxation policy design (Zheng et al. 2022) based on a two-tier MARL system. At the microlevel, autonomous agents, representing workers, firms, or households, interact in a simulated economy, generating income through labor and trade. These agents learn adaptive strategies to maximize individual utility under evolving tax regimes. At the macro level, a social planner (such as the government or local institutions) learns to impose tax policies that maximize a social welfare function, defined as

$$W(\mathbf{x}) = \sum_{i=1}^{N} U_i(x_i) - \lambda \cdot G(\mathbf{x}), \tag{4.1}$$

where $\mathbf{x} = (x_1, \ldots, x_N)$ denotes the income distribution, U_i is the utility function of the agent i, G quantifies inequality (e.g., Gini index) and λ controls the trade-off of equity and productivity. The planner policy π_θ is parameterized by θ and optimized by gradient ascent on the expected welfare:

$$\nabla_\theta J(\theta) = \mathbb{E}_{\tau \sim \pi_\theta} \left[\sum_{t=0}^{T} \nabla_\theta \log \pi_\theta(a_t | s_t) \cdot (W(\mathbf{x}_t) - \eta \cdot \mathrm{Var}(\mathbf{x}_t)) \right], \tag{4.2}$$

where τ is a trajectory of states s_t (e.g., income distributions) and actions a_t (tax schedules), and η penalizes income volatility. In simple words, this second formula says how the planner learns and improves tax policy, using trial and error, while balancing happiness, fairness, and stability of incomes. This dual-level optimization captures the tension between individual incentives and collective welfare, a core challenge in poverty reduction. In practice, it is implemented by multilayer perceptrons and LSTM as shown in Fig. 4.2.

In summary, the overall idea is to obtain AI-derived tax policies outperform current progressive or flat taxes system, by adapting to economic shocks and behavioral feedback from the agents. In simulations that mirror low-income countries, where we generally have high wealth concentration in few "rich agents," and many grass-root employers with little wealth, the AI system reduced the Gini coefficient by 16% while maintaining 98% of baseline productivity.

Translating these findings into real-world poverty alleviation requires addressing some gaps. Reinforcement learning approaches do not need any dataset for training (at least not the one we have introduced here). However, to translate the policy and its parameters to the real world, we would need some "scaling" with actual data. This might be complicated for the Global South, where data is often missing, as we stated earlier. Nevertheless, we already mentioned how to address the issue of integrating administrative microdata with predicted ones using other AI tools in combination.

Moreover, one of the main criticisms of machine learning models is that they are like black boxes, where it is difficult to understand the internal calculation. However, in this context, techniques such as counterfactual explanation (Wachter et al. 2017) could demystify AI-generated tax rules for policy-makers.

This approach was able to provide a set of numerical policy parameters, as marginal tax rates for each income sub-population. The process is a machine learning technique, but there was no precollected dataset of human economies or tax outcomes. This was deliberate since the goal was to explore optimal policies in a controlled, repeatable environment without real-world noise or ethical issues from policy experimentation. Not all AI solutions are performed without pre-collected data. Actually, most of them are based on pre-collected data, which introduces many issues.

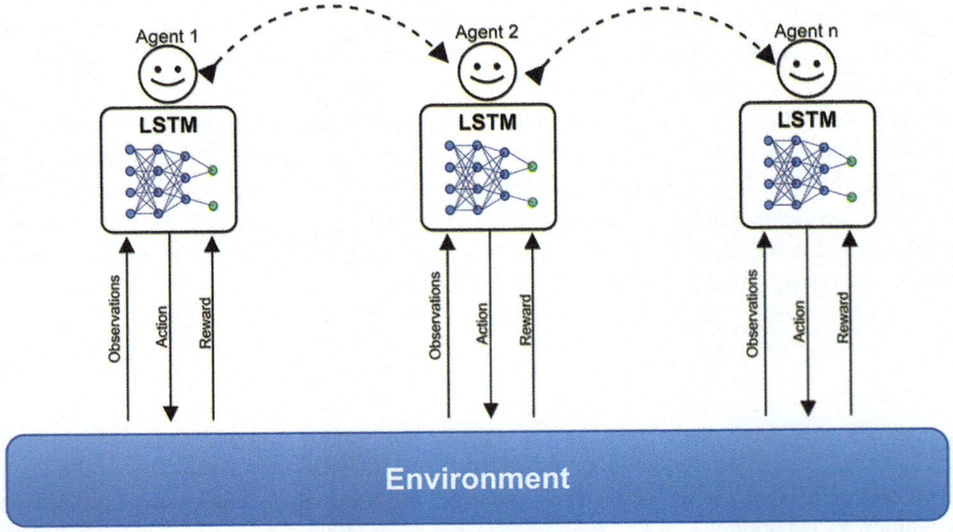

Fig. 4.2 A schematic agents interaction, the agents start with slightly different skills and, through individual learning, develop vastly different strategies and economic roles, making them heterogeneous. The environment includes also tax, the state and market behavior

There are other similar studies driven by the aim of helping policy makers design effective solutions to complex economic problems. In fact, we can say that we are at the dawn of agent-based computational economics (Axtell and Farmer 2025).

4.5 Biased Data

Despite its potential, the use of AI in alleviating poverty is not without challenges. The fundamental reason is that we have missing data to train or validate models. This could lead to the risk of biased algorithms that can perpetuate existing inequalities if not addressed with care. The concern arises from the fact that many mainstream applications, even clinical devices, are trained with data in the Global North, using white Caucasian people. The issue does not stop with physiological concerns and can also be related to cultural and intellectual restrictions. Given the impact of AI and other automations have and will have on our society, we need to mitigate this risk. We need to build and use transparent, accountable, and regularly audited models. This raises even epistemological dilemmas. A theory is called a theory if it is supported by data and empirical validation. Creating something with biased data is equivalent to a scamming theory.

Several academic articles have shown that biased datasets can lead to inaccurate and unfair machine learning outcomes, particularly affecting marginalized racial or geographical groups. The oldest example is the 2018 study (Buolamwini and Gebru 2018) showing that commercial facial recognition systems performed significantly worse on darker-skinned and female faces, sometimes failing to recognize those faces. This exposes gender and racial bias, despite involuntary, it happens because the training dataset was mostly composed of white male Caucasian faces. Similarly, studies (Obermeyer et al. 2019) gave even more concerning findings that highlight racial bias in a widely used health algorithm that underestimated the needs of black patients. An underreferral to critical care programs was identified, identifying 30% cases less than those to be identified, deepening existing healthcare disparities. The same concerns have been highlighted for skin cancer detection models trained on data from predominantly fair-skinned populations that performed poorly with darker skin tones (Banerjee et al. 2020). Sometimes, it is not just an AI bias, but it can be a hardware bias. For example, some electroencephalography sensors might not be suitable for the skin with curly hair in the scalp of African and Afro-American patients (Bradford et al. 2024). The issue is not only at the research level, but also in everyday used tools; a 2024 review of 692 FDA-approved AI-based medical devices highlighted that only 3.6% reported race or ethnicity in their training data, and more than 90% did not mention any ethnic or socioeconomic consideration (Muralidharan et al. 2024).

Even in cases where algorithmic misdiagnosis or misclassification of black patients is not driven by racism, it can nevertheless have detrimental effects and exacerbate already existing social inequalities. According to the examples given, bias in the training data may be exacerbated in the predictions, perhaps excluding already marginalized groups or feeding preconceptions. Providing fair and equitable health & social care can be achieved by ongoing audits of AI models. One simple way to develop and implement inclusive AI-driven solutions is to require that the commercial or academic AI model should be as inclusive in terms of gender, ethnicity, and geography as possible. Governments, non-governmental organizations, software houses, and local communities must work together to achieve this. This involves funding studies to learn more about the particular requirements of underserved areas. Maybe the issue should even be addressed by some regulatory body as FDA or CE, which should demand demographic transparency in model approvals, demanding ethnic quota to be included, as we are doing with housing demanding some renewable energy in some construction sites. The recent European Union AI act (Parliament and Council 2024) mentions this issue, although it does not provide a strict guideline.

In this section, we introduced the issue, in the next one, we dig further into the initiative which is pushing for a more fair use of AI especially in medicine and biology, both from the point of view of more inclusive dataset, but also accessible and sustainable costs.

4.6 Finally More Inclusive Biotech

Biotechnology combining high technology, medicine, and biology has been promising in radically improving our health and well-being for decades. Instead, like other innovations, it has often accrued unequally, amplifying the disparities. From early genomics consortia that prioritized samples from wealthy populations to AI-driven drug discovery pipelines trained on incomplete datasets, biotech's infrastructure has historically reflected the priorities and assumptions of its most powerful stakeholders, and everyone who worked on a biotech lab knows the intense cost of reagents and apparently meager but expensive tools, making entire disciplines inaccessible for labs with reduced funds.

The result is a field brimming with promise, but in practice full of biases and high costs, which are manageable only by wealthy organizations. Nevertheless, in the last two decades, a countercurrent has emerged: one that insists that inclusion is not just a matter of ethics but of efficacy. Tracing the arc of inclusive biotech is to move from the fieldwork of Eva Harris to the framework of FAIR AI: Findable, Accessible, Interoperable, and Reusable. A movement that has been growing in parallel to the growth of information technology in our society (in the Further Readings Section, there is a list of the major initiatives).

Even before the AI boom, the use of biotech was elitist of rich labs. In the late 1990s, Eva Harris, then a young scientist at UC Berkeley, began asking a question largely ignored by her field: How can molecular biology serve communities where pipettes are a luxury? Her answer was not to wait for trickle-down science, but to build horizontal collaborations that respected local knowledge and built laboratory capacity where none existed. In Nicaragua, Peru and other low-resource settings, Harris pioneered community-based virology: training local health workers in PCR, WesternBlooth, or

ELISA assays, building dengue surveillance systems, and co-authoring publications with researchers from endemic areas.

The legacy was echoed by other initiatives from CRISPR DIY (Joshy 2018), to the more recent dipstick with reverse transcription loop-mediated isothermal amplification (RT-LAMP). LAMP technology emerged during the 2019 COVID pandemic (Notomi et al. 2000). It has a faster method than the more traditional polymerase chain reaction (PCR). A group of researchers belonging to the EXPANDIA network managed to miniaturize the technology into even more affordable dipsticks (Šušnjar et al. 2025). "EXPANDIA" stands for Expanding Access to Sustainable Diagnostics in Africa and is an African Laboratory Network Initiative aimed at testing and transferring cost-effective diagnostic technologies specifically designed for laboratories with limited resources. Together with other initiatives sometimes supported by the Melinda and Gates foundations, other realities are following the lead.

In response to the issues with biased dataset that we mentioned earlier, the FAIR movement has emerged. The FAIR principles, which were first developed to direct data stewardship in the life sciences, are now a focal point for inclusive innovation. They require data to be shared in ways that respect local context and allow for global engagement, in addition to being machine-readable and properly annotated. FAIR data are not a technical fix; they are a political choice, a commitment to open ecosystems, and distributed authority.

Examples from recent times demonstrate this change. Projects such as the Latin American Genomics Consortium and the African Open Science Platform are creating data repositories that encourage South-South cooperation and represent regional diversity. Meanwhile, developers outside of prestigious universities are making biomedical AI more accessible thanks to open source tools like DeepChem (Ramsundar et al. 2023) and Bioformer models (Yan et al. 2023). Deepchem is an open-source Python library aiming to democratize machine learning in drug discovery, and Bioformer is a lightweight transformer model designed for biomedical text mining, meant to run also on local machines, and, therefore, becoming more accessible to low-resource settings. Then there is the H3ABioNet, which is a pan-African bioinformatics network that promotes local ownership of African genomic data.

One promising development is the emergence of community-led ethical review boards for digital health tools. In Kenya, for example, mobile health interventions are now subject to local data ethics councils that include patients, technologists, and traditional health workers. Their input shapes how AI is deployed, not after the fact, but from the design stage. The CARE Principles (Collective Benefit, Authority to Control, Responsibility, Ethics) and other Indigenous data sovereignty groups are also redefining open research to incorporate cultural and collective rights over digital and biological data.

4.7 FarmDrive and Kilimo Salama, Agritech Case Studies

Even with all the fast-paced innovation that we have today, agriculture remains a pivotal role. Even more in sub-Saharan Africa, where agriculture remains the economic backbone of society, employing more than 60% of the population and accounting for a significant portion of national GDP. Ironically, though, this is a very vulnerable sector, a common feature also with high-income countries, where even with high standards of living, agriculture is the basis of society, as we have seen in the last COVID-19 pandemic. The vulnerability arises when farmers need loans or investments. Most small-scale farmers do not have access to real-time data, insurance, or a good history of previous loans. Traditional banks often see these farmers as high-risk, low-return customers who do not have official collateral or a steady source of income. As a consequence, agriculture remains underfunded, not so much insured, and vulnerable to climate unpredictability. In this setting, two innovations emerged: FarmDrive and Kilimo Salama, as systemic solutions and as technology products.

Two data scientists in Kenya launched FarmDrive in 2014 after seeing a paradox: Farmers were generating data daily, but none of it was being used to assist them in obtaining financing. Traditional banks required formal financial histories and fixed asset collateral, both of which most smallholders lacked. FarmDrive sought to flip this logic. By aggregating alternative data sources, including mobile phone usage, farm activity logs, GPS-based farm size estimates, weather patterns, and market transactions they built a credit scoring engine tailored to the agricultural context.

The power of FarmDrive lies in its ability to make the invisible visible. A farmer who paid their mobile bills consistently, sold produce regularly in a local market and had stable farming cycles now had a digital footprint. Through partnerships with financial institutions, FarmDrive allowed these farmers to access microloans with terms adjusted to their agricultural calendar. Repayments were aligned with harvest seasons, not monthly cycles. More than 3,000 farmers accessed credit through the platform within its first few years, many for the first time in their lives.

Kilimo Salama, which means "safe farming" in Kiswahili, sought to address climate risk, another debilitating unknown. Kilimo Salama, which was started in 2010 as a collaboration between the Syngenta Foundation and UAP Insurance, offered index-based microinsurance to farmers in Kenya and Rwanda. Smallholder markets have never been served by traditional crop insurance because it is too costly and administratively complicated. It required documentation that farmers were frequently unable to provide, as well as loss assessments on site. Kilimo Salama used an alternative model in which temperature and rainfall were assessed by satellite data and weather stations, and automated payouts were initiated when thresholds were exceeded.

This approach turned agricultural insurance into something scalable and data-driven. Farmers are enrolled in the program when purchasing seeds or fertilizers through agro-dealers. A small insurance premium was added to the cost of the product. If drought or excess rain hit their region during the growing season, the payments were automatically disbursed through mobile money—no claims, no agents, no paperwork. This simplicity was transformative. It derisked investment for farmers who had previously been afraid to spend on high-quality inputs, knowing that a single failed season could spell financial ruin.

The impact of Kilimo Salama rippled beyond insurance. By reducing climate risk, it increased farmers' willingness to adopt improved seeds and fertilizers, which in turn increased yields. Studies showed that insured farmers invested up to 20% more in inputs and saw increases in yields up to 30% (Sibiko et al. 2018). These observations also laid the groundwork for a broader conversation on climate resilience in African agriculture. When the product was later rebranded as the Agriculture And Climate Risk Enterprise (ACRE) Africa, it expanded into a full-fledged risk management ecosystem, including bundled insurance and credit products, and partnerships with development agencies and national governments.

FarmDrive and Kilimo Salama represent two sides of the same coin. Financial inclusion is built by illuminating data patterns that allow credit scoring in high-friction environments. The other creates economic stability by buffering against climate shocks. Both exemplify the potential of agritech to address systemic market failures, not by transplanting Western technologies but by reengineering tools for local constraints. They do not romanticize smallholders; they professionalize them.

Yet, these innovations also highlight structural weaknesses in other aspects. They are both highly dependent on mobile infrastructure, digital literacy, and reliable data pipelines. In regions where women's access to digital technology is restricted by gender inequality or where mobile phone coverage is uneven, adoption is still cumbersome. To scale such platforms, telecommunication companies, government organizations, private digital entrepreneurs, and well-established financial institutions must carefully coordinate. The promise of fintech and insurtech in agriculture is real, but it is not frictionless. We will return to gender-related issues in the last chapter.

There are also important questions about sustainability. FarmDrive, despite its early success, faced challenges scaling its model profitably and navigating the data-sharing landscape with financial institutions wary of outsourcing credit risk assessments. Similarly, Kilimo Salama's dependence on donor funding and reinsurance support revealed the limits of purely market-based models in regions where climate risk is escalating faster than actuarial models can keep up. The tension between innovation and subsidy is not unique to these initiatives, but is a recurring feature of impact-driven technology in emerging economies.

Given those 2 case studies, we have relevant lessons. The right insight on data is still the "king," and can de-risk the poor. Then, as in other fields, technology must align with behavioral and institutional rhythms, including harvest cycles and literacy levels. Lastly, risk aversion is not always the wisest choice and can lead to poverty, targeted solutions such as the aforementioned and microcredit can be a solution. Platforms like FarmDrive and Kilimo Salama demonstrate that small-holder agriculture can be profitable, resilient, and easy to invest in by tackling these issues.

4.8 Digital Market Places and Inclusion in Latin America

In the heads of average people around the world, Latin America is seen more positively than Sub-Saharan Africa. Indeed, the continent has not been devastated at the same level by epidemics. However, dictatorships and pronounced inequalities have always existed. Across the fragmented geographies of Latin America, digital marketplaces have emerged not merely as economic platforms, but as engines of inclusion. It has been established that standard banking models cannot overcome the region's long-standing structural inequalities, which are characterized by financial exclusion, informal labor, and unequal access to infrastructure. PDigital platforms such as ride-hailing, e-commerce, mobile wallets, and peer-to-peer financing are beginning to give millions of underbanked and unbanked people new ways to participate in the formal economy. But this shift is unpredictable and rife with contradictions. It offers real inclusion, but not without raising questions about precariousness, platform dependency, and data governance.

Latin America is ranked highly globally for having one of the highest levels of smartphone penetration alongside one of the lowest levels of traditional financial inclusion (Rubio and León 2025).

In this area, digital marketplaces have stepped in by adding financial tools to mobility and commerce. In addition to facilitating transactions, e-commerce platforms such as Mercado Libre and Rappi also offer working capital loans, embedded payment systems, and seller reputation systems that act as stand-ins for creditworthiness. Financial tools that were previously only available to salaried or officially registered users are now available to street vendors, delivery drivers managing urban traffic, and microentrepreneurs selling handcrafted goods online via QR codes.

Innovation in fintech is essential for this change. Mercado Pago, Nubank, and Ualá are rethinking financial infrastructure for the reality of Latin America, not just providing alternatives to conventional banks. Informal workers can keep money, pay bills, and get credit using Mercado Pago, a digital wallet that was created from Mercado Libre, without having to go inside a bank. The Brazilian neobank Nubank attracted millions of consumers who had previously been routinely shut out by first providing transparent, fee-free credit cards. In direct response to the needs of those employed in informal economies, these services are frequently low-cost, mobile-first, and made to handle sporadic revenue sources and scant paperwork.

This transformation is particularly significant in a region where informality dominates. More than 50% of Latin America's labor force operates outside of formal contracts, insurance, or taxation (Pereira da Silva et al. 2019). For these people, having access to digital payments, savings accounts, or credit is not only a financial issue; it is also a means of becoming more visible, resilient, and mobile. Small business expansion is made possible by financial inclusion, which also reduces dependence on unscrupulous lenders and risky cash holdings.

Despite the enormous negative impact on society, the COVID-19 pandemic accelerated some positive changes in digital transformation. Lockdowns and physical distancing measures have pushed both consumers and small businesses toward digital payments. Emergency cash transfers were widely adopted. Governments in Brazil, Chile, and Colombia used digital wallets to distribute emergency aid, often to citizens who had never previously held a bank account. In Brazil, more than 60 million people received the Auxlio Emergencial through digital platforms, revealing not only the reach of mobile infrastructure but also its potential to embed social protection into inclusive financial ecosystems (De Arruda et al. 2021).

However, new drawbacks have been introduced that have pushed the use of these digital platforms. Platform economies and fintech may provide access, but they also create new dependence. Platform vendors, gig drivers, and delivery workers frequently work in hazardous environments with no labor laws and are susceptible to algorithmic management. Because digital credit is provided with little regulatory monitoring, it could result in excessive debt, particularly if repayment plans do not align with irregular income cycles. With few options for accountability or redress, user profiles can be created using data collected through apps. In this way, security and autonomy may be sacrificed for inclusion.

Governments and regulators must make sure that the internet marketplaces encourage financial inclusion rather than exploit it. In this regard, several Latin American nations have achieved strides. The Fintech Law, passed by Mexico in 2018, created a legislative framework for crowdfunding, electronic money, and digital financial services (Government Of Mexico 2018). Brazil's Central Bank has promoted open banking and instant payment systems like Pix, which greatly reduce transaction costs and improve accessibility. These rules recognize that trust, transparency, and cost are just as crucial to inclusion as access (Banco Central do Brasil 2020).

Cooperatives and civil society groups are also focused on these issues. Digital tools are being adapted to community-based governance by indigenous-led financial cooperatives in Bolivia and Ecuador. Feminist collectives in Argentina are establishing decentralized credit circles with blockchain technology. These bottom-up strategies provide alternatives based on accountability and solidarity, challenging the platform-centric model of digital inclusion.

4.9 Water Is the New Gold, and Other Environmental AI Challenges

On the way to Togo, from Accra in Ghana you might find a little paradise called Ada Foah, it is a lagoon style set of villages where many people go and relax in peace. To reach this paradise if you drive from Accra, you might pass two ill-fated places. The Tema Port, where many electronic waste is arriving from Europe and the United States, and Agbogbloshie, an electronic dump near the Odaw River and close to the Old Fadama slum, where lost souls wander looking to extract minerals from broken computers. Since 2021, the landfill, which has also been locally called Sodoma, has finally entered a demolition phase with the goal of reducing the enormous damage to the environment caused by old PCs, servers, and other electronics wastes. However, the sustainable aspects related to AI worldwide are not very reassuring.

Today, artificial intelligence is often associated with advancement, effectiveness, and even sustainability. Smarter energy grids, precision farming, better logistics, and climate modeling with never-before-seen granularity are all promised by its algorithms. However, the ecological cost of AI itself is a parallel and escalating catastrophe that is hidden by this narrative of AI as an environmental savior. Large-scale intelligence requires enormous amounts of infrastructure, water, energy, and minerals; it is by no means inconsequential.

AI's direct and quantifiable effects include increased energy usage. Thousands of GPUs must run for days or even weeks in order to train large-scale models such as GPT, Claude, DeepSeek, etc. These data centers may or may not be powered by renewable energy sources. According to a 2019 study, the use of non-renewable electricity to train a single large language model can result in carbon dioxide emissions equal to five cars over the course of their useful life (Strubell et al. 2019). As model sizes have ballooned, from hundreds of millions to hundreds of billions of parameters, the computational and energy demands have grown exponentially. These training cycles are not isolated events; they are repeated regularly as firms fine-tune, retrain, or create successor models, each iteration leaving a carbon footprint that is rarely acknowledged by end users, and practically all efforts we have done so far for sustainability are heavily endangered.

The environmental impact persists during deployment, even after training. The continuous operation of AI applications found in billions of smartphones, smart speakers, security cameras, and industrial systems requires high-throughput data pipelines and low-latency inference capabilities. Large data centers that are operational 24/7, water-intensive systems for cooling, and high-consumption hardware for maintenance are required to support these systems. Although cloud providers have begun to report renewable energy targets, the geographic mismatch between where energy is produced and where AI workloads are run often leads to a misleading "net zero" narrative. Clean energy credits are traded on paper, while in practice many AI calculations still depend on fossil fuels (Schwartz et al. 2020).

Water usage is another hidden cost. Cooling high-performance computing infrastructure requires enormous amounts of water. In 2023, reports revealed that the OpenAI partnership with Microsoft involved water withdrawals of millions of gallons to cool their AI servers (Koeze and Metz 2023). This is especially problematic when training occurs in regions experiencing water scarcity. The environmental impact is not only about emissions, it is about the redistribution of vital resources from local communities to centralized AI infrastructure. A silver lining comes from a study on water efficiency for African data centers, where 8 of the 11 selected African countries consume less water than the global average and the United States with searches for Llama-3-70B and GPT-4 (Shumba et al. 2025). However, water consumption can be substantially higher in some African countries that have more water demands and carbon oxide production compared to the US, as shown in Fig. 4.3, causing the need for region-specific adaptations in data centers.

Additionally, the Sodoma dump in Ghana we mentioned earlier pointed out the issue of mining and refinement of rare earth elements and metals such as lithium, cobalt, and nickel, which are utilized in GPUs, batteries, and other computing components, are part of the AI's material footprint. These mining operations occur frequently in the Global South, where populations experience long-term ecological deterioration, water contamination, and displacement due to lax regulatory monitoring (Vivian 2021).

The structure of AI innovation reinforces these environmental inefficiencies. The prevailing trend is to compete on model size and capability: bigger is better, regardless of the cost. This creates a winner-take-all arms race, where the largest tech companies with the most computational resources dominate. The result is not just environmental waste, but a consolidation of power. Smaller researchers, especially those from the Global South, are priced out of frontier research, unable to afford the computational costs to participate meaningfully in the field. The environmental cost thus intersects with epistemic injustice.

To address this, several proposals have emerged, though uptake remains slow. One is the development of more efficient architectures and training strategies, such as sparse models, knowledge distillation, or quantization, that reduce computation requirements without sacrificing performance. Another is model transparency: reporting not just accuracy scores but also energy consumption, emissions, and water use. The Green AI movement argues for shifting the field's values from pure performance to efficiency and equity (Schwartz et al. 2020). Some have proposed compute caps or carbon budgets

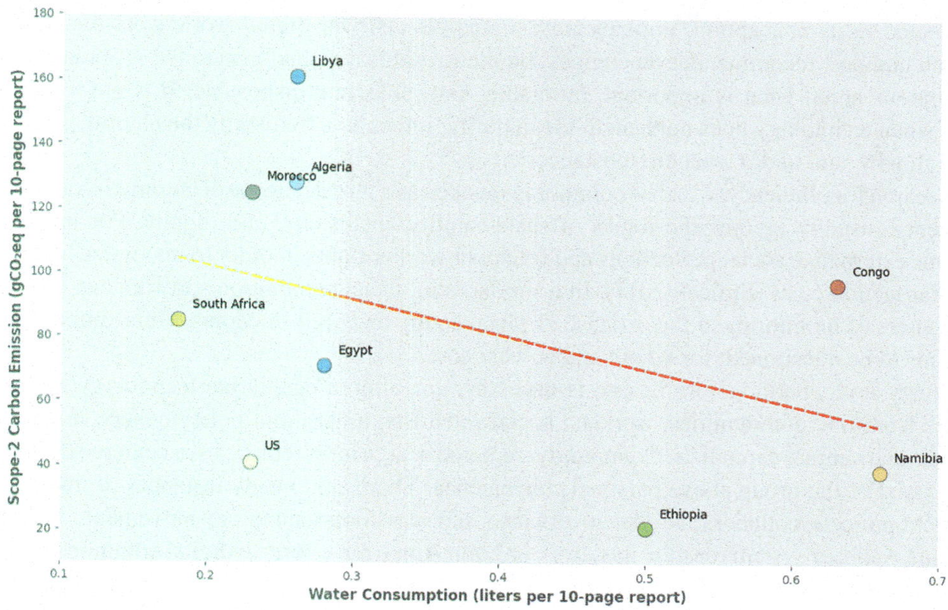

Fig. 4.3 Water consumption for cooling system and emitted pollution from some African countries compared to US, picture recreated by using the data available on Shumba et al. (2025)

for academic publications, incentivizing greener experimentation. But without industry support and regulatory pressure, these norms are unlikely to change the status quo.

Policy and governance must also step in. Environmental impact assessments should be mandatory for major AI deployments and included in procurement decisions for governments and corporations. With the approval and supervision of the community, the operation and development of the data center must be linked to local environmental circumstances. As with emissions or electronic waste in other areas, international regulation might establish baseline environmental criteria for AI infrastructure. However, current debates over AI policy frequently ignore the tangible effects of digital expansion in favor of concentrating only on bias, safety, and geopolitics.

4.10 Redirecting Technology

For a long time, the history of mankind has been supported by technological development as a straight line: from fire to steam, from letters to emails, from electricity to computers, each step purportedly bringing humanity one step closer to freedom and away from scarcity. Even in our initial age of AI, as long as retraining exists (Choi and Leigh 2024), society benefits from innovation. However, as the speed of the digital revolution increases due to biotechnology, platform economies, chatbots, and ubiquitous computing, it becomes increasingly challenging to maintain this narrative without contradiction. Not everyone in the world benefits equally from technical growth. Digital infrastructures consolidate power instead of democratizing it; algorithmic systems reinforce systemic bias; even if at the same time people in low-income countries are now learning how to use those tools. It is a contradiction, but still in equilibrium.

We need to start with a fundamental reframe in order to reroute technology toward more equitable and healthier societies: technology is neither neutral nor inevitable. Values, interests, and ideologies are reflected in its conception, implementation, and effects. Our digital world's architectures, such as search engines, recommendation engines, biometric databases, and generative AI models, encode presumptions about what is important, profitable, knowable, and disposable. It is not a flaw in the system when technology does not benefit the majority; rather, it is frequently the natural result of who created it, why, and under what circumstances.

The search for efficiency, which is commonly invoked as a moral defense of automation and artificial intelligence, usually ignores the issues of sustainability, inclusivity, and dignity. For instance, gig platforms externalize social protections and fragment worker rights in order to maximize logistics and lower transaction costs (Srnicek 2017). In a similar vein, facial recognition software can increase the effectiveness of monitoring at the expense of racial equity and civil freedoms. "Innovation" is a term that needs to be questioned: for whom and at what cost?

At every level, participatory design is necessary for a more egalitarian technology future. This includes front-line communities, workers, social scientists, artists, and policymakers, in addition to engineers and venture capitalists. Community-centered design must replace user-centered design, placing the good of the group above personal convenience. There are already instances of this in public-interest AI projects, collaborative data governance, and grassroots technology movements. Models like the Indian Aadhaar system (despite its flaws), or Latin American efforts to digital commons, show how infrastructure can be oriented around public utility rather than private capture (Mehta 2018).

The redistribution of technological power also requires a rethink of who owns and governs data. Today, the world's computing infrastructure and data pipelines are controlled by a limited number of companies, most of which are located in the Global North. This concentration makes economic domination and epistemic control possible, what is seen, spoken, or silenced. Redirecting technology for social good must involve the democratization of data, through public data trusts, community-owned datasets, and strong privacy rights. Data should not be a commodity, but a common governed with care and consent (Costanza-Chock et al. 2023).

This reorientation also involves large investments in capacity building. Technological sovereignty cannot emerge where local expertise is absent. The Global South's nations, which are frequently viewed as labor pools or passive markets, need to be considered as active participants in determining the direction of the digital economy. This involves helping community technologists, public research organizations, open-source ecosystems, and nearby universities. It involves sponsoring not only Silicon Valley AI laboratories, but also indigenous data protocols, African language models, and design paradigms with cultural roots (Massey and Kituyi 2023).

Redirecting technology must, crucially, also address its historical connections to oppressive structures. Technologies frequently replicate and expand colonial logics; they are not created in a vacuum. Whether it is labor for annotation, cobalt for batteries, or data for training, the geographies of extraction reflect historical exploitation trends. Not only do we need new tools to build a more equitable technological future, but we also need new ethics: decolonial ethics that acknowledges plurality, interdependence, and historical accountability (Mohamed et al. 2020).

Regulation will be necessary, but it must be proactive rather than reactive. Current frameworks usually focus on correcting the most serious damage after it occurs, such as deep-fakes or facial recognition abuses. Rather, we require proactive governance that prioritizes the public interest, requires transparency, and places restrictions on extractive computation. Governments must retake their responsibilities as guardians of the digital infrastructure and cease submitting to IT companies. This might involve algorithmic effect assessments based on environmental ones, required environmental audits for training huge models, or public ownership of cloud services.

There is both urgency and uncertainty surrounding the notion of an AI revolution in the Global South. It is urgent because the world's economic, political, and social systems are already changing due to AI's transformative power, endangering vast regions of the globe. The term "AI revolution" is unclear since it can refer to a variety of concepts, such as algorithmic justice, technical sovereignty, economic catch-up, or just surviving disruptions brought on by AI systems created elsewhere. In part, these are not issues limited to the global South; there is uncertainty and fear of technofeudalism in many high-income countries (?). We are all wondering to catch up with the innovations, and at the same time to align them to our society, not the other way around.

AI has the potential to reconfigure development paradigms in many fields, as we have just described. AI models can predict yields and improve fertilizer use in agriculture. Generative AI technologies can be used to customize lessons in classrooms where teachers are overloaded. Similar technologies can be used to monitor and identify diseases in public health, even in areas where there is a shortage of medical professionals. In the domains of healthcare, energy management, finance, and disaster preparedness, AI can improve accessibility, reduce risk, and improve efficiency.

Yet, the realization of these benefits requires more than access to pre-trained models or open-source tools. It requires a systemic transformation of the socio-technical ecosystem that supports AI, or better the people that are affected by its use. Most countries in the Global South lack the computational infrastructure, skilled labor force, regulatory frameworks, and capital investment necessary to develop AI systems on a scale. This asymmetry is not merely technical; it is a continuation of patterns of dependency, where knowledge and innovation flow from North to South, while data and raw use cases flow in the opposite direction. In such a system, the Global South becomes a site of deployment and experimentation, rather than of design and authorship.

To change this dynamic, we must confront the layered challenges of inclusion, access, and ownership. The first is the challenge of capacity. The Global South will continue to be a consumer rather than a creator of AI systems if funding is not allocated to AI education, research facilities, and regional talent pipelines. Universities must create an interdisciplinary context-specific AI curriculum that integrates computer science with ethics, public policy, and regional languages.

The second is the challenge of infrastructure. It takes a lot of computing power, data centers, GPUs, a steady power source, and the broadband Internet to train contemporary large-language models or vision systems. Infrastructure deficiencies in most African, Latin American, Southeast Asian, and some Middle Eastern nations make such development unaffordable. The barrier might be reduced by regional AI hubs and shared cloud infrastructures, possibly funded by development funding or international cooperation. Open-source alternatives to closed foundation models, combined with lightweight fine-tuning methods, may also allow greater accessibility without sacrificing performance.

The third is the challenge of data sovereignty. AI systems depend on data, but in much of the Global South, data is either unavailable, unstructured, or captured by foreign platforms. Satellite imagery, GIS, habits that can be connected to insurances, biometric databases, health records, and mobile phone metadata frequently leave local jurisdictions and enter the servers of multinational firms. In a fictionary (yet not far-fetched) novel of Kai-Fu Lee called "The Golden Elephant," a pervasive AI was calculating the insurance premium by looking at any minimal facet of the behavior of people: which pictures they liked on social media, which burger they ordered online, how much physical activities they were doing, and the types of online interactions with other people (Lee and Fu 2021). The insight was that certain people might engage in certain behaviors leading to health hazards, and therefore those individuals have to pay a higher insurance. This points out how tyrannical and invasive AI systems can be, oppressing and spying us in even the most intimate activity of our lives. Despite the fact that the novel is fiction and set in 2041, there are concerns even now that this will happen soon. Countries must invest in interoperable, inclusive, and privacy-preserving public data infrastructures to develop AI systems that respond to local demands. They must create data ownership and usage regulations that are representative of local values rather than simply importing them from Brussels or Silicon Valley.

And finally, there is the challenge of imagination. The AI revolution in the Global South cannot simply replicate the pathways of the Global North. Leadership and decolonization of technology must occur on a large scale. The priority on low-resource natural language processing for indigenous languages over general-purpose English-language models must be expanded. It may mean investing in cooperative data platforms, where farmers or patients co-own the data used to train systems that serve them. It may mean developing small-scale embedded AI systems that operate offline in rural areas without electricity. Innovation in this sense is not about catching up, it is about creating anew.

There are already signs of such innovation. In Kenya, companies such as FarmDrive use artificial intelligence to assess the risk of credit for small farmers based on alternative data sources. In India, the MOSIP platform supports an inclusive digital identity infrastructure open to customization by other countries. Currently, those examples and others seem still just local news while they should be the regular norm.

Decolonization is not just a challenge for the Global South, soon even in the Global North we might face inequalities at levels we cannot even foresee. Across this book, we mentioned multiple times the techno-feudalism, or Googleization. A world where we own less everyday and we contribute to online platforms, who are richer than certain governments and absorb day after day products and services. In a realistic view, it is unlikely that AI will turn against us in a ruthless way, unless the increasing power of big tech companies allows it. Decolonization is therefore also a matter concerning high-income countries. First, we need institutions and governments to take care of citizens and not be buried by powerful corporations. A solution that everyone will imagine about this is regulations. However, as we mentioned in the previous chapters, regulations often end up playing the game of strong lobbying companies, and simply killing the competitions of the big techs. We need to think more, in general, taking seriously into consideration frugal innovation and open source communities. Those are not garage projects; they might be one day our best weapons to balance techno-feudalism. Fortunately, we have many tools including software and pre-trained models, which are open and free to be downloaded. Scientists can still easily publish on platforms such as Arxiv.[1] Democracy is still alive, sharing is still caring.

The international community plays a vital role. Multilateral organizations, development banks, and charitable foundations must shift their focus from extractive innovation models to inclusive capacity building. Global North-based AI enterprises must embrace ethical engagement strategies, such as equitable data partnerships, profit sharing plans, and joint infrastructure investment. It is imperative for policymakers to ensure that digital trade agreements promote open access and mutual benefit rather than creating asymmetries. These steps require not only technical foresight but political will, and I hope I have been able to provide the big picture in this context.

4.11 AI Early Warning for Malaria, System Thinking Success Story

Putting things together and also connecting to the system thinking of the first chapter, we can actually think about several success stories. For example, in Uganda and Rwanda many early warning systems have been deployed with this mindset (Tompkins et al. 2014), I will review one here: Rwanda's Climate—Informational Malaria Surveillance System. This project, led by the Health Information Systems Programme (HISP) Rwanda in collaboration with the Rwanda Ministry of Health, the Rwanda Biomedical Centre, METEO Rwanda, and academic partners, integrates climate data into the District Health Information Software 2 (DHIS2), a national health information system aiming to improve malaria surveillance and early warning (DHIS2 2025).

[1] https://arxiv.org/.

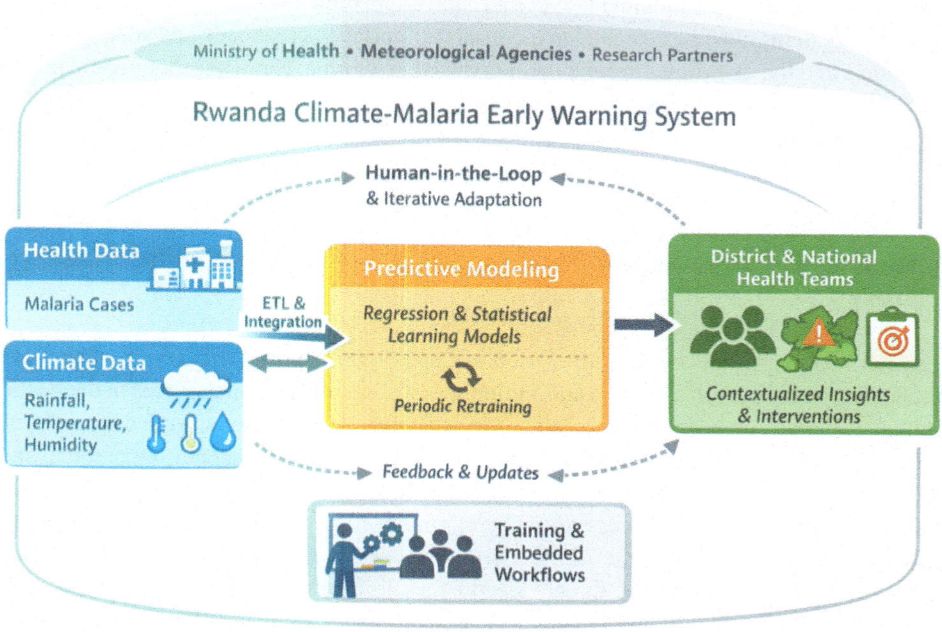

Fig. 4.4 Summary of the system thinking approach of DHIS2

The key system components can be summarized in the following list and depicted in Fig. 4.4.

1. **Integration of Multiple Data Streams**: The system combined climatic data, such as temperature, rainfall, and humidity, with time matched routine malaria case data from medical facilities. This helped to tighten the environmental determinants of malaria transmission rather than treating incidence as pure health data. More specifically, they used an Extract–Transform–Load (ETL) pipeline. to harmonize temporal and spatial resolutions across health and climate datasets.
2. **Feedback Loops and Adaptation**: Thanks to the continuously collected data which were feeding the predictive models, performance on the forecast and quick feedback to the stakeholders were possible.
3. **Human-in-the-Loop Decision Making**: Similarly, practically predictive models supported human decision-makers (district and national health teams), who interpret the results and translate them into targeted interventions, ensuring that decisions remain contextual and actionable.
4. **Capacity Building and Workflow Integration**: The results are integrated into current public health processes through training and stakeholder participation, enabling efficient adoption and understanding of the system's insights.
5. **Multi-Level Governance**: A peculiar aspect was also the coordination across national and sub-national levels. Indeed, the project involved institutions such as the Ministry of Health, meteorological agencies, and research partners, which ensured that AI insights were actually used and were providing real-world input to the governance structures.

The key lessons from the systems thinking perspective were that AI and predictive modeling should be understood as parts of a broader socio-technical system rather than as isolated, self-sufficient solutions. The relevant insight is that those are neither research projects, nor isolated tools, but their effectiveness depends on how well they are embedded in the physical and governmental infrastructures. Crucially, human actors remain central to outcomes. Predictive models can support and inform decision-making, but do not replace the judgment, expertise, and contextual awareness of trained professionals. For this reason, systems must be designed to incorporate continuous feedback and adaptation, allowing both the models and the workflows around them to evolve over time. From a technological perspective, most of the predictions were regression-based and statistical learning models that explicitly incorporate climate covariates. Feedback and adjustment occurred in the model, but rather than online learning in real time, the system used periodic re-training of the AI models (Suárez-Cetrulo et al. 2023).

4.12 Tiko Digital Behavioral Intervention for Girls, System Thinking Success Story

Tiko is an African non-profit organization based in Cape Town, South Africa, with additional offices and presence in countries such as Kenya and Ethiopia as well as international offices in the Netherlands and Portugal. Its name comes from "Tiko" comes from Kiswahili, a colloquial form derived from "iko," which means "there is/it exists/it is possible," this expression represents agency and choice, and it has been chosen by the NGO to embed its vision of behavioral change for adolescent girls. Their work provides us a further illustrative success story that aligns strongly with a systems thinking perspective. More specifically, I am referring to the *Tiko Inspiring Futures* programme (Tiko 2025). Tiko addresses what is often referred to as the "triple threat" faced by adolescent girls and young women: unintended pregnancy, HIV infection, and sexual and gender-based violence (Maughan-Brown et al. 2025). Rather than treating these outcomes in isolation, Tiko adopts an integrated, socio-technical approach that combines digital technologies, behavioral science, and local service ecosystems. The insights are to take advantage of the ubiquitous mobile system and a strong emphasis on system thinking: The programme leverages a digital platform, accessible via mobile phones, which enables girls to confidentially access sexual and reproductive health information, order health services, and connect with trusted providers. Importantly, the system is designed not merely as an information delivery tool, but as an adaptive intervention embedded within existing health, educational, and community infrastructures.

The key components of the system can be summarized as follows and are depicted in Fig. 4.5.

1. **Integration of Behavioral and Service Data**: The platform collects anonymized interaction data, including content engagement, service acceptance, and referral completion, and links these to health service delivery points. This allows behavioral signals (for example, anxious patterns of specific information online at certain times of the day, in bursts, or using multiple searches.) to be interpreted alongside service access outcomes, allowing a more holistic understanding of risk and protective factors that affect girls' health pathways. Like benevolent version of the "The Golden Elephant" of Kai-Fu Lee I mentioned earlier (Lee and Fu 2021).
2. **Adaptive Feedback Loops**: One of the core aspects of system thinking is continuous monitoring. In this case, this is achieved by looking at the user engagement and service utilization, and those enable rapid feedback to programme designers and local partners. Content strategies, outreach mechanisms, and incentive structures are iteratively refined based on observed behavioral responses, ensuring that interventions remain contextually relevant and effective over time.
3. **Human-in-the-Loop Safeguards**: Like in other approaches mentioned in this book, while digital nudges and recommender mechanisms guide users toward appropriate information and services, critical decisions, particularly those involving safeguarding, referrals for violence, or clinical care remain firmly mediated by trained human actors. Health workers, counselors, and community partners interpret digital signals and provide personalized support, preserving ethical oversight and contextual judgment.
4. **Capacity Building and Ecosystem Embedding**: The effectiveness of the platform depends on its integration into local health systems and youth-friendly service networks. Training of providers,

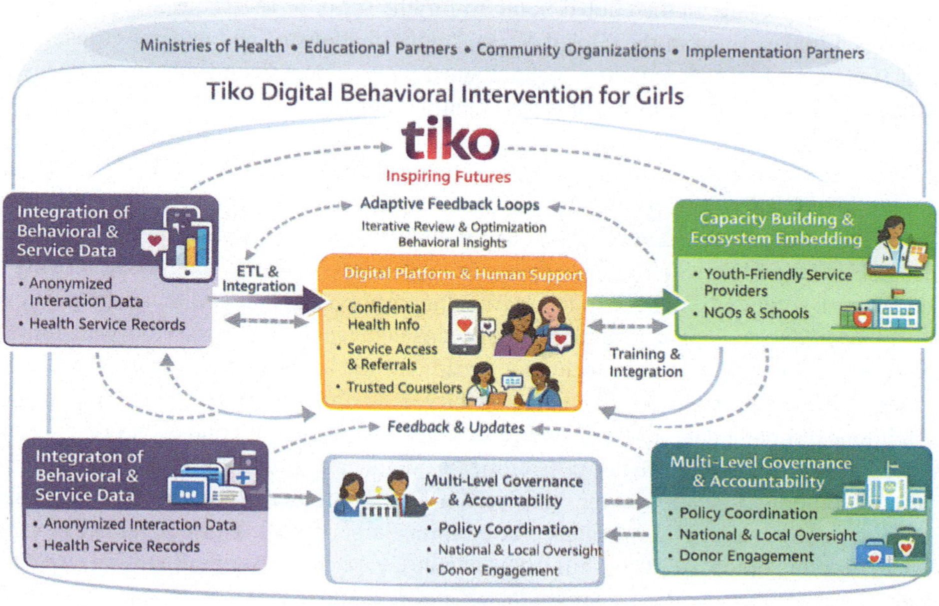

Fig. 4.5 Summary of the system thinking approach of Tiko programme for digital behavioral intervention for adolescent girls

alignment with national reproductive health policies, and collaboration with NGOs and schools ensure that digital engagement is translated into real-world access and sustained impact.

5. **Multi-Level Governance and Accountability**: Tiko operates through partnerships with ministries of health, implementation organizations and donors, enabling coordination at the local, national, and international levels. The focus is not just on the girls behavior, but also on governance structures. Hoping that the insights derived from the digital system can inform policy discussions while remaining responsive to the realities of the ground.

Therefore, from a system thinking point of view, the approach serves as an example of how digital and AI-enabled interventions work best when viewed as parts of a larger socio-technical system from the standpoint of systems thinking. Despite the health issues being not completely solved, the initiative influences the interplay of technology, human interactions, and institutional trust.

Importantly, teenage girls are active agents whose decisions, limitations, and goals influence the behavior of the system rather than passive recipients of technical solutions. The approach is yet loose, as Tiko/possible, and it is not reinforced. Program optimization can be aided by predictive analytics and data-driven targeting, but the results ultimately depend on how well these tools are integrated into ethical governance frameworks and supportive social structures. Sustained influence results from ongoing feedback, modification, and human-centered design rather than just automation, as in previous effective early-warning and prevention systems.

4.13 Summary of the Chapter

In this chapter, we navigated the complex duality of artificial intelligence, which we can frame as a force growing a new age of inequality or become a powerful engine for inclusive development, and it should be used especially in the Global South to flip the script or at least as a tool against poverty and other social issues. Even in the Global North, "cloud-feudalism" and general growing power of tech giant is creating a concentration of technological power that risks leaving the majority behind, increasing inequality even more in low-income countries. Nevertheless, so far this trajectory does not seem inevitable.

With this in mind, we can push for the shift from traditional aid to market-creating innovation, where AI is focused to solve local problems, such as providing healthcare diagnostics in regions with few specialists. Especially, since the created AI models might be strongly biased for specific regions and not easily adaptable to the Global South. This requires a decolonization of technology itself moving beyond imported Western solutions. We need to foster frugal innovation and build AI that is linguistically and culturally relevant, such as language models for African languages and dialects. Above all, those should not remain local pilot, but scale to be technology ready for the highest levels.

We can find further examples AI alleviating poverty more directly. For instance, predicting poverty using satellite and mobile data, or designing more equitable economic policies through systems like the "AI Economist." There are many possibilities to democretize upcoming technologies, yet this abundance of solutions is shadowed by significant risks, from biased algorithms that perpetuate discrimination to the immense environmental cost of training large models. Those are already examples of technolocial decolonization, Actively shift from technology transfer to supporting local, context-aware innovation. Other ideas to combat cloud-feudalism and deconolize tech can include

- Decolonize Data and Infrastructure: We can fight cloud-feudalism by funding shared computing infrastructure in the Global South that fight monopolies/oligopolies, assuming security is ensured.
- Implement Value-Based Regulation: Enact proactive policies that prioritize equity and sustainability, such as mandatory audits for impact assessments and respect for ethics.
- Foster Participation and Inclusive Design: Diverse communities, minorities, and other groups should be involved in its design and governance.

References

Adelani DI et al (2024) Irokobench: a new benchmark for African languages in the age of large language models. arXiv:2406.03368

Alemayehu C, Mitchell G, Nikles J (2018) Barriers for conducting clinical trials in developing countries-a systematic review. Int J Equity Health 17(1):37

Arruda D, Lara P, Andrade M, Lazarotto De, Falcão, Tiago, Barbosa D, Teixeira, Morgandi M (2021) Auxílio Emergencial-Lessons from the Brazilian experience responding to COVID-19. The World Bank Group

Axtell RL, Farmer JD (2025) Agent-based modeling in economics and finance: past, present, and future. J Econ Lit 63(1):197–287

Banco Central do Brasil (2020) PIX: O Sistema de Pagamentos Instantâneos do Brasil

Banerjee I et al (2020) Reading race: AI recognises patient's racial identity in medical imaging. Lancet Digit Health 2(11):e555–e556

Biallas M, O'Neill F (2020) Artificial intelligence innovation in financial services. Int Financ Corp 85(6):1–8

Bradford DE, DeFalco A, Perkins ER, Carbajal I, Kwasa J, Goodman FR, Joyner KJ (2024) Whose signals are being amplified? Toward a more equitable clinical psychophysiology. Clin Psychol Sci 12(2):237–252

Buolamwini J, Gebru T (2018) Gender shades: intersectional accuracy disparities in commercial gender classification. In: Proceedings of the 1st conference on fairness, accountability and transparency, pp 77–91

Buzaaba H, Wettig A, Adelani DI, Fellbaum C (2025) Lugha-Llama: adapting large language models for African languages. arXiv:2504.06536

Choi T, Leigh NG (2024) Artificial intelligence's creation and displacement of labor demand. Technol Forecast Soc Chang 209:123824

Christensen CM, Ojomo E, Dillon K (2019) The prosperity paradox: how innovation can lift nations out of poverty. Harper Business

Costanza-Chock S et al (2023) Data Justice in Practice: Toward a Community-Led Framework. Data & Society Research Institute

DeWitt Prat L, Ndlovu Lucas ON, Golias C, Lewis M (2024) Decolonizing LLMs: An ethnographic framework for ai in African contexts. In: Ethnographic praxis in industry conference proceedings, vol 2024, no 1, pp 46–85

DHIS2 (2025) Catalyzing climate-health data use with the DHIS2 climate app. DHIS2 Project Documentation

European Parliament and Council (2024) Regulation (EU) 2024/1689 of the European Parliament and of the Council of 13 June 2024 laying down harmonised rules on artificial intelligence (Artificial Intelligence Act). Official Journal of the European Union L 1689

Fraisl D, See L, Fritz S, Haklay M, McCallum I (2024) Leveraging the collaborative power of AI and citizen science for sustainable development. Nat Sustain 1–8

Government of Mexico (2018) Ley para Regular las Instituciones de Tecnología Financiera (Fintech Law). Diario Oficial de la Federación

Hart PE, Stork DG, Duda RO (2001) Pattern classification. Wiley, Hoboken

Joshy A (2018) CRISPR ethics & imagination: an evaluation of the role of DIY-CRISPR kit in Crispr-Cas9 deliberations. MS thesis, University of Twente

Koeze E, Metz C (2009) How much water does AI consume? More than you think. The New York Times

Lanfrica (2024) Lanfrica—the hub for African language resources. https://lanfrica.com/

Lee K-F, Qiufan C (2021) AI 2041: ten visions for our future. Crown Currency

Maatouk C, Lucero-Prisno DE III (2025) Barriers to skin cancer diagnosis and treatment in low-and middle-income countries and solutions: a literature review. Public Health Chall 4(1):e70042

MacGyver (1985) Created by Lee David Zlotoff. Starring Richard Dean Anderson

Masakhane (2024) Masakhane—machine translation for Africa. https://www.masakhane.io/

Massey A, Kituyi M (2023) Locally rooted AI: the next frontier of inclusion. J AI Soc 38(2):220–237

Maughan-Brown B, Banougnin BH, Little MT, Hertzog L, Matsha-Carpentier N, Mugambi C, Gichane H, Cluver L, Toska E (2025) Tackling the triple threat in Kenya: factors associated with protection against HIV risk, gender-based violence, and pregnancy among adolescent girls and young women. AIDS Behav 29(6):1738–1746

Mehta PB (2018) The publicness of Aadhaar. Econ & Polit Wkly 53(6):10–13

Mohamed S, Png MT, Isaac W (2020) Decolonial AI: decolonial theory as sociotechnical foresight in artificial intelligence. Philos & Technol 33(4):659–684

Muralidharan V, Adewale BA, Huang CJ (2024) A scoping review of reporting gaps in FDA-approved ai medical devices. npj Digit Med 7:273

Nesta (2024) GE ECG machine—frugal innovation. Nesta Feature

Notomi T, Okayama H, Masubuchi H, Yonekawa T, Watanabe K, Amino N, Hase T (2000) Loop-mediated isothermal amplification of DNA. Nucleic Acids Res 28(12):e63–e63

Obermeyer Z, Powers B, Vogeli C, Mullainathan S (2019) Dissecting racial bias in an algorithm used to manage the health of populations. Science 366(6464):447–453

Pereira da Silva LA et al (2019) Fintech in Latin America and the Caribbean: stocktaking. IMF Working Paper No. 19/071

Radjou N, Prabhu J, Ahuja S (2012) Jugaad innovation: think frugal, be flexible, generate breakthrough growth. Jossey-Bass

Ramsundar B, Eastman P, Walters P, Pande V, Leswing M (2023) DeepChem: democratizing deep-learning for drug discovery, quantum chemistry. Materials Science and Biology. GitHub repository

Reynolds S (1994) Fiefs and vassals: the medieval evidence reinterpreted. OUP Oxford

Roberts S (2014) Origami microscope for just 50 cents. makezine.com. Maker Media Inc

Rubio J, León M (2025) Financial inclusion as a pathway to poverty alleviation and equality in Latin America: an empirical analysis. J Risk Financ Manag 18(7):392

Samuel O, Zewotir T, North D (2021) Decomposing the urban-rural inequalities in the utilisation of maternal health care services: evidence from 27 selected countries in Sub-Saharan Africa. Reprod Health 18(1):216

Schwartz R, Dodge J, Smith NA, Etzioni O (2020) Green AI. Commun ACM 63(12):54–63

Shumba N, Tshekiso O, Li P, Fanti G, Ren S (2025) A water efficiency dataset for African data centers. In: Proceedings of the ACM SIGCAS/SIGCHI conference on computing and sustainable societies, pp 453–460

Siami-Namini S, Tavakoli N, Namin AS (2018) A comparison of ARIMA and LSTM in forecasting time series. In: 2018 17th IEEE international conference on machine learning and applications (ICMLA). IEEE

Sibiko KW, Veettil PC, Qaim M (2018) Small farmers' preferences for weather index insurance: insights from Kenya. Agric & Food Secur 7(1):53

Srnicek N (2017) Platform capitalism. Polity Press

Steele JE, Pezzulo C, Albert M, Brooks CJ, zu Erbach-Schoenberg E, O'Connor SB, Tatem AJ (2021) Mobility and phone call behavior explain patterns in poverty at high-resolution across multiple settings. Humanit Soc Sci Commun 8(1):1–12

Strubell E, Ganesh A, McCallum A (2019) Energy and policy considerations for deep learning in NLP. In: Proceedings of the 57th annual meeting of the association for computational linguistics, pp 3645–3650
Suárez-Cetrulo AL, Quintana D, Cervantes A (2023) A survey on machine learning for recurring concept drifting data streams. Expert Syst Appl 213:118934
Šušnjar U, Bitew M, Ayele S, Uršič T, Petrovec M, Carletti T, Bussani E et al (2025) Colorimetric RT-LAMP for SARS-CoV-2 detection from nasopharyngeal swabs or crude saliva: a multicountry diagnostic accuracy study in Africa. Lancet Glob Health 13(7):e1258–e1267
Sutton RS, Barto AG (1988) Reinforcement learning: an introduction. MIT Press
Tiko (2025) About Tiko–inspiring futures where girls are unstoppable forces of change. Tiko.org. https://tiko.org/. Accessed Jan 2026
Tompkins AM, Di Giuseppe F, Colon-Gonzalez F, Chirombo J, Bizimana J-P, Namanya D (2014) A dynamical climate-driven malaria early warning system evaluated in Uganda. Rwanda Malawi Malar J 13(Suppl. 1):P99
Tonja AL, Dossou BF, Ojo J, Rajab J, Thior F, Wairagala EP, Rosman B (2024) Inkubalm: a small language model for low-resource African languages. arXiv:2408.17024
Varoufakis Y (2024) Technofeudalism: what killed capitalism. Melville House
Vivian J (2021) The environmental cost of artificial intelligence. AI & Soc 36(3):715–725
Wachter S, Mittelstadt B, Russell C (2017) Counterfactual explanations without opening the black box: automated decisions and the GDPR. Harv J Law & Technol 31(2):841–887
Yan Y, Zhang H, Xu Q, Zhao J, Dai H (2023) Bioformer: a compact BERT model for biomedical text mining. arXiv:2302.01588
Zheng S, Trott A, Srinivasa S, Parkes DC, Socher R (2022) The AI economist: taxation policy design via two-level deep multiagent reinforcement learning. Sci Adv 8(18):eabk2607

5 Beyond the Global South

This chapter is leading toward conclusions, but before that it includes some elements which are more general and not particularly related to relative or absolute poverty. I still believe there is something immoral in intellectual property protection, and given these continuous fights, first Global North versus Global South, or then liberal US versus over-regulated Europe, we forgot certain structures from Asia. Let us review those points before we begin to part ways.

5.1 Is Intellectual Protection Still Evil?

When we talk about innovation, we usually refer also to its inventor: the innovator, scientist, geek working like crazy to give his or her contribution to the society. Unfortunately, our society is more prone to strange behavior, choices driven by tradition and bureaucracy, or even worse. In their quest to achieve a return on investment, many organizations have done much harm or even stifled innovation, information, and established authority. Patents and other forms of protection have been originally intended to encourage creativity and expression to compensate the inventor of his/her efforts, but often these legal tools have developed into extensive control measures that hinder rather than foster innovation and frequently put corporate interests ahead of the general welfare. In fact, analysis on number of citations of patents or related publications showed a bizarre outcome: they are often linked to the GDP of a country but not to its Gini index, suggesting that there might be an increase of average GDP but not a translation into reduction of inequality or overall increase in standard of living (Stiglitz and Greenwald 2014).

Moreover, the new advances in AI created more questions that have complicated even further legislation. We are still clarifying whether art or poetry created by large models violate copyright, but soon we will likely have all kinds of innovation being created or helped in the creation in some way by AI tools. Eventually, we might even consider the AI tool as the author of a patent. On the other hand, there will be tools that assess whether a claim can be patented, also automatically analyzing the textual description automatically. Like bots talking to each other without human interaction (Lee et al. 2021), one describes one invention and the other assesses whether it qualifies according to the USPIO standard. All for that, we are not here to discuss those cumbersome legal conundrums, we are here instead to challenge the concept of intellectual protection itself, again.

© The Author(s), under exclusive license to Springer Nature Switzerland AG 2026

A. Crimi, *Innovate for Impact*, Sustainable Development Goals Series,
https://doi.org/10.1007/978-3-032-21563-5_5

Patents are supposed to encourage research and development by giving inventors the temporary, exclusive right to their inventions. In reality, though, they have turned into instruments of obstruction: while patent trolls, which are organizations that produce nothing useful, employ ambiguous patents to embezzle funds from startups, big businesses amass patent thickets to discourage competition. The system is overburdened with these poor quality or excessively wide patents, which discourage true innovation and result in expensive litigation. According to studies, the U.S. Patent and Trademark Office frequently overgrants invalid patents because of resource limitations and incentive systems; acceptance rates are close to 97%, and the office is known to approve more claims in order to meet backlog pressures and procedural quota (Ezell 2020).

Empirical evidence shows that the patent system captures only a fraction of meaningful innovation. A study of nearly 4,500 Swedish innovations found that approximately 83% of important technical information never appeared in patent filings, and only around 8% of innovation rates responded positively to strengthened patent laws (Bessen et al. 2022). These findings suggest that the link between patent protection and innovation is, at best, tenuous and heavily overstated.

The basic idea of copyright has also been overreached. Previously a time-limited protection for writers, this protection now lasts for decades after their passing, enclosing large portions of culture in legal limbo. Teachers, libraries, remix artists, and even archivists incur unnecessary expenses as a result. Because they are too recent to be deemed public domain, but too old to be financially successful, creative works frequently find themselves in a legal limbo. In this environment, access to knowledge is reduced not by scarcity, but by legal design. However, with a large language model, the issue is more complex, as those can ingest large amount of material which is protected by copyright but in a way that is not so transparent, and produce works on request, which are different in form but are the fruit of the ingested work, substantially breaking copyrights in a very smart way.

The pharmaceutical sector illustrates the most grotesque consequences of the patent system. Major pharmaceutical firms frequently engage in "evergreening," filing dozens or even hundreds of trivial modifications to extend patent monopolies. This strategy allows companies to delay generic competition and inflate prices. Recent data show that the top-selling drugs in the US carry an average of 140 patents per product, many of which serve only to extend exclusivity well beyond the original period (Facher 2024). As a result, patients pay exorbitant sums for treatments developed with significant public funding, and countless lives are lost or compromised, not for scientific reasons, but due to the artificial scarcity enforced by law.

These harms are not new observations. In the nineteenth century, Britain saw a vibrant anti-patent movement, with inventors and economists arguing that patents created artificial monopolies and stifled competition (Machlup and Penrose 1950). The Netherlands went so far as to completely abolish its patent system from 1869 to 1912, although in 1912 a new patent act came into force (van Gompel 2019). We have experienced many successful companies based on the principles of open-source, open-hardware and open-biotech. In the software realm, critics have long contended that code is essentially mathematical in nature, and thus unfit for patenting. As many people argued, while some innovation might be discouraged without patents (Wikipedia contributors 2025b), the costs saved by eliminating litigation and legal complexity would likely outweigh the losses (Bessen and Meurer 2008).

Despite the mythology surrounding intellectual property, many of the most transformative breakthroughs in history were not born in regimes of legal exclusivity. Open protocols served as the foundation for the Internet. Peer review and cooperative research have made scientific discoveries. Much of the modern world, from Google's servers to Android phones, is powered by free and open-source software. These instances demonstrate that effect, recognition, and profitability are not negated by the lack of a legitimate monopoly.

Still, the question remains: Without patents and copyrights, how can artists and businesspeople thrive in the face of competition and imitation? In reality, there are a number of viable paths forward, all predicated on execution, transparency, and sincere relationships with communities. Artists might focus on authorship rather than copyrights and intellectual property, and in engineering, medicine, and other technical fields we have many possibilities.

Some companies embrace a model based on speed and superior execution. Being the first to market and consistently innovating are more valuable than obtaining a patent in industries that move quickly. After all, patents are offensive weapons used by large companies, they represent a considerable cost, and not necessarily are the ideal focus of an innovative startup. Nevertheless, even for large corporations, being anti-patent might be vantageous. Some corporations show their supremacy through infrastructure and brand leadership. Tesla famously made several of its electric car patents available to the public in 2014 (UBC Intellectual Property Law Blog 2024). Others rely on transparency and use free or shared intellectual property to create successful firms. Moreover, Red Hat, GitLab and others provide open access to their software code, they make money from consulting, support, and other premium services. These models function because of openness rather than in spite of it.

Direct patronage, crowd-sourcing, and community service are ways artists and producers could make money. By using websites like Patreon, Bandcamp, Kickstarter, and Substack, artists can generate steady revenue without giving up control to intermediaries. By encouraging participation and open sharing, these creators build devoted audiences rather than relying on exclusion. The electronics startup SparkFun, based in Colorado, openly invites rivals to steal its hardware innovations and expressly declines to patent them. But by fostering community trust and innovating more quickly than others can copy it, it continues to grow (Phillips 2013). These examples show that success does not need exclusion. Those who collaborate, share, and iterate quickly will be the ones driving innovation in the future, not those who keep ideas to themselves in state-approved monopolies.

Without copyrights and patents, there would still be creation in the world, there are still. In this universe, innovation is evaluated by impact rather than ownership, and creativity is unrestricted. The question is not whether humanity could live without these safeguards, but rather if we can pay the rising expenses of maintaining them. We probably need a general change of mindset, where we protect creators in a way that does not create inequality to the larger society. This is another example of the barriers to change we discussed in previous chapters, because relying on patents is strongly motivated in the current social system rather than real need.

5.2 The Laffer Curve

Moreover, we could also consider if the circumstances are favourable for an economic activity to flourish. If there is no labour, there are no employees, regardless of whether they are exploited or allowed to grow financially. The Laffer curve, introduced by the American economist Arthur Laffer, depicts the relationship between the tax rate and governmental revenues (Laffer 2004). The idea is to propose the quest of an optimal level of taxation within a country. Looking at the curve also depicted in Fig. 5.1, we can conclude a couple of things. First of all, if taxes are too low, many companies and many jobs will be created, but at the same time, the State will earn little and will not be able to offer services to citizens. For instance, Switzerland is organized in this trend, though for a series of other policies, the country works like a well oiled machine. On the other hand, if taxes are too high, the risk is the opposite, i.e., those who earn more will stop producing and relocate their company to another country, thus decreasing business volumes, jobs, salaries, etc. Then there is the risk of incentivizing evasion, making capital flee abroad, and certainly not attracting new ones. The ideal solution is in the

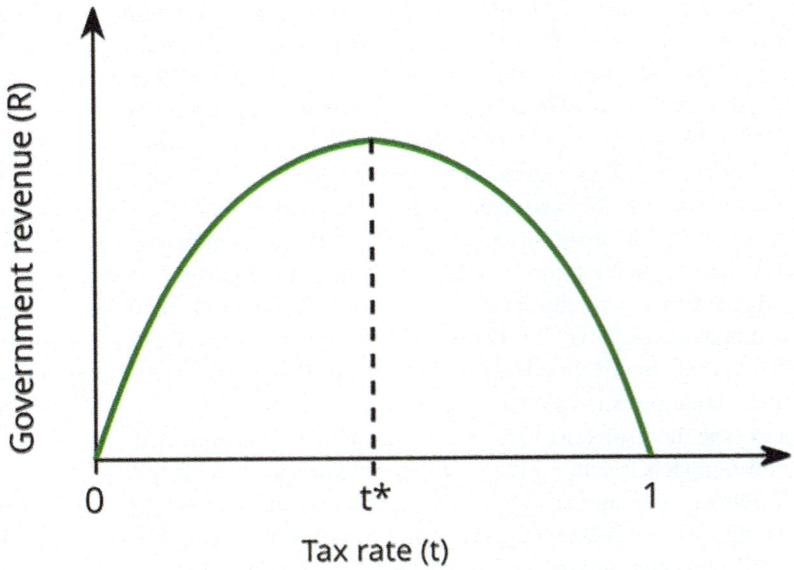

Fig. 5.1 A typical representation of a Laffer curve, with the two extremes, 0 taxation rate in a country on the left tail, 100% taxation of all revenue on the right tail, and an ideal taxation rate at the point t*

middle. The problem is that to define this middle we need to take into account several variables, and it is easier said than done.

A startup can consider the Laffer curve when selecting a location for incorporation or tax optimization. However, it is not everything about tax. Startups and established companies need to attract and keep talents, plus there might be financial aid for disadvantaged areas, or other sort of reason for establishing a company in an area with high taxation. Moreover, it has been shown that Sub-Saharan nations—as well as other low-income countries on other continents—present an Aid-Laffer curve and a Debt-Laffer curve. In the sense that debt or foreign aid can have economic outcomes in a nonlinear relationship with similar bell curves. The *Debt Laffer Curve* suggests that there is an optimal level of debt beyond which the negative effects of debt begin to outweigh the benefits. The famous saying if I owe 10,000 USD to someone I have a problem, but if I owe 1,000,000 USD to someone, someone has a problem. In essence, by funding profitable ventures, borrowing can initially spur economic growth. But as debt grows, so does the expense of paying off that debt (via interest) (Megersa 2015). This could result in a situation where taking on more debt becomes detrimental to the economic progress of both sides.

Similar to this, the *help Laffer Curve* suggests that there is a threshold for foreign help that optimizes its beneficial effects on economic expansion. After this, further assistance may become ineffective or possibly have declining results. Although, identifying the underlying cause might be cumbersome, such as corruption or moral hazard. Excessive aid can lead to dependency, reduce the incentive for domestic resource mobilization, or create governance issues such as corruption (Lensink and White 1999).

Obviously, aid and debt dependencies are complex problems, and it might be an over-simplification to look for those ideal optimal values as for other Laffer curve representations (Crimi 2024). However, understanding where a country lies on these curves is relevant for both domestic policymakers and international donors, as well as for founders of companies to have an idea of the impact of local taxation.

5.3 Chaebols and Keiretsu at the Time of AI

In the late twentieth century, the economic rise of South Korea and Japan was shaped by distinct corporate forms: the Chaebols and the Keiretsu (Ferris et al. 2003). Those are large, family-controlled business conglomerates which went on the rise during postwar reconstruction and Cold War geopolitics in those Asian countries. Economist have often neglected studying them, as we have always focused on liberal US and over-regulated Europe, though nowadays they might give us some insight on how to survive this algorithmic era, and they can be of inspiration for raising low-income countries.

Chaebols in South Korea such as Samsung, Hyundai, LG, and the SK Group are family-controlled conglomerates that expanded rapidly with state backing during the economic start-up of South Korea. They are actually at the core of the revolution that moved Korea from a low-income country to one of the most advanced countries today. They achieved global dominance in semiconductors, electronics, cars, and chemicals by combining access to foreign financing, technological licensing, and scale manufacturing. To direct growth into areas deemed strategic, the South Korean government employed protectionism, credit allocation, and selective industrial strategy. In less than 50 years, the result was astounding: from rural poverty to technical dominance. However, the dominance of multiple sectors in the hands of a unique powerful family is something that can appear oligarchic, and in fact the South-Korean government has tried to limit their influence. Indeed, such a huge colossus might represent discouraging competition for small- and medium-sized businesses, which are only left with the option of being absorbed.

Fast-pacing to our AI-driven days, they nevertheless represent scary approach: They could control multiple layers of production, from raw materials to final product: production of chips, data centers, algorithms, consumer electronics, and even lines of distribution. Samsung Electronics has actually made significant investments in edge computing and AI research, creating its own extensive models for language and vision and incorporating them into gadgets and manufacturing processes. Meanwhile, SK Hynix and SK Telecom are focusing on AI infrastructure, such as memory chips that are designed for inference and model training. Hyundai is diversifying its product line beyond cars with internal combustion engines by integrating AI into robotics and autonomous driving. There is a trend to these actions: rather than replacing current verticals, AI is being integrated within them to strengthen technological advantage.

Chaebols benefit from their sheer scale. They possess global manufacturing capacity, captive datasets from consumer electronics, and R&D labs with deep engineering talent. But their hierarchical culture and risk-averse decision-making can stifle the iterative experimentation that AI development often demands. Startups iterate faster. Open-source communities evolve more quickly. And the frontier of AI, especially in foundation models, is increasingly driven by talent density and distributed collaboration rather than capital alone.

The problem is significantly more severe in Japan. Despite being a leader in industrial automation, robotics, and sensor technology, Japan's big businesses have been slow to adopt fundamental developments in artificial intelligence. Although Japan lacks a definitive national leader in large-scale AI models comparable to OpenAI, DeepMind, or even Baidu, companies like Toyota and Sony are experimenting with AI integration. Once praised for their long-term focus, the Japanese Keiretsu culture is now at risk of falling behind due to structural inertia. It is more difficult to defend audacious investments in risky technologies due to their decentralized decision making and consensus-driven management style. Yet, not all is stagnant. Businesses in Japan are taking advantage of their competitive advantages. NEC and Fujitsu have introduced AI platforms designed for business use, frequently focusing on compliance and explainability, features that are in line with Japanese regulations. The Silicon Valley-based Toyota Research Institute (TRI) is heavily interested in reinforcement learning and robotics. Furthermore, embodied AI systems that need to integrate perception, action, and reasoning may find a suitable testing ground in Japan's capabilities in robotics, mechatronics, and sensor-rich surroundings.

The state plays a critical role in both contexts, in the initial days it was more than lobbying, it was literally a transparent collaboration between government and those large industrial conglomerates. South Korea's government has launched national AI strategies focused on research funding, data infrastructure, and public-private partnerships. Japan has done the same, with initiatives from the Ministry of Economy, Trade and Industry (METI) and the Cabinet Office focused on 'Society 5.0', a vision of data-driven, human-centered innovation. However, compared to the U.S. and China, these strategies face structural limits. Neither country has a digital platform economy on the scale of American Big Tech or Chinese super-apps. Their AI ecosystems remain dependent on foundational models from the western world, especially in natural language.

A key variable in this equation is the data. Chaebols and Keiretsu historically succeeded in controlling physical production and optimizing logistics. But in AI, the locus of value shifts to training data, model weights, and computation. This transition undermines the traditional advantages of vertical integration and engineering scale. Firms must now cultivate data governance, model interpretability, and algorithmic fairness, concepts alien to their original business logic. They must also engage with open source communities and academic researchers whose methods of discovery and sharing differ radically from corporate secrecy. Nevertheless, their size and differentiation among different markets make them less scary than American giant tech advancing as the new kings in the upcoming techno-feudalism.

Global South AI economies are generally entrenched by different cultures which are very different from South Korea or Japan; moreover, it opens many ethical discussions whether concentrating so many industrial and economical power in a family/dynasty is an ideal solution. However, low-income countries that want to raise can borrow the Chaebol speed of execution for initial infrastructure build-up, but need Keiretsu collaborative webs to prevent overconcentration and foster long-term ecosystem diversity.

5.4 The Elite Bargain

A Nash equilibrium in game theory is a condition in which no player can obtain a better outcome by changing their strategy, assuming that the strategies of other players remain constant (Holt and Roth 2004). In daily life, very few people make decisions like this where there is an equilibrium between political class, business leaders, and average people, or even run game theory simulations. Even in politics and economy, many things are driven by ideology or preexisting power conditions, unfortunately sometimes even contradicting internal cost-benefit analysis. In Chap. 1 we introduced the issue of external barriers to change, given by potential lobbies between existing regulations, companies, and other structures. In Chap. 2 we mentioned that indeed stagnating institutions might create poverty traps and not allow development, or at least not at a fast pace like it should. In fact, we have evidence with very similar geography, epidemiology, and socially alike, where purely institutions were producing completely different impacts such as North and South Korea, Arizona and Northern Mexico (Robinson and Acemoglu 2012). Nevertheless, as we mentioned in the previous section, some large-scale lobbying mostly related to powerful families has produced bounces in technology with a positive effect, as observed in Korea and Japan. This opens the doubt that not all lobbyings are bad.

Some development studies have described this circumstance as *"elite bargain", or "political settlement"* (LeVeck et al. 2014), *"development bargain," "growth coalition,"* (Cox 1999) *"inclusive pact," "development bargain"* (Dercon 2022), or other similar ways. In plain terms, those in power decide to "gamble" on a growth-oriented future instead of continuing the status quo of protecting their interests. "Those in power" is a vague definition. It can be a Keiretsu in South Korea, the current political leadership in a country, a combination of interest groups, or even a military power switching to more peaceful business. In practice, when political and economic elites collectively agree that investing in inclusive economic growth is in their long-term interest, even if it requires concessions or risks. It is like a bet: elites give up some immediate control or extraction to unlock greater prosperity. Stefan Dercon in fact called it "gambling" (Dercon 2022), and in his book cited examples, such as the Chinese agriculture rural reforms, then even expanded into information revolution, which paradoxically cannot be discussed with Deepseek as I tried (Dercon 2022): the Communist Party faced eroding legitimacy post-Cultural Revolution, and initiated economic reformers market-oriented policies from 1979 onward to boost growth and legitimacy. They started those changes in only some areas, such as Anhui and Sichuan, and then expanded, demonstrating calculated risk taking within the Party. Giving 20 or more years, the result was a more liberal society (though still under the control of the Party), with a blooming economy and research and development competing with the rest of the world. Other examples can be found throughout the world, even in Sub-Saharan Africa (Dercon 2022).

The question remains: When do the elite decide to opt for the development bargain? When do they decide to gamble on the solution that might reduce their own power for global wealth? There can be internal factors as serious crises as wars, famines, forcing the elites to reorient toward a broader bargain because the status quo becomes unsustainable. However, this is not obvious. Some governments or elites may continue on their path with self-detrimental policies. The ball might be back in the court of the civil society; as we previously discussed, entrepreneurs and non-profit organizations might organize themselves, even pushing mass protests or reformist movements, pressuring the elites. Unfortunately, a deal works only if the elites believe that long-term development aligns with their own survival. If a political group, influential business leaders see reforms as a serious decrease of power, they will resist or sabotage it. This is why changes from the bottom are possible, though "normal people" should be aware of the difficulties involved. Alternative views are given by "elite rupture," as in the French revolution, the Arab Spring (Sofi 2016), or the *"Mani Pulite"* movement in Italy at the beginning of the 1990s. Until the 1990s, Italy had the largest communist party in Europe (PCI), mostly due to the charismatic leadership of Enrico Berlinguer, who was proposing a "Third Way" taking distance from both Soviet Marxism and extreme liberalism, and proposing a blending between First World and Second World ways, an ideal empowerment of people even financially.

Due to the rivalry First and Second World, US and NATO had at the highest interest to keep in power the opposite party Democrazia Cristiana (DC) (translated from the Italian "Christian Democrats") and their allies at all costs. However, DC and Partito Socialista Italiano (PSI) (Italian socialist party) built vast patronage networks, distributing state resources in exchange for loyalty, even in more informal ways than how described in Chap. 1. Businesses through kickbacks and bribes financed the parties, and politicians maintained control of appointments and contracts, a system that was further deployed in Sicily by the mafia criminal organization Cosa Nostra (Della Porta et al. 1994). Everyone knew that the system was corrupt, but it was tolerated because it guaranteed political stability and kept communists out of the government, even if it meant working in conjunction with large criminal organizations (Guzzini 1995).

When the Cold War ended, the strategic need to keep the old order afloat disappeared. The communist party (PCI) was no longer a threat, Berlinguer died in 1984, his ideas were never really put into practice, and foreign external support for the DC disappeared as well. The investigation of the corrupted DC and PSI system was carried out by magistrates and lawyers by the so-called "Mani Pulite" movement, which translated means "clean hands." In those days a tragic yet powerful event occurred: The homicide of Giovanni Falcone, who in parallel was investigating Cosa Nostra in Sicily. His homicide was the catalyst for the elite rupture of Mani Pulite as it created great public outrage. I was still a child, and I remember people screaming in the street of Palermo when it happened, and unrest at the funeral of Falcone's bodyguards. 4,000 policemen were unable to handle tens of thousands people invading the funeral, as politicians were present at the funeral. It was clear to people the connection between mafia and politics behind the homicide of Falcone and his bodyguards, and riots were everywhere.

These examples or others are not bargains, since they occur after violent or disruptive events such as riots and shocks. In fact, the political shock of Mani Pulite and the relative disruption of Cosa Nostra did not translate in Italy into real change, since Transparency International reports only small improvements, and also the increase in production and GDP have been minor compared to other countries; the only visible positive effect was the reduction in power of Cosa Nostra in Sicily (Transparency International 2025). A similar scenario was seen in the Arab Spring protest of 2010, where after all the riots only Tunisia introduced some reforms, and the other countries returned more or less to their original status (Sofi 2016).

In contrast, next to Italy a few years earlier, we had in Spain the *Pacto de la Moncloa*, which is widely considered a successful elite bargain (Encarnación 2001). The Moncloa is a building in Madrid that serves as the official residence of the Prime Minister.

Even after 40 years of Franco's dictatorship, Spain was still a young democracy, facing high inflation, fiscal imbalances, and labor unrest. Political elites, business leaders, unions, and regional representatives negotiated a pact to stabilize the economy and democratize simultaneously. Eventually, with time, the inflation decreased from more than 30% to around 10%. Although Spain's economy is still far from ideal, it escaped the long-term stagnation like Italy. We could summarize the difference in the diagram in Fig. 5.2.

In 2025, if we look at innovation and startup creation, Spain is generally perceived as more favorable than Italy, even if both countries have their own challenges. Both countries have some cities seen as startup hubs, but Spain has a more mature scene due to government incentives and leaner tax attracting large venture capital (VC) funds, which are "scared" in Italy by the unnecessary bureaucracy and tax system. All factors also pushing a brain drain in Italy, which does not seem to decrease. Recent studies also pointed out a strong correlation with the aforementioned lack of transparency in Italy to its brain drain (Morano Foadi 2006). Those lessons remind us that even in countries in the Global North, where living standards are relatively high, lack of transparency, inefficient institutions, lack of elite bargain might seriously slow down innovation and change, and even drive people toward poverty traps. A strong call to action for policy makers, civil society, and entrepreneurs. Paraphrasing the way of thinking of Giovanni Falcone, who you can see depicted together with his colleague Paolo Borsellino in Fig. 5.3, to be a hero it would be enough to be honest and brave in our daily business and deeds. This is a lesson that perhaps current generations of NGOs and activists have learned.

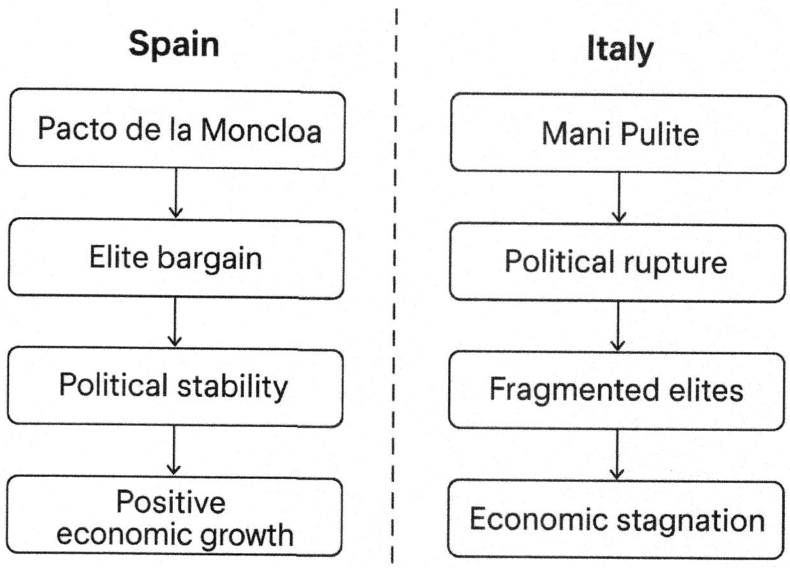

Fig. 5.2 The different dynamics of elites bargain and elite rupture in Spain and Italy

5.5 Engineering the Bargain, A Practical Framework When Possible

The preceding analysis establishes the elite bargain as a critical juncture, a moment when powerful groups, driven by crisis, foresight, or force, choose to exchange some degree of exclusive control for a more inclusive and stable prosperity. Yet, to treat this as a historical curiosity or a fortunate accident is to abandon the project of deliberate social change. If we accept that development is often a political settlement before it is an economic outcome, then we must move from description to a more prescriptive, if cautious, analysis. Therefore, we are now going to consider this in a more mechanistic and consistent way. An elite bargain is not a single event but a dynamic and often messy process, one that can be mapped across three phases: the *Trigger*, the *Negotiation*, and the *Institutionalization of Trade-offs* (Khan 2010).

The Trigger Phase shakes the foundations of the status quo, creating a credible threat to elite (either political, or private sector, or both) and their interests that outweighs. These triggers are seldom purely economic; they are socio-political frictions that render the existing system untenable. They can be exogenous, such as the military defeat as happened in Japan at the end of World War II (Dower 1999), where the sudden withdrawal of a patron state overwhelmed the state capacity. More commonly, they can be endogenous: a fiscal crisis so severe that it bankrupts the patronage machine, a widespread popular uprising that threatens revolutionary overthrow, or a prolonged civil war that exhausts all parties, as seen in the long road to Colombia's 2016 peace accords (Flores and Nooruddin 2016). The key is the perception of existential risk. Elites do not bargain because they have a change of heart; they bargain because the alternative appears worse.

Fig. 5.3 Giovanni Falcone and Paolo Borsellino smiling in Palermo's harbor, a mural by Rosk & Loste inspired by Tony Gentile's well-known photograph

The Negotiation Phase is where interests are translated into pacts. We say negotiation because there must be an interaction between those in power and some groups proposing an alternative to the crisis. Groups can be an organized civil society, NGOs or even ordinary people protesting. For example, in the South African negotiated end of apartheid (the early 1990s), the apartheid-state elites were given by national Party political leadership (e.g., F.W. de Klerk), white economic elites (mining, finance, industry), and senior military and security officials. The "other side" pressing for civil rights was represented by African National Congress (ANC) leadership (such as Nelson Mandela, Oliver Tambo), Congress of South African Trade Unions, and the black South African mass population on the ground which created ungovernability within the country (Reddy 2006). As for the South African case and the others, negotiation is not concluded in a single meeting, but rather is a long and often opaque process that involves protests in the streets, threats, promises, and coalition-building. Negotiation typically involves two parallel tracks. The first is an *intra-elite bargain*: resolving conflicts between different elite factions (e.g., industrialists vs. agrarian landowners, military vs. civilian leaders). This often requires side-payments, guarantees of amnesty for past extraction, or the creation of new, sanctioned avenues for wealth accumulation. The second is the elite-masses bargain: offering a credible commitment to broader inclusion. This is a strategic concession to secure stability and legitimacy. The terms might include land reform as for the Taiwan case (Tai 2022), the legalization of labor unions, constitutional guarantees for minority rights inclusion (South African Government 1996) and political power (Barnes 2008) in South Africa, or the opening of educational and economic opportunities in other cases. The critical ingredient is the presence of a *reform coalition* within the elite, a faction that sees its long-term future tied to productive investment and its ability to forge a temporary alliance with mobilized civil society groups.

Finally, the Institutionalization of Trade-offs phase locks in the bargain. Abstract promises are codified into laws, independent agencies, and protected budgets. The trade-offs are concrete: elites accept stronger property rights and antitrust laws in exchange for a larger, more stable market. They submit to a more independent judiciary and greater transparency in exchange for investment that depends on credible rules. They permit higher taxation on capital to fund public education and infrastructure that grow the collective pie. The Chilean "Concertación" governments after Pinochet exemplified this, using consensus-based politics to lock in macroeconomic stability and poverty reduction, thereby securing elite acceptance of democracy (Boeninger 1985).

The optimistic scenario of a crisis-induced bargain fails when elites are so entrenched, ideologically rigid, or personally vested in a impunity and control system that they would rather oversee a controlled collapse than risk a loss of power. Here, bottom-up action must become a strategic contest for power, employing a repertoire of methods calibrated to the regime's specific vulnerabilities. In cases of thief or predatory states, where the state is a vehicle for personal enrichment, the focus must shift to external pressure and internal disruption of rent flows. This involves supporting transnational civil society networks to trace illicit financial flows (Rotberg and Hampson 2024), advocating for targeted sanctions, and building alliances with non-elite business sectors strangled by the crony economy. The goal is to raise the operating cost of predation, fostering fissures within the ruling coalition. Against ideologically rigid regimes, where power is sustained by a closed belief system, strategy is necessarily long-term and is focused on information permeability and elite socialization. Supporting independent media that break the state's monopoly on truth and engaging second-tier technocrats in international exchanges can plant seeds of alternative thinking. For fragile or failing states where elite power is fragmented among warlords or local oligarchs, the primary challenge is building a sequence of local pacts that can aggregate upward. This is the painstaking work of "institutional grafting" using traditional conflict resolution mechanisms and local business councils to create islands of stability, as seen in parts of Somaliland (Renders and Terlinden 2017), thus creating a constituency for order that can eventually pressure regional power-brokers.

A one-size-fits-all approach to confronting anti-developmental elites is doomed. Effective action requires a clear diagnosis of the dominant pathology of state capture, which requires tailored strategies. For predatory kleptocracy (ruling of the thieves), where the state is a "cash machine" for a narrow group, the primary strategy must be financial transparency, asset recovery, and sanctions to disrupt rent flows, aiming to make predation less profitable. For the ideological fortress, maintained through doctrinal purity, strategy must center on information campaigns and careful external engagement with technocratic tiers to erode doctrinal monopoly. In a fragmented patronage Network, where power is dispersed among competing groups leading to volatile extraction, the focus should be on supporting local-level institutional pacts and sub-national governance to build upward from islands of stability.

Perhaps, the strategy must be to empower domestic reform coalitions with technical expertise and international connections to tilt the internal balance of power toward productive interests (Khan 2010). This framework demystifies the elite bargain. It is not a magical occurrence, but a political process that can be analyzed, influenced, and, in some contexts, catalyzed. Each case is different. The task is to accurately diagnose the political economy, identify leverage points, and deploy a strategy that raises the cost of exclusion while offering a credible and preferable alternative. The bargain is forged in the intersection of pressure, persuasion, and the hard, pragmatic work of building new institutions that make cooperation more rewarding for the elite. As mentioned in the previous section, there is no absolute guaranty that a bargain can happen, and in some cases extreme riots and revolutions might even pave the way for more chaotic resolutions.

5.6 Gender, Technology, and Empowerment

We have discussed through this book many times about between-countries inequality and poverty, mentioning often the gap between the Global North and Global South. However, any conversation about technology and poverty that ignores gender is based on a crucial blind spot. A blind spot which is not specific to the Global South.

Poverty is not a gender-neutral experience in many nations due to social norms and unequal power dynamics; rather, it is deeply gendered and begins with disparities in access to resources such as education. Even in high-income nations, where institutions do not adequately support children and the elderly, women and girls are disproportionately affected and often do most of the care (Budlender 2008). They have limited access to formal education and employment and face barriers to financial and land ownership. In many countries, women do not have the same legal rights as men to own or inherit property. For example, Chile, Ecuador, Cameroon, and many in South East Asia are the main laws against women for marital control.

The gender wage gap still exists in many nations, despite the fact that many are closing the gap. The World Economic Forum 2025 report described that with current actions it will take 123 years to fully close it (World Economic Forum 2025). New technologies are now prevalent in many aspects of education and career. Consequently, technology, be it a mobile phone, farming apps like FarmDrive, or even AI algorithms, does not place them on a level playing field. Enter this complex gendered reality, where it has the dual potential to perpetuate existing inequalities or become a powerful tool for empowerment. The path it takes is not predetermined, but is a direct result of conscious design and policy choices.

This contradiction is best shown by the effects of artificial intelligence. AI systems run the risk of automating and scaling gender bias because they are trained in large data sets that represent historical and social reality (West et al. 2019). The use of hiring algorithms to lower curriculum vitae that contain words like "women's" or the name of an all-women's college is a well-documented example. These algorithms can be trained on data from industries that are dominated by men (Bolukbasi et al. 2016). In the context of development, this could appear as artificial intelligence that uses past financial data to rank credit and deny loans to women, so perpetuating the very inequality it is intended to alleviate (Prasad 2021). Furthermore, the global data deficit on women. Generally, women are still less represented in everything from clinical trial data to geospatial mapping in those countries, means that AI models are often built on an incomplete picture of humanity, leading to products and services that are less effective for them. We previously described issues related to the Global South and data, providing biased dataset. Given these considerations, gender imbalance can also be present in Global North AI models for the same reason.

However, this same technology can be deliberately harnessed to close the gender gap. The design principle must shift from gender blind to gender intentional. For instance, women can have direct access to the markets through digital platforms, eliminating traditional male-dominated middlemen and keeping a higher percentage of their earnings (Mastercard 2019). The financial autonomy and privacy offered by digital wallets in Latin America and other places, and mobile banking, can be extremely advantageous for women who have limited influence over their household finances (Un Women 2020). Although women represent a significant part of the agricultural workforce and sales force, they may have less access to services than their male counterparts (Polson 2019). Hopefully, agritech solutions like those discussed previously can provide anonymity and avoid stigmatization by overcoming these circumstances.

In summary, it is essential to include women in all stages of the technology lifecycle, from identifying problems and designing solutions which are appropriate and more accessible, jointly to improving the local legislation. Initiatives to promote women only technology hubs are just the beginning; in theory, we should require gender-balanced stakeholder panels and participatory workshops. This inclusive approach should go beyond the narrative of just including women as users by empowering them as creators and leaders of the digital revolution, ensuring that technology matches their particular needs and circumstances. Ultimately, creating technology that helps women is not a niche problem; rather, it is a necessary prerequisite to develop just and practical solutions that actually reduce inequality for everyone, not only in the Global South (Biermann et al. 2022).

5.7 Summary of the Chapter

This chapter broadens the scope beyond the Global South, which has been the main focus of the previous chapters, to examine systemic structures and power dynamics that shape innovation and inequality on a global scale.

More specifically, we considered intellectual property as a potential creator of inequality. Patents and copyrights have frequently become tools of obstruction that stifle progress and uphold monopolies rather than fostering creativity. Although originally patents were introduced to protect the inventors of an idea, they are now more a detrimental apparatus, mostly damaging low-income countries. We might propose an open-source model and other systems that openly push creativity-based communities.

Power dynamics shape development. It contrasts the concentrated, state-aligned conglomerates of South Korea and Japan with the concept of the "elite bargain," where ruling groups consciously gamble on inclusive growth for long-term stability. This negotiated reform, as seen in Spain's post-Franco transition, is shown to be more effective than disruptive but shallow "elite ruptures," as those happened in Italy during the "mani pulite" revolution.

Lastly, we need to remember that technology cannot be impartial. AI systems run the risk of automating current gender biases and global data gaps as those mentioned in the "racist" dataset of the previous chapter, but more in relationship to current social gaps, where women can have a better participatory role rather than just underdog users. Restructuring the underlying ownership, power, and participation systems that underpin innovation globally is ultimately necessary to achieve equitable progress.

References

Barnes C (2008) International isolation and pressure for change in South Africa. Aaron Griffiths and Catherine Barnes. Powers of persuasion: incentives, sanctions, conditionality in peacemaking. Accord, London, pp 36–39

Bessen JE et al (2022) Innovation in the absence of patents: evidence from Swedish industrialization. arXiv:2210.04102

Bessen J, Meurer MJ (2008) Patent failure: how judges, bureaucrats, and lawyers put innovators at risk. Princeton University Press

Biermann F, Hickmann T, Sénit CA, Beisheim M, Bernstein S, Chasek P, Vijge MJ (2022) Five governance challenges for the sustainable development goals. Earth Syst Gov 100006

Boeninger E (1985) The Chilean road to democracy. Foreign Aff 64:812

Bolukbasi T, Chang KW, Zou JY, Saligrama V, Kalai AT (2016) Man is to computer programmer as woman is to homemaker? debiasing word embeddings. In: Advances in neural information processing systems, vol 29

Budlender D (2008) The statistical evidence on care and non-care work across six countries. United Nations Research Institute for Social Development (UNRISD)

Cox KR (1999) Ideology and the growth coalition. In: The urban growth machine: critical perspectives two decades later, pp 21–36

Crimi A (2024) Ignite global change. Rethink Press

Della Porta D, Vannucci A, Holman C, Mershon C (1994) Politics, the mafia, and the market for corrupt exchange. Ital Polit 165–183

Dercon S (2022) Gambling on development. Hurst Publishers

Dower JW (1999) Embracing defeat: Japan in the wake of world war II. W. W. Norton & Company

Encarnación OG (2001) Labor and pacted democracy: post-Franco Spain in comparative perspective. Comp Polit 337–355

Facher L (2024) Big pharma's patent abuse is driving a drug pricing crisis. TIME Mag Feb 6 2024

Ferris SP, Kim KA, Kitsabunnarat P (2003) The costs (and benefits?) of diversified business groups: the case of Korean chaebols. J Bank Financ 27(2):251–273

Flores TE, Nooruddin I (2016) Elections in hard times: building stronger democracies in the 21st century. Cambridge University Press

Guzzini S (1995) The "long night of the first republic": years of clientelistic implosion in Italy. Rev Int Polit Econ 2(1):27–61

Holt CA, Roth AE (2004) The Nash equilibrium: a perspective. Proc Natl Acad Sci 101(12):3999–4002

Khan MH (2010) Political settlements and the governance of growth-enhancing institutions. University of London, SOAS

Laffer AB (2004) The Laffer curve: past, present, and future. Backgrounder 1765(1):1–16

Lee J-A, Hilty RM, Liu KC (eds) (2021) Artificial intelligence and intellectual property. Oxford University Press (UK)

Lensink R, White H (1999) Is there an aid Laffer curve?. CREDIT Research Paper 99/6

LeVeck BL, Hughes DA, Fowler JH, Hafner-Burton E, Victor DG (2014) The role of self-interest in elite bargaining. Proc Natl Acad Sci 111(52):18536–18541

Machlup F, Penrose E (1950) The patent controversy in the nineteenth century. J Econ Hist 10(1):1–29

Mastercard (2019) The mastercard index of women entrepreneurs 2019. https://www.mastercard.com/news/media/1ulpy5at/ma_miwe-2019-report.pdf

Megersa KA (2015) The Laffer curve and the debt-growth link in low-income Sub-Saharan African economies. J Econ Stud 42(5):878–892

Morano Foadi S (2006) Key issues and causes of the Italian brain drain. Innovation 19(2):209–223

Phillips J (2013) The open-source hardware company that's turning ten. Wired Mag

Polson J (2019) For female farmers, a smartphone can be the key to the harvest. Bloomberg. https://www.bloomberg.com/news/articles/2019-03-07/for-female-farmers-a-smartphone-can-be-the-key-to-the-harvest

Prasad A (2021) The algorithmic automation of poverty: the case of the Indian public distribution system. The politics of automation. Springer, Cham, pp 53–73

Reddy T (2006) Higher education and social transformation in South Africa since the fall of apartheid. Cahiers de la recherche sur l'éducation et les savoirs 5:121–145

Renders M, Terlinden U (2017) Negotiating statehood in a hybrid political order: the case of Somaliland. Dev Chang 48(2)

Robinson JA, Acemoglu D (2012) Why nations fail: the origins of power, prosperity and poverty. Profile, London

Rotberg RI, Hampson FO (eds) Grand corruption: curbing kleptocracy globally. Taylor & Francis

Sofi MD (2016). The Arab Spring: pathways of repression and reform. J North Afr Stud 21(4)

South African Government (1996) The constitution of the republic of South Africa. Act no 108

Ezell SJ (2020) Delinkage debunked: why replacing patents with prizes for drug development won't work. Information Technology and Innovation Foundation

Stiglitz JE, Greenwald BC (2014) Creating a learning society: a new approach to growth, development, and social progress. Columbia University Press

Ta, H-C (2022) Land reform and politics: a comparative analysis. University of California Press

Transparency International (2025) Italy—corruption perceptions index. https://www.transparency.org/en/countries/italy

UBC Intellectual Property Law Blog (2024) Tesla's open source revolution: balancing corporate strategy and public good. https://iplaw.allard.ubc.ca/2024/12/21/teslas-open-source-revolution-balancing-corporate-strategy-and-public-good/

UN Women (2020) Leveraging digital finance for gender equality and women's empowerment. https://www.unwomen.org/en/digital-library/publications/2020/10/issue-paper-leveraging-digital-finance-for-gender-equality-and-womens-empowerment

van Gompel S (2019) Patent abolition: a real-life historical case study. American University International Law Review, vol 34, no 4, pp 877–922

West SM, Whittaker M, Crawford K (2019) Discriminating systems: gender, race, and power in AI. AI Now Institute, pp 1–33

Wikipedia contributors (2025) Criticism of patents. Wikipedia, the free encyclopedia. https://en.wikipedia.org/wiki/Criticism_of_patents

Wikipedia contributors (2025) Software patent debate. Wikipedia, the free encyclopedia. https://en.wikipedia.org/wiki/Software_patent_debate

World Economic Forum (2025) Global gender gap report 2025. World Economic Forum, Geneva. https://www.weforum.org/publications/global-gender-gap-report-2025

6 Conclusions

6.1 Review of the Developmental Roadmap

Throughout this book, we have mentioned a few times the risks related to innovation, mostly related to the fact that innovations are often related to automation and subsequent increases in damages to the environment and social inequalities. Anyway, novel technologies can also be used to reduce poverty.

If we would like to have an overview of the economic theories about poverty mentioned so far, we could draw a summary diagram as in Fig. 6.1. The design combines some of the most prominent points of view into a network of concepts that highlight the potential and constraints of development interventions. Development, poverty alleviation, and economic growth have been the subject of intense theoretical discussion.

The Big-Push Aid paradigm, which Jeffrey Sachs famously promoted in The End of Poverty, is located on one side of this conceptual network. We all feel that those ideas arose from the idealistic sense of making a structural adjustment to an unbalanced world with foreign aid or a program. We did not know that things were more complex than that. Sachs' idealism maintained his view that massive, well-coordinated expenditures in infrastructure, education, and health could lift countries out of poverty and start a positive feedback loop (Munk 2013). Despite its ambition and good intentions, this approach has drawn criticism for assuming that financial means alone can transcend institutional and political obstacles. Economists such as William Easterly (2009) and Dambisa Moyo (2014), who lament that foreign aid may inadvertently empower political elites, encourage dependency, and distort local markets. Their point of view emphasizes that the institutional and political problems that the aid aims to solve cannot be separated from its evaluation, but these criticisms are also extreme and cannot provide the final answer.

The work of Abhijit Banerjee and Esther Duflo emphasizes the significance of Micro-Level Interventions based on evidence-based experimentation at a more detailed level. The development economy must meet the behavioral economy. We need to understand the lives of the poor, and we need rigorous studies with randomized trial controls, looking at poverty interventions as we look at the effectiveness of a vaccine. By assessing small, context-specific interventions, often through randomized controlled trials, they demonstrate how even little changes can improve health, education, and economic results when appropriately tailored to local circumstances. However, these microinterventions are not immune to the constraints imposed by institutions and elite bargain, as they have to navigate the same political and institutional circumstances that affect larger-scale aid programs. Everything boils down to the government trap, the idea of bad institutions ruining everything, developed by James Robinson and Daron Acemoglu, is the basis of this network. Their study shows that the character of a country's

© The Author(s), under exclusive license to Springer Nature Switzerland AG 2026
A. Crimi, *Innovate for Impact*, Sustainable Development Goals Series,
https://doi.org/10.1007/978-3-032-21563-5_6

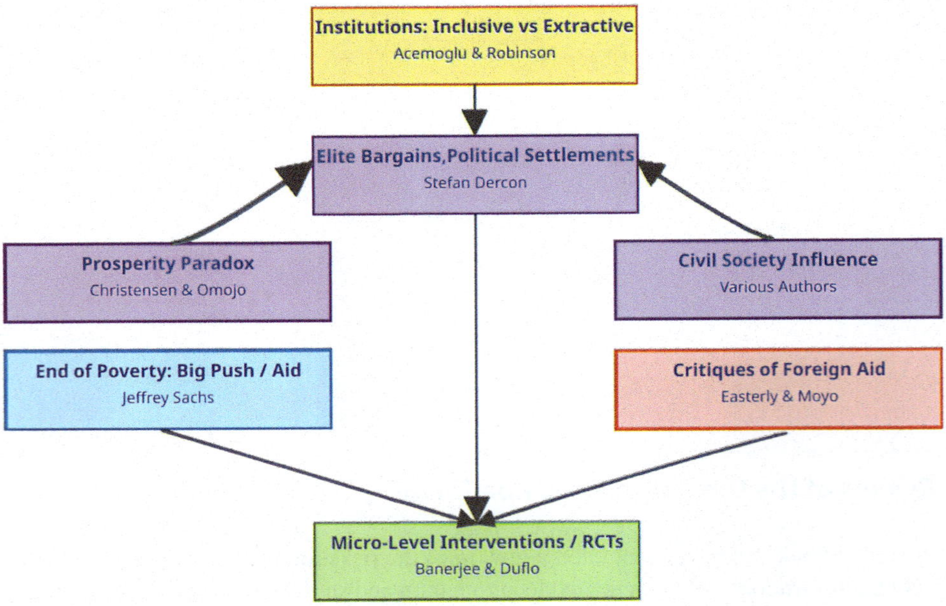

Fig. 6.1 Graphic summary of the main economic ideas reviewed across this book

institutions has a significant impact on its long-term course (Robinson and Acemoglu 2012). Innovation, investment, and sustainable growth are facilitated by inclusive institutions that uphold property rights and share political power widely. Extractive institutions, on the other hand, stifle opportunity and prolong poverty cycles by consolidating power in the hands of elites. This creates inequality and it is the poverty trap we are all sure exists. In simple words, great institutions and governments create stable societies and vise versa despite all other things in place. This is a naive simplification, which unfortunately highlights the most critical aspect of why some nations prosper and others fail.

Stefan Dercon's concept of elite bargains and political settlements, which highlights the unofficial agreements between political and economic elites that dictate the distribution of resources, policies, and opportunities, stems from this fundamental insight (Dercon 2022). These underlying agreements frequently determine who truly benefits from development initiatives, even when official institutions seem inclusive on paper. The network demonstrates how both internal societal dynamics and foreign ideas impact elite settlements. Christensen and Omojo's Prosperity Paradox (Christensen et al. 2019), for instance, shows that broad-based development is not always the result of economic growth on its own. Rather, growth must be transformed into inclusive progress by focused investments, strategic interventions, and supportive policies. We cannot expect that change comes from the top; from malfunctioning institutions, we need to invest in market-creating innovation to build new markets and new jobs, assuming this is done ethically and from the bottom. Similarly, civil society actors, such as community organizations, NGOs, and grassroots movements, are essential in influencing the conduct of the elite. This is the bottom-up approach that we should follow when government and institutions are not doing their job.

Taking all this together, the network communicates that development is far more than just a question of money or technical know-how. It is the result of a confluence of interrelated factors, institutional frameworks, elite bargaining, calculated actions, and public involvement. Designing effective and long-lasting policies and initiatives that help countries escape poverty cycles and achieve inclusive growth requires understanding these links. In a world on the brink of entering a new form of capitalism forged by techno-feudalism and Google-crazy (Varoufakis 2024; Suleyman 2025), we need more than ever both inclusive institutions, as well as sustainable businesses and effective NGOs.

6.2 A Call to Action for Scientists, Entrepreneurs, Policymakers, Activists and Everyone

The journey through these pages has not been merely an academic exercise. It has been a map of the battlefield against poverty and inequality. I proposed a catalog of the weapons at our disposal: technology, education, systemic thinking, and, most importantly, human ingenuity. There is a bright future, which we believe is not a solar-punk fantasy. It is a plausible reality waiting to be built. But it will not build itself. We need a symphony of change; each of us plays a distinct but interconnected instrument in this. Here is how you can contribute.

To the Scientists and Researchers:
Your work in the lab is the genesis of transformation, but the journey cannot end there. We call on you to embrace the complexity of the real world. There are collaborative programs in the Global South. I described AIMS, but there are other pop-ups. Including European and American collaborative grants. Mentor the next generation of scientists from the Global South not as assistants, but as future leaders and principal investigators. Empower them to set the research agenda for their own communities.

To Entrepreneurs and Technologists:
You are the engines of innovation and the bridge between invention and impact. We call on you to build with, not for. We have not taken advantage of all the possibilities of frugal innovations. Affordability and simplicity are key components of elegance, and "frugal innovations" are still fascinating, and at least they represent the beginning, we need to start from somewhere. The most revolutionary technology is not the most trendy, but rather the most widely available. Can the solution be maintained with local skills and spare parts? Like the Fair-phone which can be replaced in all its parts like battery, screen, etc. very easily (Fairphone 2025).

To avoid further expansion of corporations based on cloud-feudalism, we need more local and fair solutions decolonizing innovation and AI.

To Policymakers and Government Leaders:
You have the ability to establish the conditions necessary for change to thrive or fail. You are urged to create supportive circumstances. Make unrelenting investments in the main pillars of prosperity: Nutrition, healthcare and education, and obviously the new addition to Maslow's pyramid *digital infrastructures*. These are necessary conditions for private innovation and economic development, not costs. Protect your populace without inhibiting creativity. "Death by Regulation" should be replaced with evidence-based, flexible regulatory sandboxes that enable the safe testing of novel concepts.

To the Activists and Community Leaders:
You are the moral compass and the connection to the grassroots, ensuring that change is equitable and just. You are urged to hold everyone responsible. We need to encourage institutions, entrepreneurs, and scientists to collaborate with the communities they plan to serve to develop solutions. This is system thinking, this is an elite bargain. Make sure that the opinions of women, other under-represented groups, and for people who think that they have no voice in our society are respected. You need to keep telling stories that transform statistics into human outcomes and innovation into dignity and better quality of life, not sum GDP and more fancy gadgets. Everyone should be reminded that the objective is a better life, not merely greater technology.

To Everyone:
foster South-South Collaboration, break down bureaucratic barriers to trade and knowledge sharing between emerging economies. The solution to a problem in Ghana may already exist in Colombia. Facilitate these connections. Measure impact, create jobs, or start your own company, prevent disease, and think both local and global.

6.3 A Hopeful, Realistic Vision for the Future

Across these chapters, a pattern has emerged, one not defined by acceleration or spectacle, but by the tensions between power, technology, and justice. The overall idea is to reach poverty reduction, being this absolute or relative, often referring to inequalities. The overall idea is that we can reach this by supporting social change bottom-up, namely coming from entrepreneurs and NGOs; but also promoting the right programs for education and healthcare. The paradox of automation, such as AI and novel technologies, is that it often supports elitist groups, while we actually need it to focus more on the people in need.

In the context of technology, leapfrogging refers to a situation in which a country or region adopts a more advanced technology, skipping older intermediate technologies that are commonly used in other parts of the world. Often, this is related to a need and geographic context in which those older technologies have never been installed due to lack of funding. In the Global South, we have experienced this in many circumstances, with the mobile phones penetrating areas where no landline phones were present, or the surge of digital micro-finances in places where no traditional banks existed. Yet, it is a Red Queen race. Everyone must run to stay in the same place. Everybody must constantly adapt and evolve to survive in a changing environment, especially when faced with competition from other species or other societies from our species. The other aspect we cannot ignore is the trajectory of the entire planet resembling more and more the theory of Malthusian growth. Whether we are attained with degrowth or with better technologies and policies, we need a serious change in our relationship with economic growth; otherwise, every idea described in this book will be increasingly cumbersome to implement.

With the elite bargain, we pointed out that until stakeholders, government, and institutions proactively engage in improving the circumstances with the anticipation of some temporary reduction of their personal interests, there is little to do. Nevertheless, if this does not happen, civil society and entrepreneurs must hold governments responsible and recognize the need to prioritize results over merely retaining power through corruption and patronage. Examples include encouraging activism to alter laws or policies, allowing the public to closely examine policies or their effects, and requiring budgets, their distribution, and their results to be transparent. Activists' interventions don't have much of an influence if individuals in positions of authority lack the political will to act on them. Riots and ruptures might destabilize the current government, but if they are not translated into permanent reforms and a change of cultures, things might go back as before.

What this book has tried to show is that another trajectory is possible. It is not AI that has to be aligned with human beings, but stakeholders and decision makers should have a more balanced approach. A shift in institutional structures, funding priorities, educational paradigms, and global cooperation. Introducing effective regulations limiting the impact of big tech, and not being the results of overloading bureaucracy to average people or innovators.

From the emerging AI capacity of the Global South to Latin America's experiments in digital marketplaces, from feminist and decolonial approaches to data to climate-conscious development models, the seeds of new digital futures are already being planted. These futures are not utopian; they are difficult, uneven, and politically contested. But they are also hopeful. They suggest that intelligence, whether human or artificial, can be re-imagined as relational, accountable, and reparative.

Independently of social stratifications that will probably always exist, reduction is inequality, and a more balanced society is possible. This is probably more needed in some countries than others. The basic ideas discussed in this book are that we can achieve this yet with policies focused on health, nutrition, and education, all empowered by AI tools, taking care of the complexity between interest groups, existing powerful institutions, politics, environmental impact, and human nature. If necessary, we need to take a bottom-up approach in which civil society or companies fill the gaps left by their governments or institutions. We all want a better world after all.

References

Christensen CM, Ojomo E, Dillon K (2019) The prosperity paradox: how innovation can lift nations out of poverty. Harper Business

Dercon S (2022) Gambling on development. Hurst Publishers

Easterly W (2014) The tyranny of experts: Economists, dictators, and the forgotten rights of the poor. Basic Books

Fairphone. Reuse and Recycling — Fairphone. Fairphone. https://www.fairphone.com/en/category/reuse-and-recycling/ (accessed 11 November 2025)

Moyo D (2009) Dead aid: why aid is not working and how there is a better way for Africa. Macmillan

Munk N (2013) The idealist: Jeffrey Sachs and the quest to end poverty. Anchor

Robinson JA, Acemoglu D (2012) Why nations fail: the origins of power, prosperity and poverty. Profile, London, pp 45–47

Sachs JD (2006) The end of poverty: economic possibilities for our time. Penguin

Suleyman M (2025) The coming wave: AI, power, and our future. Random House

Varoufakis Y (2024) Technofeudalism: what killed capitalism. Melville House

Further Material

Chapter 1

Books on Lobbying and Advocacy

- Pat Libby & Laura M. Aslam. *The Lobbying Strategy Handbook: 10 Steps to Advancing Any Cause Effectively* (2011).
- Brian Lamb. *Grassroots Advocacy and Health Policy: Changing the World from the Bottom Up* (2017).
- Amy Sample Ward & Afua Bruce. *The Tech That Comes Next: How Changemakers, Philanthropists, and Technologists Can Build an Equitable World* (2022).

Toolkits and Online Resources

- International Society for the Systems Sciences (ISSS) https://www.isss.org—Research community on systems thinking.
- Donella Meadows Project
  https://donellameadows.org/systems-thinking-resources/
- IRIS= Better Evaluation tools
  https://www.betterevaluation.org/tools-resources
- Open Government Partnership (OGP) https://www.opengovpartnership.org—Advocacy and transparency tools for civic actors.
- Participedia https://participedia.net—Global knowledge base for public participation methods.
- ChangemakerXchange https://changemakerxchange.org—Network of social innovators and changemakers.
- MobLab https://mobilisationlab.org—Digital campaigning and advocacy strategies.
- Ashoka https://ashoka.org—Global network of social entrepreneurs.
- Changemakers https://www.changemakers.com—Online community powered by Ashoka.
- Skoll Foundation https://skoll.org
- Echoing Green https://echoinggreen.org—Fellowships and seed-stage funding for social innovators.
- MIT Solve https://solve.mit.edu—Marketplace for social impact innovation.
- Global Innovation Fund https://www.globalinnovation.fund
- OpenIDEO https://www.openideo.com—Collaborative platform for human-centered design.
- Impact Hub https://impacthub.net

© The Editor(s) (if applicable) and The Author(s), under exclusive license
to Springer Nature Switzerland AG 2026
A. Crimi, *Innovate for Impact*, Sustainable Development Goals Series,
https://doi.org/10.1007/978-3-032-21563-5

- UNDP Accelerator Labs https://acceleratorlabs.undp.org
- Acumen https://acumen.org—Foundation tackling poverty.
- Catapult Design https://catapultdesign.org
- Greenhouse Capital https://greenhouse.capital
- Target Global https://targetglobal.vc
- Oxfam International https://www.oxfam.org/en/research—Inequality Reports and Campaigns.
- CIVICUS https://www.civicus.org/—State of Civil Society Reports.
- OpenDemocracy https://www.opendemocracy.net/—Activism and Political Change Resources.
- Protest and Coercion Database (PCDB) https://protestdatabase.org/—University of Michigan.

Graph Theory

- Diestel, R. (2017). *Graph Theory* (5th edition). Springer.
- West, D. B. (2001). *Introduction to Graph Theory* (2nd edition). Prentice Hall.
- Pastor-Satorras, R., Castellano, C., Van Mieghem, P., & Vespignani, A. (2015). Epidemic processes in complex networks. *Reviews of Modern Physics*, 87(3), 925–979.
- Kiss, I. Z., Miller, J. C., & Simon, P. L. (2017). *Mathematics of Epidemics on Networks: From Exact to Approximate Models*. Springer.
- Wang, Y., Chakrabarti, D., Wang, C., & Faloutsos, C. (2003). Epidemic spreading in real networks: An eigenvalue viewpoint. *22nd International Symposium on Reliable Distributed Systems*.
- Holme, P., & Saramäki, J. (2012). Temporal networks. *Physics Reports*, 519(3), 97–125.
- Chen, W., Wang, Y., & Wang, S. (2010). Scalable influence maximization for prevalent viral marketing in large-scale social networks. *Proceedings of the 16th ACM SIGKDD International Conference on Knowledge Discovery and Data Mining*, 1029–1038.
- Bansal, S., Grenfell, B. T., & Meyers, L. A. (2007). When individual behavior matters: Homogeneous and network models in epidemiology. *Journal of the Royal Society Interface*, 4(16), 879–891.

Chapter 2

Measuring Poverty

- GapMinder www.gapminder.org
- World Bank PovcalNet https://povcalnet.worldbank.org/
- World Inequality Database https://wid.world/
- Luxembourg Income Study https://www.lisdatacenter.org/
- OECD Income Distribution Database https://www.oecd.org/social/income-distribution-database.htm
- Our World in Data https://ourworldindata.org/poverty
- GINI Project http://www.gini-research.org/
- UNDP Human Development Reports https://hdr.undp.org/
- World Bank Shared Prosperity Database https://www.worldbank.org/en/topic/poverty/brief/global-database-of-shared-prosperity
- ILO Income Inequality Data https://ilostat.ilo.org/topics/income-inequality/
- Commitment to Equity Institute (CEQ) https://commitmenttoequity.org/
- Brookings Institution—Poverty and Inequality https://www.brookings.edu/topic/poverty-inequality/
- PolicyLink Equity Tools https://www.policylink.org/resources-tools

- World Economic Forum—Inclusive Growth https://www.weforum.org/reports/the-inclusive-growth-and-development-report-2017
- Kende-Robb, CM. *Can the Poor Influence Policy? Participatory poverty assessments in the developing world* (The World Bank, 2002).
- Exploring Economics https://www.exploring-economics.org/en/.

Chapter 3

Academic links

- Rise-MICCAI https://rise-miccai.org/
- Deep Learning Indaba https://deeplearningindaba.com
- AIMS Ghana https://aims.edu.gh/
- Savery, J. R. (2006). "Overview of Problem-based Learning: Definitions and Distinctions." *Interdisciplinary Journal of Problem-based Learning*, 1(1), 9–20.
- Barrows, H. S., & Tamblyn, R. M. (1980). *Problem-Based Learning: An Approach to Medical Education*. Springer.
- Schmidt, H. G., Rotgans, J. I., & Yew, E. H. J. (2011). "The process of problem-based learning: What works and why." *Medical Education*, 45(8), 792–806.
- Research4Life https://www.research4life.org/—Provides free or low-cost access to academic content.
- AuthorAID https://www.authoraid.info/en/—Support and mentoring for researchers in LMICs.
- INASP https://www.inasp.info/—Supports equitable knowledge ecosystems in the Global South.
- HINARI Programme https://www.who.int/hinari/en/—Access to biomedical and health literature.
- WHO and Research4Life partnership to support capacity building in LMICs.

Chapter 4

Frugal Engineering

- MIT D-Lab https://d-lab.mit.edu
- Silicon Cape Initiative https://siliconcape.com
- Stanford Byers Center for Biodesign https://biodesign.stanford.edu
- Twende https://twende.or.tz—Accelerating Social Innovation.
- Wennovation Hub https://wennovationhub.org
- Frank's Hospital Workshop https://frankshospitalworkshop.com
- Global Disability Innovation Hub https://disabilityinnovation.com
- Hackteria https://hackteria.org
- Richards-Kortum, R. *Biomedical Engineering for Global Health* (Cambridge University Press, 2009).
- Werner, D., Thuman, C., & Maxwell, J. *Where There Is No Doctor: A village health care handbook* (Hesperian Foundation, 1977).

AI, General Tools and Applications

- Sutton, R. S., & Barto, A. G. (2018). *Reinforcement Learning: An Introduction* (2nd edition). MIT Press.
- Li, Y. (2017). Deep Reinforcement Learning: An Overview. *arXiv preprint arXiv:1701.07274*.

- Mnih, V., et al. (2015). Human-level control through deep reinforcement learning. *Nature*, 518(7540), 529–533.
- Kamilaris, A., & Prenafeta-Boldú, F. X. (2018). Deep learning in agriculture: A survey. *Computers and Electronics in Agriculture*, 147, 70–90.
- Liakos, K. G., et al. (2018). Machine learning in agriculture: A review. *Sensors*, 18(8), 2674.
- Wolfert, S., et al. (2017). Big Data in Smart Farming—A review. *Agricultural Systems*, 153, 69–80.
- Box, G. E. P., Jenkins, G. M., Reinsel, G. C., & Ljung, G. M. (2015). *Time Series Analysis: Forecasting and Control* (5th edition). Wiley.
- Hyndman, R. J., & Athanasopoulos, G. (2021). *Forecasting: Principles and Practice* (3rd edition). OTexts. https://otexts.com/fpp3/
- Zhang, G. P. (2003). Time series forecasting using a hybrid ARIMA and neural network model. *Neurocomputing*, 50, 159–175.
- Makridakis, S., Wheelwright, S. C., & Hyndman, R. J. (1998). *Forecasting: Methods and Applications* (3rd edition). Wiley.
- Ahmed, N. K., Atiya, A. F., Gayar, N. E., & El-Shishiny, H. (2010). An empirical comparison of machine learning models for time series forecasting. *Econometric Reviews*, 29(5-6), 594–621.

Data Sets

- ENDURABLE https://sites.google.com/lbl.gov/endurable/home—Benchmark datasets and AI models with queryable metadata (DOE).
- The Common Fund Data Ecosystem https://commonfund.nih.gov/dataecosystem—NIH-funded discovery platform for FAIR datasets.
- BioDataCatalyst https://biodatacatalyst.nhlbi.nih.gov—FAIR data for heart, lung, and blood research (NIH).
- Garden https://thegardens.ai—FAIR Framework for AI Models (NSF).
- Braid https://anl-braid.github.io/braid/—Data Flow Automation for FAIR Science (DOE).
- HPC-FAIR https://hpc-fair.github.io/—HPC data management framework (DOE).
- FAIR Surrogate Benchmarks Initiative https://sbi-fair.github.io—Develops AI surrogates and benchmarks (DOE).
- Materials Data Facility (MDF) https://www.materialsdatafacility.org—FAIR materials data (NIST).
- Neurodata Without Borders (NWB) https://www.nwb.org/—FAIR data standard for neurophysiology (NIH).
- Materials Research Data Alliance (MaRDA) https://www.marda-alliance.org—Promotes open data in materials science.
- PUNCH4NFDI https://www.punch4nfdi.de—German NFDI consortium for physics.
- ESCAPE https://www.projectescape.eu—European Science Cluster for Astronomy & Particle Physics.
- Awesome Materials Informatics https://github.com/tilde-lab/awesome-materials-informatics—Tools and best practices for Materials Science.
- Eco2AI https://github.com/sb-ai-lab/Eco2AI
- Kohler, C. "Ways To Repurpose Bitcoin Miner Heat" The Bitcoin Manual. https://thebitcoinmanual.com/articles/repurpose-bitcoin-miner-heat
- Africa Data Centres Association. "Data centres in Africa focus report 2024." https://africadca.org/en/data-centres-in-africa-focus-report-2024, 2024.

Chapter 5

- Dercon, Stefan. *Gambling on Development: Why Some Countries Win and Others Lose*. Hurst/Oxford University Press, 2022.
- North, Douglass C., John Joseph Wallis, Steven B. Webb, and Barry R. Weingast (eds.). *In the Shadow of Violence: Politics, Economics, and the Problems of Development*. Cambridge University Press, 2013.
- Khan, Mushtaq H. "Political settlements and the governance of growth-enhancing institutions." *Research Paper Series on Governance for Growth*. SOAS, University of London, 2010.
- Carothers, Thomas, and Saskia Brechenmacher. *Closing Space: Democracy and Human Rights Support Under Fire*. Carnegie Endowment for International Peace, 2014.
- Tarrow, Sidney. *Power in Movement: Social Movements and Contentious Politics*. Cambridge University Press, 2011.
- Tilly, Charles, and Sidney Tarrow. *Contentious Politics*. Oxford University Press, 2015.
- Mounk, Yascha. *The People vs. Democracy: Why Our Freedom Is in Danger and How to Save It*. Harvard University Press, 2018.
- Levitsky, Steven, and Daniel Ziblatt. *How Democracies Die*. Crown Publishing, 2018.
- Giovanni Falcone, Marcelle Padovani. *Cose di Cosa Nostra*. Rizzoli, 1991.
- Francesco La Licata. *Giovanni Falcone*. Rizzoli, 1993.
- Gianni Barbacetto, Peter Gomez, Marco Travaglio. *Mani pulite. La vera storia*. Editori Riuniti, 2002.
- Alexander Stille. *Nella terra degli infedeli. Mafia e politica nella Prima Repubblica*. Mondadori, 1995.

Glossary

AI	Artificial Intelligence
AI4D	The Artificial Intelligence for Development (in Africa)
AIMS	African Institute for Mathematical Sciences
ARIMA	Autoregressive Integrated Moving Average
BMGF	Bill and Melinda Gates Foundation
CARE	Collective Benefit, Authority to Control, Responsibility, Ethics
CBA	Cost-Benefit Analysis
CCB	Creative Capacity Building
CLTS	Community-Led Total Sanitation
CRISPR	Clustered Regularly Interspaced Short Palindromic Repeats
CZI	Chan Zuckerberg Initiative
DC	Democrazia Cristiana (Christian Democrats)
DALY	Disability-Adjusted Life Year
DHIS	District Health Information Software
ELISA	Enzyme-Linked Immunosorbent Assay
ETL	Extract-Transform-Load
FAIR	Findable, Accessible, Interoperable, and Reusable
GIIN	Global Impact Investing Network
GIS	Geographic Information Systems
GDP	Gross Domestic Product
GPS	Global Positioning System
GPU	Graphic Processor Unit
HDI	Human Development Index
HINARI	Health Inter-Network Access to Research Initiative
HISP	Health Information Systems Programme
ICER	Incremental Cost-Effectiveness Ratio
ICGEB	International Centre for Genetic Engineering and Biotechnology
IDRC	International Development Research Center
IT	Information Technology
KPI	Key Performance Indicator
LLM	Large Language Model
LSTM	Long- and Short-Term Memory
MARL	Multi-agent Reinforcement Learning
M&E	Monitoring & Evaluation

© The Editor(s) (if applicable) and The Author(s), under exclusive license
to Springer Nature Switzerland AG 2026
A. Crimi, *Innovate for Impact*, Sustainable Development Goals Series,
https://doi.org/10.1007/978-3-032-21563-5

METI	Ministry of Economy, Trade and Industry
NFTE	Network for Teaching Entrepreneurship
NGO	Non-governmental Organization
NRLM	National Rural Living Mission
OSAT	Open Source Appropriate Technology
PBL	Problem-Based Learning
PCR	Polymerase Chain Reaction
PDI	Power Distance Index
PRA	Participatory Rural Appraisal
QALY	Quality-Adjusted Life Year
R&D	Research & Development
ROI	Return On Investment
RT-LAMP	Reverse Transcription Loop-Mediated Isothermal Amplification
SDG	Sustainable Development Goal
SIDA	Swedish International Development Cooperation Agency
sROI	Social Return On Investment
STEM	Science, Technology, Engineering, Mathematics
TRI	Toyota Research Institute
UBI	Universal Basic Income
UHC	Universal Health Coverage
USD	United States Dollar
VC	Venture Capital
WASH	Water, Sanitation, And Hygiene
WHO	World Health Organization

The Author

Dr. Alessandro Crimi is both a biomedical engineer and a health economist. He alternated research in neuroimaging with projects on healthcare management in low-income countries. He was born in Italy, more specifically Palermo, growing up during the peak moment of violence of Cosa Nostra. During his youth, he was involved in organizations that promoted social change in the city.

He earned an MBA in healthcare administration from the University of Basel (Switzerland) and a Ph.D. in machine learning applied to medical imaging from the University of Copenhagen (Denmark) after completing his engineering studies at the University of Palermo.

Alessandro held postdoctoral positions at the University Hospital of Zurich, the Technical School of Switzerland (ETH Zurich), the Italian Institute for Technology (IIT), and the French Institute for Research in Computer Science (INRIA). He worked mainly in the field of computational neuroscience at these institutes. Dr. Crimi spent time teaching and working on in-field healthcare management initiatives in Ghana and other sub-Saharan nations in between his postdoctoral years at the European institutes. He oversaw multiple MSc theses while teaching the machine learning in medicine course for eight years at the African Institute for Mathematical Sciences (AIMS) in Ghana and South Africa. He cofounded a biotech company that operates between Switzerland and Ghana.

He is currently a professor at the AGH University of Krakow, where the majority of his teaching responsibilities are related. Using cutting-edge technology such as machine learning, image processing, and social engineering, his efforts in sub-Saharan Africa dealt with HIV management, diabetes, malaria, and maternity care. Dr. Crimi is currently working on technology transfer projects for young scientists and campaigns to encourage entrepreneurship among women and people of immigrant backgrounds.

© The Editor(s) (if applicable) and The Author(s), under exclusive license
to Springer Nature Switzerland AG 2026
A. Crimi, *Innovate for Impact*, Sustainable Development Goals Series,
https://doi.org/10.1007/978-3-032-21563-5

The manufacturer's authorised representative in the EU is Springer Nature Customer Service Centre GmbH, Europaplatz 3, 69115 Heidelberg, Germany. If you have any concerns regarding our products, please contact ProductSafety@springernature.com

Printed and bound by CPI Group (UK) Ltd, Croydon, CR0 4YY
17/09/2026
02218451-0011